Unworkable

SUNY series, Insinuations: Philosophy, Psychoanalysis, Literature
———————
Charles Shepherdson, editor

Unworkable
DELUSIONS OF AN IMPLODING CIVILIZATION

FABIO VIGHI

Cover image from Adobe Stock.

Published by State University of New York Press, Albany

© 2022 State University of New York

All rights reserved

Printed in the United States of America

No part of this book may be used or reproduced in any manner whatsoever without written permission. No part of this book may be stored in a retrieval system or transmitted in any form or by any means including electronic, electrostatic, magnetic tape, mechanical, photocopying, recording, or otherwise without the prior permission in writing of the publisher.

For information, contact State University of New York Press, Albany, NY
www.sunypress.edu

Library of Congress Cataloging-in-Publication Data

Name: Vighi, Fabio, author.
Title: Unworkable : delusions of an imploding civilization / Fabio Vighi.
Description: Albany : State University of New York Press, [2022] | Series: SUNY series, Insinuations: Philosophy, Psychoanalysis, Literature | Includes bibliographical references and index.
Identifiers: ISBN 9781438487250 (hardcover : alk. paper) | ISBN 9781438487274 (ebook) | ISBN 9781438487267 (pbk. : alk. paper)
Further information is available at the Library of Congress.

10 9 8 7 6 5 4 3 2 1

Contents

Acknowledgments — vii

Prologue. Loss of Gravity in the Capitalist Galaxy — ix

Chapter 1. Labor, Value, and Other Capitalist Delusions — 1
    Dialectical Totalities — 1
    Brief Encounters — 5
    Setzung der Voraussetzungen — 9
    Hegel after Marx — 13
    The Fantasy of Surplus-Value — 17
    Hegel in and out of Political Economy — 20

Chapter 2. Implosion of the Work Society — 25
    Modernity's Self-deployment — 25
    Self-caused and Self-realized Reason — 29
    Real Work and Labor-time — 33
    Calling the Bluff — 36
    André Gorz's Critique of Work — 39
    Disaster Economics — 42
    The Difficulty of Letting Go — 46

Chapter 3. The Missing Cause — 51
    Chronic Constipation — 51
    A Worldless Discourse — 54
    The New Master — 58
    Colonization of the Productive Mind — 61
    Clouds of Impotence — 64

Labor as Vanishing Presupposition	67
Marx's Teleology	71
The Transcendental Schema of Capitalist Time	77
Beyond Exploitation	80
Chapter 4. Dialectical Short Circuits	**85**
The Catastrophe of Liberation	85
Blindness of the Automatic Subject	89
Hegel: Being as Self-mediated Groundlessness	93
The Speculative Breakthrough	99
The Labor Decoy	103
Big Data and the Fanaticism of Breathing	107
Chapter 5. The Financial Demon	**111**
Shackled by Nostalgia	111
Capitalist Bulimia	116
The Anatomy of Finance Is the Key to the Anatomy of the Real Economy	121
Genie out of the Capitalist Bottle	123
Neoliberal Perversions	130
Populist Symptoms	136
Viral Simulations	139
Epilogue. Emergency Capitalism and the Exhaustion of a Form of Life	**145**
Notes	151
Works Cited	177
Index	187

Acknowledgments

Chapters 3 and 5 contain sections revised from earlier articles: "The Hegelian Moment: From the Withering Away of Labour to the Concrete Universality of Work," *Continental Thought and Theory* 2, no. 4 (2019): 83–107; "Genie out of the Bottle: Lacan and the Loneliness of Global Capitalism," *Crisis and Critique* 6, no. 1 (2019): 390–415.

Prologue

Loss of Gravity in the Capitalist Galaxy

This book discusses the ongoing implosion of the work society from three distinct angles: the dialectic of capital and labor (Hegel and Marx), our societies' loss of symbolic efficiency (Lacan and Gorz), and the ideology of simulation (Baudrillard). The overarching aim of my three-pronged approach is to show that our implosive condition is rooted in the unstoppable dissolution of our shared labor narrative, as well as in a pervasive ideological structure preventing us from confronting the cause of such dissolution. To this end, Hegel and Lacan are engaged as thinkers of the 'empty cause,' which needs to be endorsed if we are to find a way out of the current stalemate. Marx, on the other hand, is situated between radical critique and appraisal of labor as modernity's ontological horizon. Finally, Baudrillard is introduced to illuminate the insidious ideological text of our time, where the evaporation of the social bond is obscured by the imposition of viral hyperreality.

While the book's central themes return in each of its five chapters, I start from the analysis of the capitalist dialectic and end with a critique of contemporary ideology. Much of the book is an attempt to unravel capitalist accumulation as an exhausted mode of production that is now approaching its *redde rationem*. My opening gambit is to show how capitalist implosion can be properly appreciated only by supplementing Marx's critique of political economy with Hegel's speculative dialectics. The only way to think labor dialectically is by endorsing its speculative identity with capital. In this regard, the critical discussion of labor is cross-fertilized with the assessment of technological automation's role in undermining our world's reproductive capacity. Notwithstanding the devastating impact of automation since the third industrial revolution, I argue that capitalism continues to reproduce itself by the sheer force of its ideology, namely, by *simulating* conditions that are no longer available.

⁓

Our time is dominated by the perception that we are descending, as if in slow motion, into a nightmarish realm where life is no longer supported by the presupposition of shared symbolic values, and the future ceaselessly relapses into a claustrophobic present. This descent is as real and irreversible as the global sovereignty of capital, a self-enhancing drive for profit-making that is now liquidating its own basis in value production, while relegating entire populations to misery and abjection. We can picture the collapse of our civilization as the irresistible gravity of a black hole. As we approach it, it begins to strip the outer layers of the work society, spelling the end of the transcendental field of capitalist space-time. Yet, we continue to disavow such an insight, choosing instead to believe in the eternal renewability of our socioeconomic narrative, even though such metafiction is now evaporating before our eyes.

As a discourse based in the reciprocal mediation of money and labor, capitalism conquered modernity and installed itself as the invisible density of our world, the form of life we are immersed in from cradle to grave. Its history cannot be understood without taking into account the way in which it established a system of symbolic relations among countless possibilities, organizing and directing all significations toward a single belief system based on the dogma of labor and the delusion of endless productivity. By inundating all social spheres and subjecting them to its language and rationality, capitalism invented the work society, the most powerful apparatus ever conceived by human beings. Despite the ongoing dissolution of our value-producing machine, however, we are unable to break out of capital's metaphysical spell. The wearing out of symbolic significations would seem to condemn us, at best, to a protracted state of stunned acquiescence within a decaying social link now consigned to the sleights of hand of the financial industry. This book probes the extent to which it is possible to grasp the breakdown of contemporary capitalism as a self-dissolving dialectic. While capital was always reconciled with its social antagonist (wage labor), this relationship is now past its expiration date, the historical tipping point at which the contradiction stops working for capital and begins to destroy its social foundation.

PROLOGUE

Within an economy now permanently driven by the self-reflexive logic of finance, capital emerges for what it always was: the unbroken accumulation of its fetish-signs. With the melting away of its social mask, we have a chance to observe the elementary form of profit-making, which is simultaneously the measure of capital's freedom and undoing. Today, then, we have come full circle: with the abolition of labor as 'subject of value,' capital unwittingly calls its own bluff and reveals its true colors, the fanatical passion for the reproduction of its insignias. Of course, capital never cared for labor. Rather, it employed it to fuel its own gargantuan appetite, while establishing a value system where that appetite could find social justification. Capital's parasitic disposition, then, does not merely concern the exploitation of surplus labor-time, but especially the retroactive definition of time itself as the social time of labor. However, the referential universe of labor, as we have known it throughout the twentieth century, is now disappearing. Capital, in other words, is reaching the stage that Hegel called *negation of negation*, the dialectical figure where a notion is negated in order to affirm *not* some positive content beyond it, but the intrinsic negativity of the notion itself. If the crisis of contemporary capitalism is to attain the properly Hegelian status of self-relating negativity, we need a collective political will to recognize it as such.

The replacement of labor by the purely differential logic of the capitalist signifier proves that labor valorization was always a structural ruse concealing the univocal vocation of capital. With the vanishing of the law of value, capital has to rely on the efficacy of its timeless drive for self-replication, the unconscious matrix of our world. And this, it would seem, requires us to relinquish the last remnants of critical consciousness and embrace our fate like lemmings jumping off a cliff. While this book is about the implosion of our world, it also argues that the immediate outcome of this process is the rise of "zombie capitalism,"[1] whose more current version is what I call "emergency capitalism." Having reached the end of its journey, capitalism will continue to drag its putrefied body around the globe like a revenant we are unable to shake off. For the foreseeable future, it is likely to survive its structural demise by feigning undeadness, with the support of precarious labor subjectivities and an aggressive ideology that simulates the existence of common values that are no longer there.

If the destruction of the ecosystem represents the *external* limit of our mode of production, the dissolution of the law of value represents its *internal* limit. The fourth industrial revolution will only exacerbate the breakdown of the capital-labor dialectic, now reduced to the bare bones of its contradiction. Ultimately, however, external and internal limits amount to the same *absolute* limit to the production of surplus-value. For the latter now emerges for what it always was, the black hole sustaining the gravitational field of modernity. Especially over the last two decades, this absolute limit has been disguised by various global emergencies that are managed ideologically.

The more swiftly that socially necessary labor is eliminated, without any possibility of being reabsorbed, the more our global civilization condemns itself to delusion and barbarism. Yet, whether we care to admit it or not, an absolute barrier to capitalist expansion is being reached, beyond which there are no economic miracles awaiting us (no Green New Deals or other pious illusions), but a future riddled with dystopian scenarios. In the preface to the *Philosophy of Right*, Hegel wrote that the task of philosophy is to reveal "a form of life grown old,"[2] which as such has exhausted its historical possibilities. We should now give priority to this mission, because the mediation that socialized us for centuries is vanishing, and the ground beneath our feet is giving way. We are at dusk, and the owl of Minerva must prepare to take flight.

But while our shared history is growing increasingly fragile, we remain unable to let go of its framing assumptions. Our anxiety originates in our inability to articulate the terms and stakes of our epoch's contradictions. Confronted by this impasse, the first Hegelian step to take, if we are to turn anxiety into enthusiasm, is to abandon all false hopes and throw ourselves *rationally* into the emptiness of our condition. In Emil Cioran's words, we need to rein in our palpitations and cool down our ardors, in the awareness that all this continues only "because our desires beget that decorative universe which a jot of lucidity would lay bare."[3] Lucidity, however, requires dialectical thinking. We need to grasp our world not as a diverse conglomeration of lifestyles and cultures, but as a totality of social relations overdetermined by the capitalist signifier, the tacit coalition of an increasingly sterile life around a "mass of desires and convictions superimposed on reality like a morbid structure."[4]

Our Hegelian moment, then, is neither a time for hope nor one for wisdom. What it calls for is a cunning sense of fatalism,[5] which alone might help us to relinquish the injunctions that condemn our winded civilization to its credulity. The modern idol of economic value—the metafiction in which all other values are rooted—lies unmasked in front of us, and yet we persist in enslaving ourselves to it, because by renouncing value we would renounce our identities. Our caged restlessness is symptomatic of the strength we lack when facing the prejudice that binds us to our historical destiny. Fanatics without conviction, we are lured on by the wreckage of a flickering world, as we crawl before its altar half-knowing that it exists only for our dispassionate gaze. And yet, "we shall not be able to sustain the ceremony of our contradictions much longer."⁶

From a psychoanalytic standpoint, this book concerns itself with the historical impasse of the civilization that emerged with the modern invention of labor-time. As a discursive phenomenon, the capitalist process of signifying labor is ambiguous. On the one hand, it oversees the liaison between money and labor, establishing the omnipotence of the value-form. On the other hand, however, it gestates that highly enigmatic entity that we call, following Marx, surplus-value. The ambiguity of the capitalist discourse can be dissected through dialectical categories that expose what lies at its core—not merely labor-time but rather lack. Borrowing from Jacques Lacan's psychoanalytic theory, the central assumption here is that a *signifier of lack* occupies the heart of the capitalist narrative. This signifier is none other than surplus-value, a strictly speaking *meaningless* remainder of surplus labor-time that sustains capitalism as a retroactive process of signification. From this perspective, it is the centrifugal force of the capitalist dialectic that, up until the current impasse, has prevented us from falling into the black hole of surplus-value.

As a manifestation of the inconsistency of surplus-value, capital is ambivalent, oscillating between its concrete determinations (salary, profit, interest, rent) and the emptiness from which its relentless dynamism derives. To generate a social anthropology, this dynamism needs both to engage and obfuscate its negative core, which is why wage labor as social category had to be invented. Wage labor is what made capital possible by socializing it into capital*ism*; it is the human mask of capital, its sign and condition of possibility. Capitalism as social discourse requires us to believe that wage labor is the naturalized substance of our lives. Contrary to what Marx thought, however, the dialectic between the forces and the relations of production does not lead to the workers' freedom. Rather, it leads to the unilateral triumph of capital over labor (globalization), and eventually to the disintegration of our form of life. Whatever form postcapitalism will take, it will have to replace the current *mode of production* with a *mode of living* where humans learn to make a different use of the useless.[7]

In psychoanalytic terms, if you take away labor from capitalism you get the capitalist symptom. This book argues that our world is rapidly withdrawing into capital as symptom, which barely conceals its self-destructive drive. Let us recall Lacan's illuminating passage from Seminar 22: "I define the symptom as the way each of us enjoys the unconscious, insofar as the unconscious determines us."[8] If capital is the pulsating enjoyment of its "mad dance," then capitalism was always the ideological fantasy obfuscating the traumatic volatility of its symptom. This fantasy coincides with our social narrative, a bond that relies both on the drive for profit-making and the desire for commodity consumption.

A dialectical approach, however, reveals that the cause of capitalist wealth is not simply a positive substance that gets pumped out of someone who works. The worker as such does not possess value, and value as wealth has no relation with work. Rather, the opposite is true: capital acquires social life because work as wage labor produces nothing but entropy, a *negative* substance around which our societies reproduce themselves. Ultimately, however counterintuitive this may seem, capital acquired social validation through the repetition of its *failure* to gain value. The ideological mask of capitalist power, which affirms itself in circulation, retroactively conceals not merely the exploitation of labor, but especially the radical inconsistency of surplus-value.

In this light, labor-time was always the ruse through which capital covered up the embarrassment of its own impossibility. The signification of work as wage labor is meant to allow us to orient our lives at a safe distance from the blind violence of the capitalist drive. In Lacanian terms, it amounts to *symbolic castration*, the alienating intervention of (capitalist) language that shields us from life's intrinsic volatility. While Marx discovered surplus-value as the leading character in the capitalist fiction, he did not grasp that its truth lies in its being a point of entropy, a productive impasse whose lacking is denied so that it can be possessed as profit. The movement of capital presupposes this passage through surplus-value as signifier of lack. The creation of this signifier via the correlation of money and labor-time allowed capitalism to acquire a socially synthetic language that both hides and engages its negative substance.

If surplus-value is the capitalist cause insofar as it is not there, then labor is, truly, "absolute poverty,"⁹ a *subject without value* posited as *subject of value*. Labor as human praxis, in other words, is rooted in the vitally resilient laboring of the unconscious. And this uncountable, valueless human substance is now resurfacing while the architecture of the work society remorselessly collapses. The unstoppable elimination of labor-power delivers work from its capitalist use, forcing us to confront the elementary inoperability of the human condition. The differential logic of financial capitalism is itself merely a symptom of such inoperability. However, the implicitly traumatic and potentially revolutionary encounter with the symptom of capitalist modernity is neutralized by the formidable 'ideology of simulation' that increasingly saturates our lives, as perfectly exemplified in today's infosphere. A digitized feudalism is in the making, promoted by the new masters of the class struggle, such as the Silicon Valley Tech Giants, Big Pharma, and Wall Street's Mutual Funds. Yet, financialized capitalism is now *unworkable*, bearing in its bosom the very contradiction of its moribund mode of production. It is from this contradiction that we shall begin.

Chapter 1

Labor, Value, and Other Capitalist Delusions

Dialectical Totalities

The starting point of Marx's critique of political economy is the claim that capitalism is a dialectical relation. Just as for Hegel and Aristotle, his major philosophical influences, for Marx the world could only be explained as a self-developing totality rather than as a series of isolated, empirically accountable phenomena. The priority of the whole over its parts means that reality is constituted through dialectical interrelations, which philosophy has a chance to reveal. If history proved Marx wrong on many counts, his compulsive urge to dissect the "real abstraction"[1] of the capitalist relation, which began to haunt him in the 1850s, remains the decisive orientation for any enquiry that wishes to examine the terminal malady of contemporary society, with a view to elaborating the outlines of a new discourse that might correspond with a postcapitalist anthropology. But to begin to carry out this task, we need to delve into the presuppositions of Marx's critique, namely, Hegel's dialectical system.

Marx inherited from Hegel the persuasion that human beings are responsible for creating organic systems of dialectical correlations whose magnitude proves to be greater and more formidable than any of their individual components. In capitalism, this systemic whole is grounded in the *Wertform* (value-form), an intangible entity constituted by the performative interrelation of the commodity-, money-, and capital-forms of value, logical moments of a tirelessly repetitive process. These moments presuppose and feed into each other in a circular and synchronous progression: once capital is in motion, its stages and temporalities merge into one.[2] In its hyperactivity, capital informs its subjectivities by presupposing them as its cause. For this reason, we should reclaim the Hegelian core of Marx's inspiration. Hegel's ambition to capture the dialectical form of a given historical constellation is what qualifies most enduringly Marx's critique of political economy.

The only correct way of understanding the relevance of Marx's critique of political economy for today's world is therefore the Hegelian one: we must abandon the narrow perspective of the *particular* capital, the *particular* enterprise, and the *particular* worker, in order to apprehend capital as the (increasingly polluted) air that we all breathe, or the (increasingly poisoned) sea in which we all swim. We need to perceive capital both as *substance* (the objectivity of political economy) and as *subject* (our social participation in, and validation of, such substance). By starting with Hegel, we have a chance to appreciate how, in capitalism, subject and substance are two sides of the same coin—if you take one away, you lose the other too. This in turn exposes a subtle form of disavowal: whenever we claim independence of thought through adherence to spiritual, political, or ideological values—as typical of all bourgeois societies—we conveniently forget that modern subjectivity is fundamentally *sequestrated* by the totalizing form of value generated by capital's self-expansion. The more the latter's role is denied, the more emphatically it imposes its domination upon us.

Since its inception, bourgeois thought ontologized political economy by naturalizing its foundational categories. While classical liberalism mobilized sets of values that exceeded the apparatuses of direct economic valorization, including such noble sentiments as honesty, solidarity, and respect for the law, this terrain of shared morality was nevertheless legitimized from the start by the production of economic value. Put differently, any narrative of solidarity evoked by liberal discourses old and new is strictly correlative to the institutionalization of the capitalist dogma of profit-making. Far from merely capturing a cynical attitude, this observation allows us to begin to think critically about our condition.

The embedding of political economy as the abstract universality of the modern world is our starting point. While it is clearly discernible in Adam Smith's eternalization of production and exchange as matters of immediate sensible experience and undisputable knowledge, it is also announced in John Locke's dehistoricization of private property and David Hume's utilitarian desocialization of human nature. Historically, the progressive extension of capitalism over other modes of production meant that social life became increasingly dependent on economic valorization. In this regard, as demonstrated by Domenico Losurdo's detailed analysis of liberalism, the philosophical and political tradition concerned with the liberty of the individual—best represented by the writings of John Locke, Hugo Grotius, Adam Smith, and Benjamin Franklin—coincided with a history of violent confiscation, racial genocide, and mass exploitation: "There is no doubt that, along with black enslavement and the black slave trade, the rise of the two liberal countries either side of the Atlantic involved a process of systematic expropriation and practical genocide first of the Irish and then of the Indians."[3]

While aware of the Great Transformation introduced by political economy,[4] Hegel remained fundamentally opposed to liberal individualism, as much as he was opposed to a view of the world where external reality is reduced to a set of measurable and exchangeable entities organized in a system of wants. If in his *Philosophy of Right* Hegel underscored the universal appeal of modern political economy, this appeal concerns the sphere of abstract understanding (*Verstand*) rather than dialectical reason (*Vernunft*). For Hegel, political economy corresponds to a "science that has sprung from the soil of modern times," where "[l]abour has as its aim to satisfy subjective particularity." While "reconciling the opposite elements of the finite sphere," the new science has to do with "principles belonging to the understanding."[5] In other words, Hegel's holistic dialectical thought cannot be squared with (Lockean) liberalism, where the chief function of the state is to protect *homo economicus*'s freedom to maximize self-interest within modern civil society.[6] For both Hegel and Marx, individual freedom is not a natural given, but the historical product of dialectical relationships within the community that are not immediately intelligible.

Hegel's influence on Marx began to prove decisive with the *Grundrisse* (1857–58).[7] After the uncertain settling of accounts with his predecessor in the last chapter of the 1844 Manuscripts (aptly entitled "Critique of the Hegelian Dialectic and Philosophy as a Whole"),[8] Marx started to gravitate toward Hegel again in his quest to unveil the inner logic of capitalism, where self-valorizing value (captured by Marx with the general formula M-C-M') emerged as money's attempt to overcome its historical impasse as simple mediator of commodities (C-M-C'). Marx's narration is well known: to actualize itself as capital, money (wealth accumulated in precapitalist times, as well as money created ex nihilo by the new banking system) began treating labor as a special commodity for market exchange. Once bought, sold, and put to work, the labor-commodity started laying golden eggs, generating surplus-value as the engine of the system's self-reproductive capacity.

With this transition, money upgraded its status from passive *means* of circulation (C-M-C') to active *end* of exchange (M-C-M'), thereby restyling itself as capital. In the former case, money merely mediated the circulation of commodities, whose cause resided outside the valorization process, in social conditions of demand and supply. In the latter case, however, "value becomes its own end rather than mediator of other relations; that is to say that with capital we have before us an individual 'subject.'"[9] One way in which Marx described the difference between the two types of money-form was by borrowing from Aristotle's distinction between *economics* (whose purpose is the creation of use-values) and *chrematistics* (whose purpose is the limitless expansion of wealth).[10] With *chrematistics*, value spins out of control by hijacking the human drive to boundless expansion: the impersonal, anonymous, automatic compulsion to repeat the same circuit of self-multiplication. In the *Grundrisse*, Marx captured the essence of general wealth in capitalism as a self-propelling drive:

> Thus, growing wealthy is an end in itself. The goal-determining activity of capital can only be that of growing wealthier, i.e. of magnification, of increasing itself. [. . .] Fixed as wealth, as the general form of wealth, as value which counts as value, it is therefore the constant drive to go beyond its quantitative limit: an endless process. Its own animation consists exclusively in that; it preserves itself as a self-validated exchange value distinct from a use value only by constantly multiplying itself.[11]

Insightfully, Chris Arthur reads this passage through Hegel's notion of "bad infinite":

> In every measure of itself it finds only its existing limit, which, under the imperative of valorisation, is a restriction to be superseded. Marx argued in his *Grundrisse* as follows: hooked on the general form of wealth (money), capital has an unrestrained and limitless urge ("*schranken- und masslose Trieb*") to go beyond its bounds ("*Schranke*"); every limit ("*Grenze*") necessarily appears as a barrier ("*Schranke*") for it to pass. Capital is so structured that its truth lies not within itself but always beyond itself—a case of Hegel's bad infinite.

The dialectic of *Grenze* and *Schranke* suggests that the capitalist form engages the vital contradiction of the human psyche, for it conceives value both as the rational knowledge of a given measure and as its mad self-expansion, whose Freudian name is death-drive (*Todestrieb*). Or, to use Gilles Deleuze and Felix Guattari's felicitous definition: "Everything's rational in capitalism, except . . . capitalism itself."[12]

Brief Encounters

Let us quickly ponder the historical genesis of capitalism, the passage from the ancient tributary economies of feudal society to mercantilism as initial iteration of the modern world. What matters here is the *dialectical* constitution of the modern world around the two poles of money and labor, which mediate each other to form capital as a dynamic totality. For Marx, labor as producer of use-values is "the everlasting, nature-imposed condition of human existence, and it is therefore independent of every form of that existence, or rather it is common to all forms of society in which human beings live."[13] In Hegelian terms, however, work cannot be merely framed as an eternal necessity that, independent of all social forms, mediates all exchanges between humanity and nature. Rather, precisely as a social form and productive capacity, work is always historically mediated.

If Marx posits labor as the single force that mediates all human existence, a Hegelian reading needs to emphasize the *mediatedness* of this universal power of mediation—the fact that every social constellation has to invent a symbolic role for the productive capacity of human praxis. In this respect, capitalism emerged precisely when work was provided with a new declension of its social function, one that befitted the capitalist mode of production. If work as abstract labor emerged as capitalism's necessary precondition, work as universal capacity exceeds the modern realm of economics. This question was alluded to by Herbert Marcuse in his 1933 essay entitled "On the Philosophical Foundations of the Concept of Labor in Economics," where he claimed that

> labor is not at all primordially a phenomenon of the economic dimension, but is rooted in the process [*Geschehen*] of human existence itself. Precisely through the concept of labor economics is led back to deeper spheres that provide its foundations. Thus, any fundamental treatment of the concept of labor by economics refers to these spheres which constitute its foundation while at the same time transcending economics.[14]

The "deeper spheres" which political economy taps into in order to determine its foundations, are the central character of this book. Marx's theory of value has more to do with them than it is generally assumed. So-called primitive (or original) accumulation, as described by Marx in the final chapters of *Capital* volume 1, corresponds to the historical period when the obscure, intrinsically undefinable potentiality of work was redefined by force to suit the capitalist narrative: a dialectical moment where the role of labor was framed in economic terms. Primitive accumulation no doubt marked the point at which the opportunity for the capitalist revolution materialized. If, as Marx argued, it is "the historical process of divorcing the producer from the means of production,"[15] whereby laborers became "sellers of themselves only after they had been robbed of all their own means of production, and all the guarantees of existence afforded by the old feudal arrangements,"[16] a Hegelian approach should also emphasize how primitive accumulation formalized the liaison between money and wage labor.

While the history of human expropriation that ended feudalism and prepared the ground for capitalism "is written in the annals of mankind in letters of blood and fire," as "[t]he starting-point of the development that gave rise both to the wage-laborer and to the capitalist was the enslavement of the worker,"[17] what remains decisive is the extraordinary fact that the lives of the new masses of 'free proletarians,' once separated from the means of production, suddenly came to be defined by a new historical entity: wage labor. Marx captured this passage very clearly:

> For the transformation of money into capital, therefore, the owner of money must find the free worker available on the commodity-market; and this worker must be free in the double sense that as a free individual he can dispose of his labour-power as his own commodity, and that, on the other hand, he has no other commodity for sale, i.e. he is rid of them, he is free of all the objects needed for the realization [*Verwirklichung*] of his labour-power. [. . .] One thing, however, is clear: nature does not produce on the one hand owners of money or commodities, and on the other hand men possessing nothing but their own labour-power. This relation has no basis in natural history, nor does it have a social basis common to all periods of human history. It is clearly the result of a past historical development, the product of many economic revolutions, of the extinction of a whole series of older formations of social production.[18]

Although the new connection between 'free labour' and money proved to be a form of *enslavement*,[19] the figure of the wage laborer nevertheless represented a paradigm shift in terms of work relations. Unquestionably, the genesis of capitalism was a slow process that lasted three centuries, during which "political coercion played a major role": autonomous economic markets only "emerged after a long apprenticeship under the protection of the state."[20] However, this should not prevent us from stressing the importance of the *formal* shift that affected work as the essential precondition for the constitution of capital.

Despite proclaiming himself both a Marxist *and* an anti-Hegelian thinker, Louis Althusser framed the origins of the capitalist mode of production by reading the latter through his "materialist theory of the aleatory encounter," which accurately describes the structural conditions for the Hegelian dialectic to unfold. Against Marx's teleological penchant, Althusser, already in his first book, *Montesquieu, la politique et l'histoire* (1959), but especially in later unfinished writings, upheld the view that for a mode of production to come into existence there must be a thoroughly contingent, fortuitous encounter between autonomous historical elements "*in a 'floating' state*"[21] such as 'free money' and 'free labor.' All of a sudden, for no teleological reason whatsoever, these elements find a way not merely to connect, but more crucially to hold on to that connection by reproducing it socially.

This is how the anti-Hegelian Althusser mobilized the emphatically Hegelian theme of the 'necessity of contingency' in relation to the problem of the origins of capitalism. As he put it, such an encounter must not merely *take place*, but especially *take hold* through its repetition, thereby becoming

> the accomplished fact of this encounter, inducing stable relationships [. . .]. What matters about this conception is less the elaboration of laws, hence of an essence, than *the aleatory character of "taking hold" of this encounter which gives rise to an accomplished fact* whose laws it is possible to state.[22]

Or, in more explicit terms, "that encounter must last; it must be, not a 'brief encounter,' but a lasting encounter, which then becomes the basis for all reality, all necessity, all Meaning and all reason. But the encounter can also not last; then there is no world."[23] For Althusser, the conditions for capitalism to settle were already there prior to its actual occurrence, such as in Italy's Po Valley during the thirteenth and fourteenth centuries, "where there were certainly men who owned money, technology and energy (machines driven by the hydraulic power of the river) as well as manpower (unemployed artisans)"; however, in that instance the encounter simply "failed to 'take hold.'"[24]

Somewhat ironically, Althusser's materialism of the (aleatory) encounter, which he dubbed a nonphilosophy, enjoys a rich philosophical genealogy: from Epicurus (*clinamen*, or theory of the swerve) to Spinoza, Machiavelli, Cournot, Canguilhem, down to Deleuze's notion of virtuality. It was also heavily influenced by psychoanalytic theory (Freud and Lacan), and as such it returns in contemporary theories of the event (Badiou and Žižek). Crucially, the key philosophical category in Althusser's materialism of the encounter is *retroactivity*: in order to produce a new social order, the encounter has to proceed backwards (like in rugby where, to move the ball forward, it has to be passed backwards). As Althusser put it, "no determination of these elements can be assigned except by working backwards from the result to its becoming, in its retroaction."[25] On this point, however, Althusser was too vague, failing to explain how one should understand the retroactive logic of the encounter; or, put differently, how such retroactive movement turns contingency into necessity. Ultimately, Althusser was unable to theorize the powerful Hegelian figure of the *posited presupposition*, which, as we shall see, involves creating the future by changing the past.

In our case, the object of dialectical retroactivity is work: in order to establish itself as a new social bond (when 'free labor,' i.e., impoverished masses, became available in conjunction with money being released from its feudal role), value in money-form managed to posit wage labor as its capitalist precondition. This was a forceful act of positing that effectively changed contingency into necessity by transforming the old (feudal) determination of work into the new (capitalist) one. From that moment on, earlier socializations of work started being overdetermined by wage labor, which is how the brief encounter between money and work morphed into a lasting love affair, the passionate liaison we call, after Marx, capitalist mode of production.

To put it in Althusser's (French) terms, this is how the *surprise* (the chance encounter) became a *prise* (it took hold).[26] Here it is once again crucial to emphasize the priority of form over the material brutality with which wage labor was imposed historically, since it is the formal act of positing that created its necessity. While contingent material conditions, as Althusser rightly pointed out, had been available prior to their capitalist overdetermination, it is only when wage labor was affirmed as presupposition of self-valorizing money that the ruthless regimentation of labor-power found its ontological legitimacy. And the success of this new totalizing structure depended on its ability to project its own labor-cause onto the past, so that previous configurations of work suddenly appeared overshadowed by the new labor-capital dialectic. The fact that we treat wage labor as an eternal category of human life only confirms capitalism's retro-performative capacity to establish itself as modernity's unsurpassable ontological horizon by reconfiguring, in its own image, previous forms of societal reproduction.

Setzung der Voraussetzungen

What supports capitalism since its inception is a dialectic that mobilizes a *social whole*, a complex system of interrelations whose logic functions precisely because, when we are engaged in it practically, we struggle to make sense of it. In psychoanalytic terms, *it involves our symptomatic or unconscious attachments*, which constitute our contradictory nature as human beings. If that is the case, then the history of labor movements, at least in the orthodox Marxist tradition, is characterized by their fundamental blindness toward their own role in the discourse they attempted to resist or subvert. A Hegelian reading of capitalism should focus on disclosing the constitutive contradiction of labor as subject of value.

The transition to capitalism was enabled by the structural alteration through which work was no longer treated as a relatively obscure subjective capacity to produce things that the wealthy owner of the means of production would enjoy or exchange on the market. Instead, work acquired center stage by morphing into labor-power as *quantifiable* activity. By becoming amenable to value, labor-power became the foundation of modernity. If to understand capitalism we need *a theory of value representation*, since empirical calculations alone miss the target, then the same principle applies to labor as source of value. Labor, in other words, needs to be seen as a *sign* in a narrative, a *character* in a story whose meaning emerges dialectically. At a certain point in our history, work began to function like yeast does in baking,[27] namely, as a leavening agent that converts the fermentable sugars present in dough into carbon dioxide, thus causing dough to expand (no wonder 'dough' is another word for money). Only at that point was the worker granted the prestigious rank of "possessor of the value-creating substance."[28] The main condition for this promotion was that the production process be regimented within a new narrative based on the monetary retribution of labor-time, which—this is the central stake of Marx's critique—included the vampiric extortion of *surplus* labor-time. For capital is, essentially, a vampire that feeds off our time.

This means that the capitalist mode of production attained ontological cogency only when a new narrative concerning the *computability of labor* was installed within the social fabric. When the worker morphed—to use Marx's accurate expression—into "time's carcass,"[29] a new social form based on the valorization of labor as pure motion in time had already imposed itself. The *temporal representation* of labor—no doubt a filiation of the coeval discourse of scientific objectivity—was the *invention* through which capitalism began it course. As such, it marked the beginning of a new social ontology dominated by the ubiquitous yet intangible presence of value. What allowed the value-form to attain dominance in our societies was the gradual normalization of its fetish character: as understood by Marx, we do it (we engage in commodity fetishism) "without being aware of it."[30] Psychoanalysis tells us that the role of the fetish is to cover a lack. More precisely, the fetish is the sentry that patrols the lack of foundations upon whose denial the social is built. The capitalist relation was therefore produced through the unconscious normalization of value-fetishism. The latter in capitalist societies is not the symptom of a pathology, but rather a sign of great health (healthy production, healthy exchange, healthy consumption, and so on).[31]

The central hypothesis advanced here is that the elementary function of the relation between capital and labor—a dialectic of *forms* if ever there was one—was to *conceal* and at the same time *engage* the negative, self-contradictory status of economic value in modern societies. Since we started living under the shadow of the capital-labor relation, value has provided us with ontological cover, a common point of symbolic identification. A Hegelian approach to the critique of value should conceptualize the value-form as a totalizing social representation that functions by mediating itself through labor as its posited presupposition. Put differently, capitalist autopoiesis (self-creation) needed to assert labor-power as its fictional cause. Wage work is a modern invention, which has provided humanity with a shared temporality and, therefore, an existential horizon. Especially since the advent of industrial society, work exchanged on the market and organized into time units has become for us the primary form of alienation/socialization.[32]

From this perspective, Hegel's *Setzung der Voraussetzungen* (positing the presuppositions) ought to be regarded as the crucial dialectical figure of modernity. Its role is to reveal how the capitalist discourse began to thrive by establishing labor as antagonist, whose role in the modern theatre of illusions is to be scientifically valorized and exploited. As André Gorz put it concisely in 1980: "In its struggle with capital, the proletariat takes on the identity capital itself has given it."[33] This identity is, precisely, a presupposition, a representation whose social consistency derives from its solidifying into a specific spatial and temporal magnitude. And, as anticipated, its ultimate role is both to conceal and engage the cause of capitalist accumulation, namely, the fact that *there is no such thing as value*. In other words, at the heart of the valorization narrative there lies a properly speculative paradox: only because there is no such thing as value can value be created as fictional substance of capital; only because living labor is not value can it be conceived as a measurable entity. Or, in Michel Henry's words:

> The impossibility of exchanging labor—that is to say, subjectivity—[. . .] *is the decisive fact that gave birth to this universe and made its invention necessary.* The economic universe is an invented universe; economic reality is an invented reality. What does this invention consist of? Since it is not possible to measure the living force that creates use values and since such a measure is what permits them to be exchanged, the only solution is to replace the unrepresentable and unquantifiable subjective activity with an equivalent that can be measured—with something quantifiable and calculable.[34]

The value-form is what ties capital to its *lacking* substance, making this relationship profitable as the endless quest for a mythical measure that would fill the gap, square the circle, turn impossibility into plenitude. But precisely because value as substance of capital is by definition lacking (thus, a *negative* magnitude), that moment of plenitude is endlessly deferred. While Marx, especially in the *Grundrisse*, came close to grasping this speculative point, eventually he embraced a *positive* articulation of labor-power as substance of value, thereby indirectly endorsing the founding act of the capitalist fiction. As Chris Arthur put it:

> Value is not the social recognition of labour's success at producing a good, but of capital's success in producing a commodity through alienating labour to itself, producing value through exploiting "counterproductive labour" during the working day. Thus, whereas at the start of *Capital* Marx assumes there is no problem about labour appearing as (reified in) value, we now discover [in the *Grundrisse*] that this is consequent only on the success (partial and always contested) of the struggle to subsume labour under capital.[35]

Another way of approaching this issue is by observing how workers were from the start socialized by capital as *value-making machines*. In production, workers are merely nuts and bolts within the mechanism that pumps out surplus-value. This is clearly acknowledged by Marx: "The worker's activity, reduced to a mere abstraction of activity, is determined and regulated on all sides by the movement of the machinery, and not the opposite."[36] As cogs in the apparatus of capital, wage workers play the lead role in its grand narrative, to the extent that, borrowing again from Gorz, "[w]orking-class demands have turned into consumerist mass demands."[37] The entire process of valorization presupposes the transformation of the subjective, pulsating, *unconscious* quality of work into a measurable and therefore *objective* quantity of human energy, which is abstractly equalized to a given amount of money. This foundational process threatens to disable the working class's potential for self-transcendence: "Workers' capacity to recognise the difference between their objective position as cogs in the productive machine and their latent potential as an association of sovereign producers is not inherent in the proletarian condition."[38]

The accumulation cycle begins with a practical monetary transaction that authorizes the labor presupposition of the new mode of production, which in turn hinders workers from redefining their condition outside the valorization process. It follows that there are no autonomous, subversive, or revolutionary subjectivities within the capitalist relation, except for capital itself as *the* subject of modernity, whose power resides in constituting itself as totality by determining its own conditions of possibility. On the one hand, then, capital produces subjective mass subordination by setting up and coordinating an antagonistic relation with exploited labor-power, from which it profits; on the other hand, it reproduces its own viral contradiction in the form of an anonymous force that automatically regurgitates its own semantics, irrespective of changing historical contexts. With capital, the subjective power of self-creation merges with a blind compulsion to accumulate abstract wealth.

The above consideration would seem to disqualify the assumption—voiced with force, for instance, by Italian *operaismo* (workerism)—that within capitalist relations there exists a collective capacity for radical political emancipation. The elementary problem with these assumptions, evidenced for instance in Mario Tronti's classic text *Workers and Capital* (originally published in 1966), consists in conceiving *labor-power* as *autonomous power*, which as such would bypass the dialectical role it plays from the start in the capitalist fiction. The theoretical mistake, with significant political consequences, lies in assuming that when Marx writes of labor as *not*-capital and *not*-value, the negative can be translated into revolutionary antagonism. On the contrary, as summarized by Riccardo Bellofiore, "[l]abour not only *counts* as abstract in commodity circulation, when it is already *objectified*, but it *is* already abstract in production, as *living* labour."[39] Production, in other words, is always-already form-determined by capital. If exchange values are embedded within the principle of universal exchangeability, this is also what qualifies the sphere of production as constitutive of value.

In Hegelian terms, then, it can be seen how, through an act of self-externalization, or *self-othering*, capital gave birth to itself by fashioning a dialectical correlation with labor, thus instituting the socio-ontological boundary within which its mode of production began to proliferate. This eminently *porous* boundary between capital and labor was installed by a narrative concerning the computation of work. One should be able to appreciate the Hegelian logic involved in this move: the inherently fetishistic and self-contradictory status of monetary value in premodern times (when the mode of production was essentially tributary) found a way out of its historical deadlock by externalizing its contradiction onto labor qua antagonistic 'character mask,' which resulted in the epochal invention of the social narrative we call capitalism. This is how a fetish (money) turned into a self-valorizing fetish (capital). We should be very precise apropos this dialectical passage: it is not merely that capital posits the labor presupposition, but that in doing so it presupposes its own positing activity—it presupposes itself as capable of positing its own inverted or alienated substance (labor), so as to ground itself dialectically.

The above act of self-mediation remains, ultimately, as much sovereign as it is ungrounded, for it implies the reciprocal transubstantiation of capital and labor as two speculatively identical moments of the same value-creating process. This suggests that if "[*l*]*abour becomes productive only by producing its own opposite*,"[40] as Marx claimed, by the same token capital exists only by transubstantiating into labor as its alienated other.[41] One cannot reduce the dialectic to the assertion that labor produces a value that is expropriated by the capitalist—the 'exploitation narrative' advanced by most variants of Marxism in the twentieth century. While Marx repeatedly asserted that labor is the substance of value, he also qualified it as a dialectical category incessantly (re) produced by capital. Marx's ambiguity on this crucial speculative matter should not be shirked but assumed as the symptom of his greatness as a thinker.

Hegel after Marx

It is with his notion of the value-form that Marx demonstrates his debt to Hegel, principally because the *forms of value* (commodity, money, capital) are abstract categories resembling the *forms of thought* in Hegel's system. Marx's value-form is as intangible and totalizing a concept as Hegel's Idea. Only as such does it retain a "purely social" function, since "[n]ot an atom of matter enters into the objectivity of commodities as values."[42] Through its "phantom-like objectivity,"[43] value colonizes all social relations inscribed within its remit and can only be recognized by its effects. Here, however, we should also highlight the fundamental difference between these two types of abstraction. While in Hegel the totality of the dialectical forms of thought is unconditional, thus enjoying ontological primacy over material reality, what inspires Marx is the *critique* of the abstraction of the value-form, whose totalizing power is played out against the materiality of labor as producer of use-values. In Hegel, reality coincides with the dialectical self-determinations of the Idea. These determinations are not reality's abstract veil but the necessary formal representations in which anything real and substantial appears. Reality can be experienced as *concrete* only as a formal determination. Hegel's dialectic, in other words, has nothing to do with the external application of logical arguments to objective reality. Rather, it concerns the *Auslegung der Sache selbst*, the dialectical self-development of a specific content.

The main point to highlight about reality's self-development is that *there is no external force determining its content*, since what is at stake is the immanent self-movement of a given reality intended as a unified organic whole.[44] That is to say, the central methodological argument in Hegel, and especially in the *Science of Logic*, is that the concrete can only be derived immanently from the abstract, for the simple reason that there is no concrete reality for us without a modicum of abstraction. This correlation also implies that abstract universality—contrary to what typically naive readings of Hegel assume—cannot sustain itself as an all-encompassing, neutral, all-mediating totality; instead, abstract universality owes its specific determinacy to the relationship it sets up with the particular reality it gives substance to. The implication is that the universal is speculatively identical with the particular insofar as the particular is informed by a universal bias or antagonism. Put differently: the deadlock inscribed in universality, its impossibility or self-difference, qualifies the contradictory and finite character of the particular insofar as each particular is nothing but an attempt to provide an answer for a universal deadlock.

In Marx, on the other hand, the Hegelian dialectic of abstract and concrete, or universal and particular, is framed by a binary opposition between the alienating abstraction of the value-form and the liberating materiality of labor-power, ultimately incarnated by the proletariat as revolutionary subject.⁴⁵ That is to say: while the historical role of the proletariat is conceived dialectically (by antagonizing the capitalist mode of production the proletariat leads humanity to the communist society, where the labor theory of value is finally abolished), the struggle of this particular subject coincides with the struggle of the *materiality* of labor-power against capitalist *abstraction*. Dialectical materialism, in other words, engages with the universal deadlock of human existence not only in the name of a spurious universality liberated from conflict (communism as the classless society of associated producers), but especially as the concrete power of labor over the alienating, phantom-like reign of exchange-values (commodities).

In fact, it is the axiomatic opposition of the liberating materiality of labor to the alienating abstraction of the value-form that authorizes the teleological and intimately theological vision of communism as the heavenly kingdom to come.⁴⁶ The framing of the class-struggle in materialistic terms is informed by a fundamentally undialectical understanding of the fight against capitalist alienation. This is because, as we have seen, the concrete (or particular) can only be conceived dialectically as form-determined, and only as such does it embody the *concrete* 'impossibility' of abstract universality. If, on the other hand, the proletariat stands for the power of materiality over value-abstraction, its revolutionary endeavor can only result in a struggle *against itself* as particular embodiment of that abstraction.

It should not come as a surprise, then, that while Marx did acknowledge Hegel's influence on his critique of political economy, he never explained exactly how Hegel's dialectical ontology assisted him in articulating his materialistic dialectic. Perhaps it is worth conjecturing that if he had tried to make sense of Hegel's influence on his work, he would have had to rethink the political claims of his philosophy. Whatever the case, it remains significant that Marx developed his mature critique of capital after reacquainting himself—as he wrote to Engels in January 1958, while he was compiling the *Grundrisse*—with the method established in Hegel's *Science of Logic*.⁴⁷ It is therefore incontestable that, at least since the *Grundrisse*, Hegel became a central reference for Marx.⁴⁸ While I am not interested in the philological reconstruction of the Hegel-Marx relationship, my aim here is to explore the extent to which Hegel's dialectic informed Marx's critique, as I believe that such investigation can throw new light on what is truly at stake in Marx's analysis of capitalism. In this context, the often-cited line from the postface to the second edition of *Capital* volume 1—where Marx claims that Hegel's dialectic "is standing on its head" and therefore "must be inverted, in order to discover the rational kernel within the mystical shell"⁴⁹—would seem to make sense only if conceived as an attempt to establish the priority of matter over form.

My view is that while Marx did intend to "invert" Hegel (from 'idealistic clouds' to a material reality that had to be accounted for scientifically),[50] he did so by applying Hegel's dialectical method to an object that was largely neglected in Hegel's philosophy: the capitalist mode of production. It is for this reason that *Capital* begins with the analysis of the commodity, "an elementary material phenomenon," rather than with "a basic concept—value."[51] Marx detected an affinity between the Hegelian system and the mystifying forms of appearance of capital, which he aimed to demystify through the employment of "the Hegelian 'contradiction,' which is the source of all dialectics."[52] As stressed by Maurice Merleau-Ponty, among others, for Marx it is "a question of annexing Hegel's logic to the economy."[53] Just as Hegel, in his *Logic*, shows Essence to be a dialectical self-determination of the immediacy of Being, so too Marx wants to demonstrate that the sphere of circulation, which appears incontestable in its immediacy, is dialectically interconnected with, and dependent on, the sphere of production. And just as Hegel develops Essence into Concept as the realization of the self-determination of the Idea, so too Marx wants to show that the relation between circulation and production unlocks the logic of capital as the self-valorization of value.

Thus, Hegel's Being-Essence-Concept triad would appear to mirror Marx's Circulation-Production-Capital triad, or the formula M-C-M', where the money-form found in circulation (M) dialectically relates to the labor commodity (C) to engender capital as a new form of money (M'). This influence of Hegel's *Logic* on Marx's critique is at its most explicit in the *Grundrisse*, particularly where Marx makes use of Hegel's notion of essence as containing within itself its own negation (the contradiction between money as capital and living labor), which enables its development (the self-movement of capital).[54] As in Hegel, essence here is both its contradictory self-identity, and the overcoming (sublation) of this negative ground through compulsive self-expansion. Thus, it can be argued that the processual nature of Marx's definition of capital (its 'becoming') is derived from the processual nature of Hegel's notion of essence.

In what follows, however, I argue that Marx's use of Hegel's method remains marred by a formidably consequential misreading through which Marx, paradoxically, ends up confirming the fundamental assumption of the dialectical logic of capitalism: the accreditation of capital's own ideological secret—the productivity of labor-power—with a revolutionary finality. This is what, paradoxically, makes Marx's reversal of Hegel inherently idealistic, inasmuch as it entrusts the productive forces with a Promethean potential they do not possess. This is the "great delusion"[55] of which Paul Lafargue (Marx's son-in-law) wrote in the incipit of his pamphlet against work. The target of Lafargue's critique is the productivity dogma of capitalists and proletarians alike: "Work, work, proletarians, to increase social wealth and your individual poverty; work, work, in order that becoming poorer, you may have more reason to work and become miserable. Such is the inexorable law of capitalist production."[56] The prophetic import of this passage is undeniable. But before going any further on this side of the argument, let us first focus on what would appear to be the theoretical limit of Marx's materialist dialectics.

The Fantasy of Surplus-Value

As anticipated, discovering the rational kernel of Hegel's dialectic implied, for Marx, the task of inverting not only Hegel's logic, but especially the way in which capital itself appears through the lens of Hegel's logic. For the Hegelian centerpiece and key narrative twist in Marx's critique is no doubt his exposing the *substantial* role of production (the exploitation of labor-power) within the seemingly self-sufficient realm of exchange-values (the market). While it is in the sphere of circulation that the value-form is at home, Marx's central argument in *Capital* is that, if one is to grasp the logic of value, one must connect the shiny universe of circulation with the darker sphere of production. Circulation alone cannot explain how profits are made, since they emerge only through the mediation/exploitation of labor. The ambiguity of Marx's Hegelianism, however, resides precisely in the way he posits labor as substance of value. While in the rough draft of *Capital* Hegel's dialectic of the posited presuppositions is engaged in considerable complexity,[57] in *Capital* Marx tends to authorize an ultimately non-Hegelian understanding of the labor-substance as a value-creating category that enjoys a *positive material autonomy* over the abstracting *telos* of capital. This is probably what prompts Merleau-Ponty to claim that,

> [i]n the second preface to *Capital*, what Marx calls dialectic is "the affirmative recognition of the existing state of things." In his later period, therefore, when he reaffirms his faithfulness to Hegel, this should not be misunderstood, because what he

looks for in Hegel is no longer dialectical inspiration; rather it is rationalism, to be used for the benefit of "matter" and "ratios of production," which are considered as an order in themselves, an external and completely positive power.[58]

In the *Grundrisse*, however, despite naively claiming that "Hegel fell into the illusion of conceiving the real as the product of thought,"[59] Marx's substantialist assessment of labor would seem to be destabilized by the dialectical argument that, in order to produce value, labor needs to be *negated* as noncapital and nonvalue:

> Labour itself is *productive only* if absorbed into capital, where capital forms the basis of production, and where the capitalist is therefore in command of production. [. . .] Labour, such as it exists *for itself* in the worker in opposition to capital, that is, labour in its *immediate being*, separated from capital, is *not productive*.

This is probably the closest Marx gets to conceptualizing labor as a negative determination, that is to say as an object that stands for the *failure* of the subject to achieve a positive identity and therefore a stable place in phenomenal reality. In this respect, "negative determination" is the obverse of the Hegelo-Marxian notion of "determinate negation" [*bestimmte Negation*], understood as the immanent potential for antagonism inscribed in a given situation.[60]

This would suggest that there is nothing *immediately* subversive in labor, for in order to generate change as determinate negation, it has first to withdraw into its own groundless substance. Only as a negative self-relation *without* content (which corresponds to Hegel's figure of the 'negation of negation,' or 'double negation'), can labor aspire to be resymbolized within a new signifying chain or ideological order. While in the next section I will return to this question of labor's potential for self-sublation (*Aufhebung*) by referring to Hegel's notion of concrete universality, for the moment let us stay with Marx's critique. Even as "non-productive labour"—or labor as "purely subjective existence [. . .] stripped of all objectivity," "absolute poverty"[61]—Marx's concept of labor remains characterized by an *affirmative* Aristotelian potential that exceeds capitalist subsumption, which is why it fails to act as determinate negation of capitalism. In other words, the dialectical-materialist antagonism that Marx accords to labor is framed in advance by its positivity qua ideal producer of use-values. As a determinate negation and source of contradiction (Marx, like Hegel, underscores the importance of Spinoza's dialectical principle *"omnis determinatio est negatio"*),[62] Marx's labor misses the dialectical point that negativity is, fundamentally, self-relating, which is why dialectical development does not coincide with evolutionism as something predicated upon a preexisting potential. By the same token, any dialectical transition needs to endorse the indeterminacy of its own presupposed content.

This idealization of labor ends up informing also Marx's concept of surplus-value. For Marx, the contradictory essence of capital is expressed as the surplus-value extracted from labor-power through its exploitation. While surplus-value as such (i.e., not "in the particular forms of profit and rent" but as an abstract totality),[63] captures a dialectical contradiction that enables the self-expansion of capital in general, it remains for Marx a positive entity rather than, literally, a creation out of nothing. As he claims, quoting Lucretius's *De Rerum Natura*, "'*nil posse creari de nihilo*,' out of nothing, nothing can be created."[64] On this key point, then, Marx hardly goes beyond the assumptions of the political economy he critiques.

In defining surplus-value as a function of surplus labor-time—an amount of labor-time that exceeds *necessary* labor-time (necessary for the reproduction of both the worker and capital)—Marx also states:

> During the second period of the labour process, that in which his labour is no longer necessary labour, the worker does indeed expend labour-power, he does work, but his labour is no longer necessary labour, and he creates no value for himself. *He creates surplus-value which, for the capitalist, has all the charms of something created out of nothing.* [. . .] It is just as important for a correct understanding of surplus-value to conceive it as merely a congealed quantity of surplus labour-time, as nothing but objectified surplus labour, as it is for a proper comprehension of value in general to conceive it as merely a congealed quantity of so many hours of labour, as nothing but objectified labour.[65]

By claiming, ironically, that for the capitalist surplus-value appears to be created ex nihilo, Marx is arguably closer to the truth than he thinks. The same can be said about the section of the *Grundrisse* where it is discussed how circulation alone cannot be a source of value-creation:

> Nothing more absurd, then, than to conclude that [. . .] *capital* can make something out of nothing, make a plus out of a minus, make a plus-surplus value out of a minus-surplus value, or out of minus-surplus labour time, and that it possesses, therefore, a *mystical* wellspring of value independent of the appropriation of alien labour.[66]

Although Marx was right in claiming that surplus-value only emerges through "the appropriation of alien labour," at the same time his theory of exploitation misses the connection between the 'minus' of surplus-value and the 'minus' (negative substantiality) of labor itself. What needs to be stressed, then, is that capital as a self-expanding turbine depends on this minus qua *negative* determination, which makes things tick precisely because it fails, therefore escaping dialectical mediation. And, to take the argument a step further, it is precisely on account of labor as negative determination that the commodity acquires its metaphysically mystifying character, as described in the opening chapter of *Capital* volume 1—which, as accurately noted by Adorno, is "truly a piece from the heritages of classic German philosophy."[67]

While labor was characterized by Marx (and especially by his followers since Engels's and Kautsky's sponsorship) as a liberating force of revolutionary opposition (dialectical materialism), it is more accurate and auspicious to conceive it as 1) a dialectical mediator that is *retroactively posited* as the *presupposition* of the self-valorizing loop of capital and 2) the negative substance that constitutes the core of the capitalist dialectic of positing/presupposing, *precisely as a minus that, in capitalism, functions as a surplus*. This allows me to claim not only that every class relation is under the sway of the capitalist dialectic of forms, preformatted by its immanent assumption. More crucially, it also suggests that the 'substantialist paradigm' should be rethought in light of the argument that, paradoxically, the strength of labor-power lies in its self-contradictory status as self-relating negativity. Ultimately, it is labor as negative determination that qualifies surplus-value as cause within the capitalist dialectic.

Hegel in and out of Political Economy

The precondition for my approach to value-critique is the assumption that every social formation is constituted by logical abstractions engaged in dialectical struggle not merely among themselves, but more fundamentally with their own negative core. With the installation of the capitalist mode of production as the ontological horizon of modernity—whereby wealth acquires a specific social value in the commodity-form, which contains "congealed quantities of homogeneous human labour"[68]—labor emerged as integral to the new social narrative. In Hegelian terms, I take labor-power to be a historically specific abstraction of the *concrete universality* of work, to which capital accords determinacy via its employment by the means of production.[69]

It should be added that this understanding of work as concretely universal has nothing to do with Marx's notion of concrete labor as producer of use-values, for, to my mind, the latter makes sense only within the universality of labor-power as capitalist abstraction.[70] More generally, my argument relies on a point that Marx came close to making but eventually shied away from: all sociohistorical determinations of labor qua physiological expenditure of "human brains, muscles, nerves, hands etc.,"[71] are necessarily *abstract* in their own *particular* ways; that is to say, they achieve a social form thanks to a specific correlation with their negative cause, which is what I call the *concrete universality of work*. Contra Marx, a Hegelian approach to labor privileges the negative relation between subject and matter, insofar as it shapes the object as much as the working subject, thus uniting them in their intrinsic self-difference. From a Hegelian viewpoint, work is creative not because it produces values, but because it expresses a singular concreteness that, in its fundamental inconsistency, is universal.

For this reason, work as universal is, for Hegel, on the side of the slave (bondsman): in his/her work qua negation of meaningless materiality, the slave attains the necessary degree of self-mediation. The *Bildung* of work implies, for Hegel, overcoming the state of nature. This is what Hegel has in mind when he defines the slave's work, in the *Phenomenology of Spirit*, as "desire held in check, fleetingness staved off," immediately adding that the "negative relation to the object becomes its *form* and something *permanent*, because it is precisely for the worker that the object has independence." Work is a concrete universal in engaging and tarrying with the negative, not by overcoming it in the positive exchangeability of the object: "This *negative* middle term or the formative *activity* is at the same time the individuality or pure being-for-self of consciousness which now, in the work outside of it, acquires an element of permanence."[72] As underscored by André Gorz, the necessary alienation or self-othering involved in the Hegelian notion of work clashes with its quantitative declension: "Today, in fact, it [work] is most often bereft of what defined work for Hegel: it is not the exteriorization

(*Entäusserung*) by which subjects achieve self-realization by inscribing themselves upon the objective materiality of what they create or produce."⁷³

Let us recall that in his writings of the Jena period Hegel had distinguished between abstract mechanical labor, where "the skill of the single laborer is infinitely limited, and the consciousness of the factory laborer is impoverished to the last extreme of dullness,"⁷⁴ and the singular mastery of one's craft, which on the contrary enriches the self while achieving *social permanence*. Here, however, we should add that for Hegel the concrete singularity of work does not emerge spontaneously, as a natural propensity of the human being, but on the contrary it solidifies through a repetitive process of *self-othering*: "[I]t is a universal routine, and it becomes the skill of the single [artisan] through this process of learning; through its process of othering itself it returns to itself."⁷⁵ In a counterintuitive way, Hegel claims that the *savoir-faire* of the artisan is a result of the alienating routine of learning, the self-discipline through which the worker engages with the object in order to derive from this process a particular skill and a specific social consciousness.⁷⁶

In this sense, two forms of work-related alienation must be deduced from Hegel's account. On the one hand, the necessary alienation involved in self-disciplining, whereby the self acquires individuality by *externalizing* itself in the object of labor and *returning to itself* as self-mediated substance. On the other hand, the young Hegel denounces the numbing effect of abstract mechanical labor, where the former logic is dissolved as the self undergoes a process of dehumanizing objectification, thereby failing to accomplish the process of self-mediation. Although at the time of the 'Jena system' Germany had only been marginally touched by the industrial revolution, we can safely assume that Hegel, who possessed a copy of Adam Smith's *The Wealth of Nations*, was aware that the economy was going to play an increasingly central role in modern society.

While in his vision civil society remained organized around self-regulating corporations, Hegel underlined how the new, manifold system of needs installed by mechanical factory production was bound to realize its own historical abstraction as a form of alienating totality (the market), which he described in no uncertain terms as "a life of the dead body, that moves itself within itself, one which ebbs and flows in its motion blindly, like the elements, and which requires continual strict dominance and taming like a wild beast."⁷⁷ Although Hegel did not develop a critical theory of the capitalist mode of production, he did realize that the nascent work society was characterized by a new quantitative understanding of value based on the generalized production and exchange of a surplus:

The surplus set into indifference, as something universal and the possibility of [satisfying] all needs, is *money*, just as labor, which leads to a surplus, leads also, when mechanically uniform, to the possibility of universal exchange and the acquisition of all necessities. Just as money is universal, and the abstraction of all these, and mediates them all, so *trade* is this mediation posited as activity, where surplus is exchanged for surplus.[78]

This critical focus on the role of labor abstraction in the constitution of modern society would seem to fade, or remain marginal, in Hegel's mature works. His *Philosophy of Right*, for instance, privileges ethical and juridical frameworks over the analysis of the form of value and the dialectic of labor, thus effectively endorsing the market as a regulative (albeit unstable and contradictory) socio-ontological structure. This neglect of the self-contradictory aspects of political economy no doubt signals the limit of Hegel's social theory. In the *Philosophy of Right*, for instance, Hegel leaves the relationship between labor and value largely untheorized. Rather, he describes value as a "universal characteristic, which proceeds from the particular object and yet abstracts from its special qualities." As such, "[v]alue is the true essence or substance of the object, and the object by possessing value becomes an object for consciousness."[79] Hegel here further specifies that quality is both retained and superseded in any quantitative valorization of the object. Labor, on the other hand, is defined not in relation to the value it informs, but as "an habitual use of skill acquired by practice and implying objective conditions."

The emphasis on "training" and "habituation to an employment" confirms that for Hegel work is, chiefly, a necessary form of alienation that has to do with the worker's singular capacity to shape the object.[80] While he briefly refers to the abstraction involved in the modern division of labor and the mechanization of production, ultimately his account remains descriptive:

> The result of the abstraction of skill and means is that men's interdependence or mutual relation is completed. It becomes a thorough necessity. Moreover, the abstraction of production causes work to be continually more mechanical, until it is at last possible for man to step out and let the machine take his place.[81]

Fundamentally, then, the mature Hegel limited himself to defining labor abstraction and valorization as socially legitimate categories of modern society. However, it is important to stress that for him any abstract universal is the actualization of a process of dialectical self-deployment that remains largely unaccounted for. It is to this immanent process that I now turn my attention to.

Chapter 2

Implosion of the Work Society

Modernity's Self-deployment

Perhaps the key to grasping Hegel's failure to explore the dialectical form of the economy of his time resides in the observation that, from a certain point onwards, he became almost exclusively preoccupied with presenting the figure of *reconciliation* as the counterintuitive unity of contradiction (contingency, particularity) and its overcoming (necessity, universality). Thus, while necessary alienation in universalized social substance does not liquidate the living contradiction that universality implies—since necessity itself is nothing but the mode of *appearance* of contingency—nevertheless the emphasis falls upon the (unresolved) speculative unity of these opposites, rather than on the socially critical exposure of their inconsistent content.

Especially in the *Philosophy of Right*, the last work published during his lifetime (1821), Hegel is concerned with demonstrating the speculative coincidence of such couples as subject and substance, particular and universal, contingency and necessity. This suggests that the critical disclosure of specific substantial inconsistencies (such as the economy's) is not so much disavowed but considered immanent to the dialectical process itself. In this regard, it is significant that Hegel conceives the possibility of sharing in the general wealth produced by labor as conditional on two particular contingencies: individual skill, which varies according to natural endowment, and "capital." The claim that inequalities of wealth depend "on something which is directly the individual's own, namely, capital,"[1] should not be dismissed as a meaningless tautology, since capital here is conceptualized as *its own cause*, a category that is not external to but identical with (the unequal distribution of) wealth. That which Hegel calls "the objective right of particularity of spirit," which "produces inequality out of spirit and exalts it to an inequality of talents, wealth, and intellectual and moral education," is a figure of contradiction in both particular and universal terms, and as such it has attained *actual* social existence in modern political economy. To oppose to it "a demand for equality," Hegel argues, "is a move of the empty understanding."[2]

In discussing the modern definition of wealth, in other words, Hegel refers to a *form of universality* that, as such, deploys its unity with self-difference. While he argues that rural civilization reflects a "simple disposition unaffected by the desire for wealth," he focuses on the universal character of the new "work society," based on the dominance of the "industrial class," the "more abstract collective mass of labour," and therefore "commerce" and "money" qua "general medium of exchange." And he describes this new social totality as "a particularity which has become objective" in organizing communal life.[3]

When (in the section "Civic Community" in the *Philosophy of Right*) Hegel discusses the selfishness of the particular person who is "an end to himself," adding that, in respect of this selfishness, "[m]any modern teachers of political science have not been able to develop any other view of the state,"[4] he is describing particularity as "measureless in its excess,"[5] which as such is a threat to ethical life (*Sittlichkeit*). However, he also points out that "the principle of particularity develops of its own accord into a totality, and thus goes over into universality," where "it has its truth and its right to positive realization."[6] What Hegel calls "the infinitely subjective substantiality of the ethical life" requires that the particular achieves universality as "it gives itself limit and finitude in the natural needs and the region of external necessity."[7] This act of self-limitation performed by self-interested particularity is the necessary prerequisite for the acquisition of universality and ethical life.

In other words, Hegel is fully aware that the free development of a civil society driven by economic self-interest alone will produce wealth for some and misery for most (the rabble), as well as the nihilistic bad infinite of endless search for more wealth. And yet the point to emphasize is that, for him, the passage into modernity implies not the imposition of some external system of values alternative to those of political economy, but rather the awareness that "the particular person is essentially connected with others. Hence each establishes and satisfies himself by means of others, and so must call in the assistance of the form of universality. The universality is the other principle of the civic community."[8] In short, this is how Hegel describes the self-actualization of the modern state out of the contradictory condition of liberal civil society. What matters to him is the overlap of contingency and necessity in the processual self-deployment of modernity. Put differently, Hegel does not ask himself whether he should or should not endorse the nascent modern industrial society. This would be a methodological error from his perspective. Rather, his aim is to track the consolidation of modernity as a universal form generated by a specific self-relation of the particular.

In Hegel's view, then, the particular historical actualization of the universal idea that corresponds to modern society as a "system of wants" coordinated by the state,[9] cannot be merely negated or critiqued from a position of externality, for the simple reason that "the particular gives to the universal its adequate content and unconditioned self-direction."[10] Ultimately, insofar as it is a mode of appearance of the particular, the universal is that which "secures for itself an objective embodiment."[11] Or, differently put, that which obtains a socio-ontological form that both transcends self-difference and embodies its unity with it.

While in Hegel's political theory the self-contradictory character of civil society is both transcended and maintained in the political form of the state, what needs to be emphasized is that the state as universal representative of the subject's freedom emerges logically from within the self-contradictory "soul" of a modern civil society increasingly driven by egotistic self-interest rather than shared values. The early 'subjective' critique of economic rationality, then, is not simply dismissed here; rather, it is objectified within the idea of modernity's self-deployment. So instead of asking ourselves whether Hegel was more inclined to endorse liberal or communitarian ideologies,[12] the crucial dialectical question we should consider concerns the formal reproduction of a social bond where a particular content (the economy) achieves universal validity by actualizing its immanent contradiction, which remains at its heart.

Hegel was fully aware that the economy of his time (the nascent industrial society) mobilized its uneven particularity to achieve that universal socio-ontological character that Marx later called *Wertform*, the value-form. And the state for Hegel was the political structure where that particularity (a liberal society motivated by economic self-interest) was actualizing itself organically as universal. Whether or not we agree with Hegel, the fundamental purpose of his political theory is to demonstrate the dialectical self-deployment of modernity from family to civil society and the state, as opposed to the moralistic critique of modernity from an external perspective, which he considered as impossible as any speculation about the future. As he put it in the preface to the *Philosophy of Right*: "Philosophy is [. . .] an inquisition into the rational, and therefore the apprehension of the real and present. Hence it cannot be the exposition of a world beyond, which is merely as a castle in the air, having no existence except in the terror of a one-sided and empty formalism of thought."[13]

Hegel believed that, vis-à-vis society and politics, the task of philosophy was to chart the inner self-deployment of the idea that shapes a given civilization: "The rational is synonymous with the idea, because in realizing itself it passes into external existence. It thus appears in an endless wealth of forms, figures and phenomena."[14] So Hegel insists that his treatise of political science "must be on its guard against constructing a state as it ought to be," because philosophy is "its time apprehended in thought," and not a matter of "opinion, which gives room to every wandering fancy." Rather, philosophy reconciles with reality when reason is recognized "as the rose in the cross of the present."[15] Reconciliation therefore means aligning subjective reason (form) to the substance of the present (the "cross" as content) insofar as they both progress only via their inconsistencies. If we miss this crucial assumption—that philosophy can only proceed immanently by reconciling reason with its substantial and inherently self-contradictory actualization in reality—we miss Hegel himself. In this respect, although Hegel failed to apply his method to the immanent laws of capitalist economy, he was cognizant of the economy's central role in modern societies.

As he claims in the introduction to the *Philosophy of Right*, when he opposes his dialectical logic to the scientific method, any assumption of critical externality misses the speculative coincidence of thought and its object. Dialectics, Hegel writes,

> does not merely apprehend any phase as a limit and opposite, but produces out of this negative a positive content and result. [. . .] Hence the dialectic is not the external agency of subjective thinking, but the private soul of the content [. . .]. To consider anything rationally is not to bring reason to it from the outside, and work it up in this way, but to count it as itself reasonable. Here it is spirit in its freedom, the summit of self-conscious reason, which gives itself its actuality, and produces itself as the existing world.[16]

The role of contradiction, or self-relating negativity, remains therefore crucial for grasping the dialectical self-deployment of spirit in relation to society as a system of right. Hegel introduces his thesis that "the system of right is the kingdom of actualized freedom"[17] by according ontological priority to the universality of thought as, *in primis*, pure abstraction: "To make something universal is to think. [. . .] When I say 'I,' I let fall all particularity of character, natural endowment, knowledge, age. The I is empty, a point and simple, but in its simplicity active."[18] Similarly, "thinking itself, devoid of personality, [is] the productive subject."[19]

This initial moment of pure and blind abstraction, in which I withdraw from "all particularity of character" in order to be able to say "I" and therefore think, is upheld by Hegel as the necessary condition for "the transition from blank indefiniteness to the distinct and definite establishment of a definite content and object."[20] In other words, abstract negativity constitutes the foundational point for its own negation into a particular content, where the initial negativity is not eliminated but actualized. And in criticizing Fichte and Kant, Hegel emphasizes their inability to perform the ensuing speculative step, that is to say to "apprehend the negative as immanent in the universal."[21] Hegel's defense of speculative logic against mere understanding ("all truth, as far as it is conceived, must be thought speculatively") involves "infinitude as negativity which refers itself to itself," and as such it is "the ultimate source of all activity, life and consciousness."[22] The exercise of reason implies the self-relating negativity of the subject (qua abstract I) as condition of possibility of self-consciousness, intended as existence that finds itself in its own self-othering, that is to say in its speculative coincidence with substance.

Self-caused and Self-realized Reason

One of the most penetrating exemplifications of Hegel's speculative principle is the passage on love as "the most tremendous contradiction," which we find at the start of the section on the family in the *Philosophy of Right*. Hegel writes:

> Love is in general the consciousness of the unity of myself with another. I am not separate and isolated, but win my self-consciousness only by renouncing my independent existence, and by knowing myself as unity of myself with another and of another with me. [. . .] The first element in love is that I will to be no longer an independent self-sufficing person, and that, if I were such a person, I should feel myself lacking and incomplete.

> The second element is that I gain myself in another person, in whom I am recognized, as he again is in me. Hence love is the most tremendous contradiction, incapable of being solved by the understanding. Nothing is more obstinate than this scrupulosity of self-consciousness, which, though negated, I yet insist upon as something positive. Love is both the source and solution of this contradiction.[23]

Love, then, has nothing to do with a naive understanding of *recognition* (mutual dependency of two rational identities), which is why Hegel describes it as "the most tremendous contradiction." In love, self-consciousness coincides with its own negation qua self-othering, and the unity of self and other is reached only through the estranging experience whereby the self renounces a positive and substantial determination.

On the strength of its speculative character, love works as a powerful metaphor for Hegel's dialectical vision, where subjectivity finds itself in its self-contradictory coincidence with substance. In the *Philosophy of Right*, then, Hegel demonstrates the maturity of his thought, beyond what he came to regard as the naive critical attitude of the Jena period. Now, the negativity of a subjective attitude is shown to be inherent to the affirmative dimension of the object. This is why Hegel states, in the last pages of his work, that "world-history [. . .] is self-caused and self-realized reason."[24] Similarly, in the *Encyclopedia* the Notion (or Concept) is defined as the principle of freedom insofar as it is *self-realized substance*.[25]

These claims suggest that, for Hegel, all philosophy can do is observe how, in order to progress, humanity employs reason as the power of its own self-deployment, the capacity to generate movement out of itself—that is to say, out of its own radical insufficiency. Put differently, *effects produce the causes that produce them*: the cause does not come first; it is generated retroactively by what appears as its effect. From this perspective, transcending capitalism would mean changing its own cause via an effect that no longer works for capitalism. This, in turn, implies that transcendence is always self-transcendence: the possibility to move beyond capitalism is to be found within the logic of capital itself, more precisely within its negative core (or dialectical impasse). Historical development can only be conceived within this process of necessary self-actualization. Human reason constantly creates the conditions for its 'really existing' historical occurrence and sustenance. And the key point about this self-causative loop, or bootstrap, is reason's engagement with its negative core, for the positing of the cause can only be conceived, logically, if we assume that there is no cause to start with, no metanarrative that justifies reason's work from an external position.

It is in these speculative terms that we should grasp the dialectic of the concrete and the abstract universality of work. If indeed the elementary task of work is "creating forms endowed with duration and permanence,"[26] as Marcuse put it paraphrasing Hegel, this task is accomplished by mobilizing the radical indeterminacy of the human condition that continues to inhere in any form of duration and permanence. Or, in Marcuse's precise words, it is accomplished by mobilizing "the primordial negativity of labouring activity,"[27] which is "essential excess of being over existence"[28]—a definition that aligns neatly with my understanding of work as a concrete universal.

In the chapter titled "Teleology" of the third part of the *Logic*, Hegel emphasizes how a concrete universal, differently from an abstract universal "that only *subsumes*," owes its status to its particular self-externality, that is to say, to its "impulse to repel itself from itself."[29] This impulse, formally comparable with the Freudian drive, is precisely what abstract universals remain blind to, insofar as they exclude/negate certain concrete determinations without recognizing the self-reflexive character of such act of negation: the latter does not merely refer to the excluded determinations, but it bends backward into its self qua universal, thus making universality *concrete*.[30] This theme is indeed central to Hegel's entire 'subjective logic' (volume 2 of the *Science of Logic*), in which the concept is construed as a universal whose totality is both "absolute determinateness" and a *"negation of determinateness,"* "the diremption of its self."[31]

When Hegel discusses concrete universality in connection with the dialectical couple genus-species, for instance, he characterizes genus as a universal form that, while extending over its particular species, at the same time is itself one of its own species. As such, it is a "negative self-identity"[32] that cannot precede and subsume its determinations, but instead emerges through its correlation with one of them: a genus encounters itself in one of its species as its determination, which also means that its framing capacity is not external, but it arises from within, immanently, in its connection with a particular species. In a well-known section of *The Holy Family*, aptly entitled "The Mystery of Speculative Construction,"[33] Marx and Engels missed this speculative point when they claimed that the universal, having no content of its own, cannot derive the particular. But what Hegel means is exactly the opposite: precisely because the universal is inconsistent, it can only realize itself in a correlation with the particular. To use Marx and Engel's own example: there is no universal fruit outside the particular pear-fruit, apple-fruit, almond-fruit, and so on, since each of them embodies the incompleteness of the universal notion of 'fruit' itself. The same applies to 'capital in general,' whose negative self-identity manifests itself in the eternal conflict of particular capitals. Or it also applies to the generic concept of production, which exists only in relation to one of its determinations (for instance, the capitalist mode of production).

This speculative point tells us that what is *concretely* universal is not the diversity of various species belonging to a common genus, but the self-difference or exceptionality of each species as it coincides with the inconsistency of the genus. While "[s]pecies are contrary inasmuch as they are merely *diverse*," and "[t]hey are *contradictory*, inasmuch as they exclude one another," nevertheless "each of these determinations is by itself one-sided and void of truth." Instead, concrete universality captures the speculative coincidence of the self-disjunctive singularity of each species and their negative unity in their genus: "In the 'either or' of the disjunctive judgment, their unity is posited as their truth, which is that the independent subsistence of the species as *concrete universality* is itself also the *principle* of the negative unity by which they mutually exclude one another."[34] The exclusionary logic of diverse identities, then, is *concretely universal* only inasmuch as it embodies their self-relating negativity, since the latter captures the *universal principle* of their negative unity, thus undermining any (intrinsically identitarian) notion of abstract universality.

Slavoj Žižek provided a clear account of the disruptive potential of concrete universality:

> Abstract universality is the mute medium of all particular content, concrete universality unsettles the identity of the particular from within; it is a line of division which is itself universal, running across the entire sphere of the particular, dividing it from itself. Abstract universality is uniting; concrete universality is dividing. Abstract universality is the peaceful foundation of particulars; concrete universality is the site of struggle—it brings the sword, not love.[35]

In short, a concrete universal can only manifest itself as the partiality of an engaged stance: it is *concrete* because it shows purpose, and it is *universal* because it embodies an impossibility that is common to all subjective positions. Thus, every concrete universal expresses itself as a form of self-relating *inadequacy*: it is unable to realize itself in a particular identity; it is the self-difference, or rupture, that belies the false universality of any abstractly universal determination. To paraphrase Hegel's definition from the *Phenomenology of Spirit*, the difference between concrete and abstract universality is the *defect* of both.[36] This is because concrete universality unmasks the defect (radical incompleteness) of the abstract universality it refers to. In today's global constellation, for instance, concrete universality is represented by all those subjects who are dislocated, excluded, scarred, prevented from achieving their particular identity within the social order. Here it is crucial to insist that the inherent insufficiency of a particular identity is, literally, universal: it defines the global social order itself as inconsistent and lacking, therefore vulnerable and open to its reconfiguration.

Real Work and Labor-time

The above Hegelian topic can be translated into psychoanalytic terms through Jacques Lacan's dialectical categories—for instance, that of sexual difference. The latter is concretely universal because it signals how the impossibility of each sexual identity overlaps with the universal inconsistency of sexuality as such. In Lacan, the very difference between Symbolic and Real reflects the antagonism between abstract and concrete universality: the concreteness of the Real, its particular unruliness, coincides with the universal inconsistency of the Symbolic. In that respect, labor as working capacity falls under the rubric of the Real of *jouissance*—always the intractable *work of the unconscious*, which relates to a specific modality of enjoyment—while the valorization process is the (failed) attempt to convert this unconscious, concrete *laboring* into a sociosymbolic fiction whose legitimacy claim rests on the ideological affirmation, and policing, of the abstract exchangeability of the labor-commodity. Lacan's definition of the unconscious substance of work in nonproductivist terms is crucial for my Hegelian argument on the breakdown of the capitalist dialectic. Lacan's linking of work to knowledge and thus to the Real of *jouissance* (work as *savoir-faire*, *poiesis*, unconscious knowledge-at-work), in Seminars 16 and 17,[37] grants his theoretical position a dialectical advantage over other similar critiques of labor that emerged in France in the early 1970s, such as those of Jean Baudrillard, Georges Bataille, and Jacques Camatte.[38]

One way of capturing Lacan's notion of work as a negative substance informed by unconscious knowledge, therefore not amenable to computation and valorization, is by cross-fertilizing it with Hegel's dialectical articulation of crime as inherent to the law,[39] a clear case of infinite judgment or speculative coincidence of opposites. For Hegel, crime is not merely antagonistic to the law, but dialectically correlated with it, as it constitutes the law's foundation: to originally assert itself, the law must act as a negative (criminal) force. More precisely, crime for Hegel is the self-relating negation the law harbors as its foundation while attempting to conceal it by asserting itself as a positive set of norms. Thus, the Real intractability (negativity) of crime enjoys priority over the symbolic law, which is, strictly speaking, a secondary event that remains within the horizon of crime. The dialectical couple crime-law is therefore formally identical to the couple work-labor: strictly speaking, work is 'criminal' inasmuch as it is rooted in the antagonistic surplus of the unconscious, or in what Lacan names the Real of *jouissance*.

This is nowhere more evident than in crime films that focus on the *savoir-faire* of their protagonists. One of the best examples of this logic can be found in Michael Mann's masterpiece *Thief* (1981), the story of a safecracker and jewel thief named Frank (James Caan) whose exceptional criminal dexterity is antagonized not only by the law, as we would expect, but more significantly by ring leader Leo (Robert Prosky), who helps Frank in order to capitalize on his thieving ability (he wants Frank to work for him, thus turning his singular skill into profitable labor). The film's main battleground, then, shifts from 'Frank vs. the law' to 'Frank vs. Leo,' where we witness the figuratively capitalistic struggle to turn the unruly core of *savoir-faire* into economic value. This is brilliantly conveyed by Leo's brutal rant toward the end of the film, after his henchmen beat up Frank to coerce him into obedience:

> You treat what I try to do for you like shit? You don't wanna work for me, what's wrong with you? And then, you carry a piece, in my house! You one of those burned-out demolished wackos in the joint? You're scary, because you don't give a fuck. [. . .] You got a home, car, businesses, family, 'n' I own the paper on ya whole fuckin' life. I'll put ya cunt wife on the street to be fucked in the ass by niggers and Puerto Ricans. Ya kid's mine because I bought it. You got 'im on loan, he is leased, you are renting him. I'll whack out ya whole family. People'll be eatin' 'em in their lunch tomorrow in their Wimpyburgers and not know it. You get paid what I say. You do what I say, I run you, there is no discussion. I want you work, until you are burned-

out, you are busted, or you're dead . . . you get it? You got responsibilities—tighten up 'n' do it. [. . .] Back to work, Frank.

Here everything should be endorsed as a true representation of the work society and its violence. Capitalist universality means that *labor counts because it is counted*: the condition for its exploitation and profitability is its abstract quantification into discrete units of labor-time. This *reification of time* into valorized fragments of *labor-time* regulates all processes of socialization, while reducing time itself to a homogenous (Adorno would say 'mythical') entity to which life is ferociously subjected in its entirety. Much of the feeling of inevitability and immutability that qualifies social life under capitalism originates from this compression of the experience of time into commodified units of labor-time. Furthermore, when free time is returned to the worker, it can only return as the time of exchange-value, the temporality that presides over market exchange.

The crucial 'productive' implication here is that the indefinable character of subjective time is not only subsumed, but also *assumed* by capital, as it passes over into the acephalous process of self-valorization. Hence, the quantification of labor-time is not merely an act of computation, for it implies the vampiric extraction of the unmeasurable *quality* of time, which makes of capital "an animated monster which begins to 'work,' 'as if its body were by love possessed'" (as Marx writes quoting Goethe's *Faust*).[40] What animates the capitalist monster is precisely the production of a nonsymbolizable, nonsensical remainder out of the narrative that marries labor and money. Surplus-value is the 'less than nothing' that emerges out of valorized (symbolically castrated) labor-time, and it is this *less* that animates capital's endless search for the *more* in the self-valorization process.

This, in short, is how modern political economy constitutes itself by turning the exceptionality of work as concrete universal into an abstract universal. In this respect, capital confirms its status as a dialectic of forms that parallels Hegel's dialectic of forms of thought. However, this does not mean that Marx was right in considering Hegel a philosopher of bourgeois modernity.[41] Rather, it means that by mobilizing Hegel's dialectic we have a chance to accomplish what Marx eventually missed: the comprehension of the inner logic governing the self-reproduction of the modern forms of value (commodity, money, and capital) *inclusive of their negative, concretely universal core*. My Hegelian reading of labor as a moment of capital, emphasizes the failure of capital's tautological mechanism of self-expansion. The contradictory status of labor is precisely what capitalism 'employs,' in a risky operation that, today, is no longer working, thus heralding the collapse of our mode of production.

Calling the Bluff

Let us not forget that, for Hegel, philosophy "paints its grey in grey." When Hegel states that "[t]he owl of Minerva begins its flight only with the falling of dusk," he asserts that philosophy's fundamental task is to reveal "a shape of life grown old," the approaching end of a given form of life.[42] Hegel's philosophy, in other words, affirms the ontological priority of the inconsistent ground, the lacking presupposition, the vanishing mediation; while Marx's stands, ultimately, for the actualization of a positive substantiality. The Hegelian dialectic cannot rely on positive foundational categories. Its development is not securely grounded, for its conditions of possibility must be posited as contingent social forms. This means that the *end*, for Hegel, has always-already taken place, because the end is the insubstantial ground of any dialectical ontology based on the installation of particular presuppositions that, as such, can claim foundational value only insofar as their normative capacity continues to be antagonized by their inconsistency.

As with Freudian psychoanalysis, for Hegel the normativity of reason operates against the background of its own impossibility, with which it engages in a battle it has always-already lost. Thus, being able to reflect on the elementary indeterminacy of the human condition is reason's highest task, the point where it achieves what Hegel terms "absolute knowing," which is freedom. Never before had philosophy dared to claim that reason reaches itself the moment it loses itself. The difficult theoretical point to grasp here is that the vanishing of reason's capacity to sustain its own conceptuality, or normative power, is also *its condition of possibility*, which continues to haunt reason as its explosive truth. Impotence is the ground for any assertion of potency, as Lacan grasped when he defined the phallus as a signifier without signified, which as such—that is, as meaningless—sustains signification: it inaugurates meaning "by its disappearance."[43] This suggests that the radical *contingency* of any foundational principle that claims social normativity is both what antagonizes such normativity from within, as its grounding truth, and what makes it necessary as a fictional/ideological configuration. It is precisely this theme of the speculative coincidence of opposites that we should repoliticize today, when the capitalist mode of production, having triumphed, implodes. This, incidentally, has nothing to do with postmodernist antifoundationalism, which by opposing (or deconstructing) all claims to normativity, effectively affirms its own foundationalism in inverted form— that is to say, in the form of universally abstract relativism.

To grasp the modality of the ongoing decomposition of our social bond, we need to insist on the centrality of the capital-labor dialectic. As we have seen, capital uses labor-power as the inexhaustible dynamo for the generation of surplus-value by positing its abstract computability as necessary precondition. While labor for capital is a countable entity, in itself it remains uncountable, a negative self-relation that survives its violent socioeconomic abstraction. It is an object of calculation and exchange on the surface, but also a mesmerizing (unconscious) subjective quality. In short, it is an *abstract* and a *concrete* universal.

The volatility of the above contradiction is what capital attempts to use in its favor by positing labor as its own externality (in Hegelese, as 'external determination'). However, precisely because capital and labor overlap as speculatively identical manifestations of value, the radical heterogeneity of work as concrete universal threatens to unmask the negativity of capital itself, the fact that capital, in its deepest configuration, coincides with its own lack of determinacy. Today *labor betrays capital*, its masterminding alter ego in the pantomime of endless productivity, just as much as *capital betrays labor*. This is not as a result of labor's antagonistic (revolutionary) self-awareness as exploited class, but because the current rate of technological automation threatens to expose the devastating (Hegelian) contradiction that underlies the historically productive bond between capital and labor.

As more and more living labor is expelled from the job market, increasingly without a chance of reentering the rat race, work *formally* becomes *what it always-already was*, a negative entity that, as such, resists full assimilation within the socioeconomic matrix. Conversely, no longer supported by its internal presupposition, capitalist universality comes apart at the seams and is forced to reveal its *bluff*, the emptiness at the core of its narrative. In respect of the apparent inevitability of this explosive dynamic, Peter Fleming claims that, to prevent collapse, the capitalist state is coming to the rescue of the economy:

> The state plays an important role here as well. It has stepped in and negotiated a deal with the business world to keep the myth of employment alive, precisely by not automating everything. This would explain the recent and dramatic drop in technological

investment in the UK and elsewhere. Business agrees to the arrangement not because it is a fan of workers but due to its major stake in the status quo. Once again we notice that the capitalist state is far savvier than the business class with respect to the self-preservation of the capitalist universe. The neocons currently governing the polities in the West and Global South fully understand Marx's law of the falling rate of profit. Without labour or its vast theatre of loss, we could no longer have capitalism, for basic and obvious economic reasons.

Fleming's argument is echoed by the late David Graeber's claim concerning the creation of "bullshit jobs."[44] The system is forced to invent perfectly useless jobs to maintain a semblance of consistency and viability. From a 'work society,' our world is mutating into a 'workless society' that looks like a 'society of shitty work.' However, while the state may well—as it has always done—attempt to tame the overexcitement of capital, it cannot prevent another wave of "creative destruction,"[45] as private investment in new technologies is the only card the system can play to postpone its own collapse, irrespective of how catastrophic the creative destruction will be.

What we are facing today is the idiotic persistence of a mode of production that runs counter to its own (re)productive logic. Capital is abolishing jobs, but not their exploitation. The less work there is for everyone, the longer we are required to work, since technological unemployment depresses wages. The elementary logic of this situation was already clear to Marx, who in *Capital* argued that

> machinery produces a surplus working population, which is compelled to submit to the dictates of capital. [. . .] Hence that remarkable phenomenon in the history of modern industry, that machinery sweeps away every moral and natural restriction on the length of the working day. [. . .] Hence too the economic paradox that the most powerful instrument for reducing labour-time suffers a dialectical inversion and becomes the most unfailing means for turning the whole lifetime of the worker and his family into labour-time at capital's disposal for its own valorization. [. . .] machinery is the surest means of lengthening the working day.[46]

In Gorz's words: "Instead of liberating people from poverty, toil, stress and stupefying work, labor-saving technologies are used to strengthen the domination which capital, via the logic of markets, exerts on all aspects of people's working and living conditions."[47] Indeed, if capital has assumed totalizing power over everyone's lives, it is because wage work continues to retain its social and ideological centrality while being eliminated across all fields of employment. The ongoing obliteration of wage work points to the necessity of a radical redefinition of the macroeconomic meaning of work beyond the wage society. Marx's labor theory of value is no doubt obsolete, and yet it provides the basic coordinates for us to understand the dilemma of contemporary capitalism. It does so for a surprisingly simple reason: it shares those coordinates.

André Gorz's Critique of Work

Capitalist economy appears increasingly disjointed from the way it functions. At first glance, it would seem that we need a different economy, one that is not centered on the valorization/exploitation of labor, but that instead is able to account for a fairer distribution of what it can produce independently of the key capitalist variable of labor-time, which is dramatically fading. However, as the last four decades have shown, this is no easy task to accomplish, not least because capital is immensely resourceful in the art of ideological obfuscation and self-transcendence: while it cannot alter the elementary dialectical matrix of its mode of production, it very ingeniously projects its own decrepit logic into the firmament of human destiny. We continue to live in capitalist utopia, no matter how adept we are growing at seeing through it. Gorz grasped very clearly how utopia informs societies based in the extraction of economic value:

> The utopia which has informed industrial societies for the last two hundred years is collapsing. And I use the term utopia in its contemporary philosophical sense here, as the vision of the future on which a civilization bases its projects, establishes its ideal goals and builds its hopes. When a utopia collapses in this way, it indicates that the entire circulation of values which regulates the social dynamic and the meaning of our activities is in crisis. This is the crisis we are faced with today.[48]

Sharing many ideas with value-critique thinkers like Jean-Marie Vincent, Moishe Postone, and Robert Kurz, Gorz understood that the capitalist system undermines its own utopia by progressively making wage labor superfluous and by destroying the working class. His proposals for a concrete utopia of liberated time, intermittent employment, and guaranteed basic income, were centered on the assumption that the system would continue to provide wages with purchasing power despite the planned shortening of working time. Gorz, however, was also aware that "from the macro-economic point of view, an economy which, *because it uses less and less labour*, distributes less and less wages, inexorably descends the slippery slope of unemployment and pauperization." His proposed solution was that any loss of income would be compensated by a "second cheque," in other words a "social wage" to be drawn from a "guarantee fund," a pool of "socially produced wealth."[49] Here, however, the key issue of value production in an increasingly automated society would seem to be deferred rather than confronted head-on, for how would the social wage be financed? Gorz proposed financing it with an indirect tax on products and services, which would gradually lead to the replacement of market prices with "a system of political prices":

> As the unit costs of automatable products tend to become negligible and their exchange value is threatened with collapse, society must inevitably provide itself with a system of political prices reflecting its choices and priorities as regards individual and collective consumption. Choices as to what is produced will ultimately have to be made in terms of the use value of products and the system of prices will be the expression of these choices.[50]

It is important to emphasize that Gorz defended the emancipatory character of work as a "socially determined and remunerated" activity. In other words, he defended the social alienation of work in the Hegelian sense of the term. For him, the right to work, to participate in productivity, remains a *social duty* that is the basis of citizenship. The inevitability of reducing working time in an increasingly automated society, then, does not detract from the fact that work continues to be "governed by universal rules and relations which liberate the individual from particular bonds of dependence and define her or him as a universal individual, that is, as a citizen: her or his paid activity is socially recognized as *work in general* having a *general social utility*."[51] The Hegelian flavor of Gorz's position, which disqualifies any utopian proposal for the abolition of work, is evidenced in the following passage:

> The emancipatory character of work in the economic sense derives from this: it confers upon me the impersonal reality of

an abstract social individual, as capable as any other of occupying a function within the social process of production. And precisely because what is involved is a *function* which is impersonal in its essence, which I occupy as an interchangeable person among others, work does not, as is generally claimed, confer a "personal identity" upon me, but the very opposite: I do not have to engage the whole of my person, the whole of my life in it; my obligations are circumscribed by the nature of my occupation, by my work contract and by social legislation. I know what I owe to society and what it owes me in return. I belong to it by virtue of social capacities which are not personal, during a limited number of hours specified by contract and, once I have satisfied my contractual obligations, I belong only to myself, to my own family, to my grassroots community.[52]

From his first reflections on the unstoppable shedding of paid work, which is articulated in his 1980 book *Farewell to the Working Class*, Gorz went on to dialecticize the relationship between the reduction of working time, the obligation to work, and the expansion of the private sphere of personal autonomy within society: "The right to work, the duty to work and one's rights as a citizen are inextricably linked."[53] Although often flirting with libertarian positions, Gorz eventually championed a model based on the political mediation of the economy in a society that was supposed radically to rethink the role of subjective time outside work, while relying on wages from intermittent employment and guaranteed social income. The subordination of the economy to politics (heteronomous regulation) for the achievement of social objectives and a degree of personal autonomy, means that Gorz was perfectly aware of the necessity for social alienation, which is why he vied for the retention of both money as "a universal equivalent" and "a legal code and system, an organ of coordination and equalization, in short, *the thing we call a state*."[54]

While Gorz's proposals were tentative, and mostly meant to ignite discussions *about*, rather than provide a blueprint *for*, the future, they nevertheless reflected his conviction that the current socioeconomic model was bound to end in barbarism if left to itself: "Evading the issue and the need for radical innovations and change implies that you simply accept the fact that society, as it decomposes, will go on engendering increasing poverty, frustration, irrationality and violence."[55] Although Gorz's suggestions remain open to criticism (concerning, for instance, the feasibility of a guarantee fund for the distribution of social income in a society where wage work becomes marginal; or the retention of commodity relations in a society emancipated from work) what they stand for is, ultimately, the urge to think a transition to a form of life characterized by the reduction of working time, and therefore by the potential "to increase considerably the space available for non-commodity forms of production and exchanges of good and services."[56] In short, the Hegelian merit of Gorz's approach was to have focused on the negative substance of the work-based society; to have identified, in other words, the negative variable—the withering away of labor-power—where new preconditions to social life would have to be created.

From this perspective, what is required is not merely a new economy, but a new social relation, for a job-based consumer society deprived of its anchoring point in quantified labor-time must by necessity redefine time socially outside the work relation—a cultural transformation that requires the installation of a new set of societal habits and desires. But precisely because this transformation is *not* taking place, the objective vanishing of socially necessary labor-time continues to be disavowed through the suspension of the boundary between work and nonwork activities. In the neoliberal work society of corporate ethics and zero-hours contracts, labor-time paradoxically pervades all aspects of life.[57]

Disaster Economics

While Marx revealed his debt to Hegel by describing the transition from C-M-C (money-form of value in pre-capitalist times, where the "simple circulation of commodities"[58] does not produce surplus-value) to M-C-M' (capital-form of value, where the anticipation of money produces surplus-value), he nevertheless failed fully to unravel the grounding inconsistency of the capitalist discourse. In his materialistic adaptation of Hegel's dialectic, Marx missed the key intuition according to which, insofar as it is a logical *whole*, the self-valorization dynamic of capitalist accumulation is structured around a *hole*, a lacking or negative cause. This hole qua absent cause is the central character in the capitalist whodunit, the main ingredient in political economy's pie. This is why Jacques Lacan's discourse theory of the late 1960s, where the social bond is shown to be articulated around its lack, can be employed successfully to explore the role fulfilled by the missing cause in the structural shift from C-M-C to M-C-M'.

The hole in the capitalist dialectic, however, is increasingly difficult to locate and politicize. Individually and collectively, we continue to invest our beliefs in the obdurate capitalist fantasy by displacing its demise onto an array of negative placeholders whose role is to strengthen that very fantasy. Typically, collapse takes on different masks, from ecological catastrophe to nuclear war, global terrorism, and, recently, microbiological pandemic. The ideological function of these preventive scenarios is to make sure we do not see the inconsistency of our mode of production. Today, more than ever, we should therefore acknowledge that all debates are null and void without reference to political economy and its naturalization. Whether we lament the ascendancy of populism, the return of authoritarian ideologies or the coming environmental collapse, we would be mistaken in disconnecting the ethico-political implications of these symptoms from the implosive regime of structural violence that constitutes their global economic context.

Today, the semantics of the labor-capital narrative are regressing into their original lack of foundations. Both historically and structurally, our conundrum can be summarized as follows: the economy's drive to generate surplus-value is both the drive to *exploit* the workforce and to *expel* it from the production process. While this contradiction constitutes the lifeblood of capitalism as a mode of production, today it backfires, turning the economy into a mode of permanent devastation. The reason for this change of fortune is an *objective* failure in the structural configuration of the capitalist machine: the current, unprecedented acceleration of technological automation means that more labor-power is ejected from production than reabsorbed. The symptoms of this situation are clear to see, for the contraction of the volume of wages means that the purchasing power of a growing part of the world population is falling, while poverty and debt spread like wildfire. As less value is produced, capital seeks immediate returns in the financial sector rather than in the real economy or in long-term investment in socially constructive sectors like education, research, and public services in general.

In what is only deceptively a different context, our systemic breakdown scenario is hinted at in the 2019 miniseries *Chernobyl*. The simple yet enlightening insight provided by the series' last episode is that the failure of the nuclear reactor that led to the Chernobyl disaster of April 1986 was not, in the last instance, imputable to the plant's engineers, despite their criminal behavior in insisting to carry out a safety test without the necessary precautions being put in place. Ultimately, the reactor exploded because of a design flaw in the control rods, an elementary system failure that had to do with the backwardness of the technology employed at a time of widespread economic recession, which first Andropov (1982–84) and then Gorbachev (1985–91) unsuccessfully attempted to stem. Chernobyl therefore can be read as a metaphor for the breakdown of a mode of production that shared with capitalism the same reliance on the exploitation of the workforce. While in the 1980s Western capitalism was able to overcome its valorization crisis through a significant *salto mortale* in the financial sector, this option was not available to Soviet state capitalism, which therefore went broke. However, we are talking about the same systemic collapse originating in the formidable acceleration of automated productivity (third industrial revolution). The line between capitalist state and state capitalism is thinner than we think.

As Martin Ford put it, most jobs today are "squarely in the sights as software automation and predictive algorithms advance rapidly in capability."[59] This is true not only of the manufacturing industry, but also of other key sectors like logistics, services, and retail. Furthermore, algorithms, Big Data, and AI are quickly colonizing the knowledge industry, including areas until recently considered resistant to intelligent technologies. All this means that we are already facing the collapse of the virtuous feedback loop between production, wages, and consumption. In such a bleak context, recourse to financial prestidigitations is the only way in which collapse can be camouflaged into implosive inertia.

Let us stress that unbridled capitalism's financial overdose and credit binge are not simply destructive revenants of a more stable, rational, and healthy socioeconomic structure. Instead, they capture the essence of the capitalist dialectic insofar as it is increasingly incapable of profiting from its labor contradiction. This means that, while the financialization of our economy originates in the same ontology of self-valorization that characterized it from its inception, it is also a symptom of its exhaustion and fundamental impotence. As Robert Kurz argued back in 1999:

> Credit (i.e., the mass of the savings of society which are collected by the banking system and lent for the purpose of production or consumption in exchange for interest payments) is quite a normal capitalist phenomenon, but its importance has grown as the capitalist expansionary development accelerated. Credit implies the usage of future money revenue (and, hence, of a future employment of workers and the future creation of substance of value) in order to maintain the present operation. The development of credit since the beginning of the 20th century, and likewise the "de-substantiation" of money through the disconnection from the real substance of value (i.e., the end of

the gold standard), already indicated the immanent barrier of the process of valorization, which comes to the surface today.⁶⁰

Kurz claimed that a falling rate of profit, as predicted by Marx in volume 3 of *Capital*, could exist next to an increase in the mass of profit only if "the corresponding future money revenues were really obtained on the basis of the real substance of value (including payments of interest). But this was made increasingly impossible by the Third Industrial Revolution," and, today, by the fourth.⁶¹ The implication is that, as the route into credit and annexed "casino capitalism" becomes inevitable, the gap between the creation of fictitious capital and its basis in labor-power widens, with catastrophic consequences. When 'money that makes money work' (finance) cuts its ties with 'money that makes people work,' the result can only be a drastic devaluation of existing capital with breakdown potential. The 2008 crisis effectively confirmed Kurz's prediction (and those of others before him)⁶² that "the simulated perpetuation of the capitalist expansion starts to reach its limits."⁶³

In 2019, more than a decade after its latest devastating crisis, the world economy was still plagued by the same sickness that caused the global credit crunch of 2008, as well as the economic crises of the last forty years or so. COVID-19 has now exacerbated this situation, with global productivity growth heading toward stagnation.⁶⁴ In this setting, debt-leveraged financialization constitutes contemporary capitalism's specific line of flight, the inevitable *forward-escape route* for a model of socioeconomic reproduction that has reached its historical limit. By continuing to borrow from the future (imaginary profits to come), the economy only has one desperate aim: to disguise its own collapse.

COVID-19, then, accelerated a process of implosion *that was already underway*. The prepandemic world economy was already in the grip of a debilitating inertia with ominous deflation scenarios looming large. Most crucially, it was suffocating under an unsustainable mountain of debt, private and public. At the end of 2019, the global debt-to-GDP ratio had risen to an all-time high of 322 percent,⁶⁵ 40 percentage points higher than in 2007. Many public companies could not even generate enough profit to cover interest payments on their own debt, and were managing to stay afloat only by issuing new debt.⁶⁶ Whichever macroeconomic indicators we look at—debt, industrial production, trade, unemployment, and so on—they all tell us that the global economy was on the verge of a repeat 2008 *before* the arrival of the mighty virus. The ship, in other words, had only been steadied for the short term, and warnings that a new global slump was brewing were issued daily. All that was missing was a trigger, which, as a rule, takes the form of an accidental occurrence that sparks the inevitable explosion—just like the Lehman Brothers collapse did for the 2008 crash. In recent years, luminaries of various persuasions have debated how to stimulate an economic recovery typically characterized by rising investment creating more jobs and boosting consumption. However, regardless of the measures taken (austerity packages or expansive monetary policies), such recovery eluded us. Instead, COVID-19 arrived.

While it looked like the proverbial straw that breaks the donkey's back, the virus also carried unforeseen opportunities for those in charge of the capitalist matrix. Firstly, it allowed them to deflect the world's attention away from a morose economic system that has run out of excuses for its failures; secondly, it accelerated the concentration of wealth and power in the hands of the dominant sectors of the economy (especially the digital oligarchy, Big Pharma, and biotechnology) while strengthening the supremacy of the financial industry.[67] After all, spinning the narrative of a natural cataclysm that nobody could have predicted is much more convenient than having to answer for the devastating consequences of economic depression. The mystifying operation through which the coronavirus was turned into *the* cause of the world's suffering (World Pandemic I, as Bill Gates put it) made sure that no enquiry could be launched into the implosion of our mode of production.

The Difficulty of Letting Go

The main challenge we are facing today has to do with our inability to translate the *objectively self-destructive* character of our condition into a *subjective (political) desire* to move beyond it. This passage can only be dialectical. Any alternative to the *Aufhebung* of our exhausted historical form may well lead, sooner than we think, to global devastation. This includes the hypothesis of a *seamless* transition to postcapitalism, as argued by some optimistic commentators since the debate on labor-shedding automation has gone viral.[68] To grasp today's stakes we should perhaps resurrect Freud's quotation from Virgil's *Aeneid*: "Flectere si nequeo superos, Acheronta movebo." Freud was very fond of this line and used it as the motto for his seminal work *The Interpretation of Dreams*. It means, roughly, "If I cannot bend the heavenly powers, I will have to move the powers of hell." Read as a psychoanalytic metaphor, it points to the difficult retroactive recalibration of our unconscious attachments (modes of enjoyment) to our world as the necessary step toward collective emancipation. Simply put: if we cannot reconfigure our capitalist modes of enjoyment, it is both pointless and counterproductive to fantasize about postcapitalism.

In his book *The Brave New World of Work*, sociologist Ulrich Beck described this challenge in a series of existential questions on the attachment to valorized work:

> Along which coordinates can people's lives be structured if there is no longer the discipline of a paid job? Is its loss not the root of all evil: drug addiction, crime, social disintegration? How can people's basic existence and social status be assured if these no longer rest upon performance at work? Which ideas of justice, or even of social inequality, can serve as the measure of people's lives, if society no longer thinks of itself as "hard-working" or "industrious"? What does the state mean if one of its most important sources of tax revenue—paid employment—dries up? How is democracy possible if it is not based upon participation in paid employment? How will people's social identity be determined, if they no longer have to tell themselves and others that "what they do in life" is one of the standard occupations? What would be the meaning of governance, order, freedom—or even of society itself? Visions that work will progressively disappear as the social norm rebound off the faith that most people still have in job miracles and in themselves as citizens of the work society. Having lost their faith in God, they believe instead in the godlike powers of work to provide everything sacred to them: prosperity, social position, personality, meaning in life, democracy, political cohesion. Just name any value of modernity, and I will show that it assumes the very thing about which it is silent: participation in paid work.[69]

While Beck, the theorist of the risk society, abstains from confronting macroeconomic presuppositions—which ultimately makes his analysis superficial—we should nevertheless heed the warning contained in the just-quoted passage: in capitalist modernity, wage labor informs the totality of our subjective existence, *including its unconscious mode of enjoyment*. We should therefore go all the way in our critique: labor is the anthropomorphic side of capital. It is through wage labor that capital as automatic subject begins to become identical with the human species, attempting to subsume all (human) life under its reproductive principle. However, this also means that the more capital 'emancipates' from labor, the more humanity has a chance to emancipate from capital, although the latter may look more like a "controlled implosion," an "implosion in slow motion" in which the system feigns its own survival while continuing to impose its dominance by authoritarian means.[70]

Yet our libidinal attachment to the work society is so ingrained that it continues to define us even after the traditional notion of productivity has largely been replaced by the alchemic rituals of the finance industry. This point can be quickly summarized via another brief filmic reference. Woody Allen's *Blue Jasmine* (2013) delivers a very simple but effective punch: a precise description of the standard psychic imbalance affecting the global post-2008 subject. Jasmine (Cate Blanchett) marries a rich broker, ends up penniless after he is incarcerated for corruption, but *she still flies first class*. That is to say, she believes (literally, for she suffers from an increasingly damaging form of delusion) that, despite her sudden fall from grace, she continues to belong to the glitzy Park Avenue society of the 0.1 percent. While she knows that her economic circumstances have drastically worsened, she refuses to accept her new working-class condition, taking refuge instead in delusional fantasies, as if her identity had been torn asunder from her social context.

It would be useful to concede that, within the ongoing crisis of our *form of life*, we are all like Jasmine—we share her psychology. Despite its increasingly manifest deterioration, the Crystal Palace of the *Wertform* continues to identify us by providing the illusory sense of domesticity and everydayness we crave, thus defusing any real antagonism. Today's ideology of deterrence is preventing us from identifying any points of systemic rupture. Perhaps Fyodor Dostoevsky's Crystal Palace (together with Walter Benjamin's Parisian arcades) is still the architectural metaphor that, as Peter Sloterdijk argues, conveys more convincingly the hermeneutics of the *spell* of contemporary capitalist alienation.[71] Such metaphor "invokes the idea of an enclosure so spacious that one might never have to leave it."[72] (Or, to use a metaphor from popular culture, a Hotel California where "we are all just prisoners of our own device," since "you can check out at any time, but you can never leave").[73] Capitalist captivity owes its power not merely to appearing necessary, but to constantly evoking the openness of freedom: "It implies the project of placing the entire working life, wish life and expressive life of the people it affect[s] within the immanence of spending power."[74]

Although its artificial ether is growing toxic and unbreathable, the great palace of consumer capitalism continues to tell us who we are by shaping the flows of our desires, in a colossal effort to immunize us from its contradictions. This way, it continues to function for us as our "substance," a concept Lacan captured with the deceptively simple term big Other (*grand Autre*): the commonly shared, unwritten, and naturalized symbolic rules that confer a veneer of meaningfulness upon human life. After the wake-up calls of the 2008 credit crunch, and after COVID-19, we have once again opted to retreat in the big Other of the capitalist relation, a globalized fiction that stages the immunizing powers of the economy as our natural and indestructible habitat. But how long will our epochal delusion last? How long, in the face of the disintegration of society, will we be able to endure this stale ceremony? The next chapter delves further into the impotence of our social discourse.

Chapter 3

The Missing Cause

Chronic Constipation

I have argued that our world's loss of symbolic efficiency is caused by our growing inability to churn out the necessary mass of value required for the reproduction of the social machine. Due to escalating technological progress over the last forty years or so, capital finds itself increasingly embarrassed vis-à-vis its mission of squeezing surplus-value out of the exploitation of labor-power. With the unleashing of artificial intelligence this will truly become *mission impossible*—game over.

Lacan alluded to capital's embarrassment in a passage of Seminar 16 (session of March 19, 1969), when he stated that capitalism introduced "liberal power" in order to mask its being "against power," against any form of political power that might dare to challenge the economy. Lacan's point is simple: in modern liberal democracies, "power is elsewhere"—not in politics, but in the complete dominance of the economy over politics. While Lacan claimed that the 1917 Russian revolution was essentially a (failed) attempt to "restore the functions of power" over the discourse of the economy, he pointed out that this situation

> is not easy to hold onto, precisely because in the time when capitalism reigns, capitalism reigns because it is closely connected with this rise in the function of science. Only even this power, this camouflaged power, this secret and, it must also be said, anarchic power, I mean divided against itself, and this without

any doubt through its being clothed with this rise of science, it is as embarrassed as a fish on a bicycle now.¹

This passage is worth pondering. Lacan avers that capitalism is a form of "camouflaged power" whose intimate nature is self-destructive ("divided against itself") because of its being strictly conjoined with the epistemology of modern science. In fact, he continues, "something is happening in the science quarter, something that transcends its capacity for mastery." The embarrassment of contemporary societies driven by the "curious copulation" between capitalism and science, as Lacan will put it in Seminar 17,² lies in the fact that, all of a sudden, the big Other's capacity to provide symbolic cover for our lives weakens dramatically. Hence the significance of Lacan's (in)famous warning to the subversive students of May 1968 that all they aspire to is a new master.³ Except for the revolutionary spirit of those years, the situation described by Lacan in March 1969 is still very much our situation. The erosion of the capitalist big Other today reaches new heights due to the devastating impact of scientific innovation. To use one of Lacan's most popular mottos, we could say that the copulation between science and capital today misfires, revealing that there is 'no such thing as a sexual relationship' between them, but only awkward impotence.

In its hunger for profitability, the economy undermines the basic condition of its own reproduction, namely, the exploitation of human labor. The organic composition of capital is now so high that financial speculation is the only *logical* way forward. In an exemplary case of what Hegel called *the cunning of reason*, it is as if contemporary capitalism was desperate to show us that it does not need any revolutionary opposition: it can destroy itself much more efficiently on its own. Precisely at its point of maximum expansion and ideological triumph, capitalism unwittingly reveals its fundamental loneliness and vulnerability.

This point is by now shared by thinkers of diverse political and ideological persuasions. Jeremy Rifkin, for instance—a staunch promoter of collaborative commons—has for some time argued that "[c]apitalism's operating logic is designed to fail by succeeding," insofar as "intense competition forces the introduction of ever-leaner technology" that boosts productivity, reduces marginal costs to near zero and with it the global mass of profits. Rifkin's conclusion is disarmingly Hegelian:

> Ironically, capitalism's decline is not coming at the hands of hostile forces. There are no hordes at the front gates ready to

tear down the walls of the capitalist edifice. Quite the contrary. What's undermining the capitalist system is the dramatic success of the very operating assumptions that govern it. At the heart of capitalism there lies a contradiction in the driving mechanism that has propelled it ever upward to commanding heights, but now is speeding it to its death.[4]

As anticipated, a similar diagnosis was made by André Gorz in early 1980s works like *Farewell to the Working Class*, *Paths to Paradise*, and *Critique of Economic Reason*. Gorz's later *Reclaiming Work*, published in 1997, opens with the following enlightening passage:

> A new system has been established which is abolishing "work" on a massive scale. It is restoring the worst forms of domination, subjugation and exploitation by forcing each to fight against all in order to obtain the "work" it is abolishing. It is not this abolition we should object to, but its claiming to perpetuate that same work, the norms, dignity and availability of which it is abolishing, as an obligation, as a norm, and as the irreplaceable foundation of the rights and dignity of all.[5]

The embarrassment of which Lacan spoke in the late 1960s, then, derives precisely from the speculative coincidence of capitalist success and failure (phallic power and impotence), against the background of the seamless fit between technology and accumulation. Today, Marx's insight that "the *true barrier* to capitalist production is *capital itself*"[6] rings truer than ever, since it is not conditioned on the dream (turned nightmare) of a higher social order (communism) but on the cunning silence of reason, which allows for the free deployment of capital's full (i.e., self-destructive) potential. For Hegel, power is truly antagonized only when we "make it return into itself as movement, so that it negates itself." The "cunning of reason" (*die List der Vernunft*) implies not the art of combat in open confrontation, but the ability to bring the opponent to face the inherent contradiction of its own position. Our global economy is facing a similar destiny. The free deployment of capital's full potential is undermining its very premises. And in Hegel's words, "silence is the worst, vilest cunning"[7]—which, incidentally, is exactly what Lacan had in mind when he formulated his discourse of the analyst: the analysand, faced by the silent cunning of the analyst, talks and talks until he/she is confronted by the meaninglessness of the symptom, which he/she has a chance to assume. Here, however, the big question is: (when) will capitalism assume its symptom? Or, perhaps more pointedly: is capitalism not already its own symptom?

Let us propose the following explanation: in itself, the capitalist discourse is split between its self-destructive drive and a strategy of self-containment inscribed within its astute logic of self-valorization, whereby the value-fetish conceals the intrinsic impotence of the discourse. Lacan, as we shall see, endorsed both aspects: the peculiar type of capitalist alienation lies in its centrifugal or deterritorializing impetus coupled with the centripetal or reterritorializing logic of valorization, where every aspect of life is mediated by exchange-value. At the same time, however, he intimated that this balancing act is undermined beyond repair by the alliance with technology: capital runs very fast, "comme sur des roulettes" (as if on wheels), and yet "ça se consomme si bien que ça se consume" (it consumes itself to the point of consumption).[8] What is alluded to here has now become self-evident: automation inadvertently calls the bluff of the valorization fetish, showing how—in Lacan's terms—surplus-value (*Mehrwert*) was always surplus-*jouissance* (*Mehrlust*), the symptomatic core and potential breaking point within the capitalist logic of self-expansion.

In a brief and rare mention of automation, Slavoj Žižek liquidates the real prospect of mass technological unemployment in a couple of, ultimately, superficial lines: "But why fear this prospect? Does it not open up the possibility of a new society in which we all have to work much less? In what kind of society do we live, where good news is automatically turned into bad news?"[9] These rhetorical questions effectively work against a background of disavowal: while most of us would, at least in principle, welcome a society where there is less work to do, the point to stress is that such prospect clashes ominously with the overwhelming evidence that the capitalist valorization process continues to be imposed on us ideologically as the only possible fuel on which to run the social machine.

A Worldless Discourse

Lacan's "capitalist discourse" was meant to capture the novelty of a social formation whose fundamental purpose is to turn the potentially debilitating impasse of the social relation into a powerful engine of self-reproduction. This is how capitalism promises to deliver the modern subject from *castration*, that is to say, from the frustrating experience of lack brought in by the symbolic law (language) and consubstantial with human life. The capitalist discourse, in other words, aims to liquidate any awareness that "[w]e are ourselves only by the sum of our failures."[10]

While the promise of castration's foreclosure marks a major shift in the modern subject's libidinal economy, it also engenders a world in constant flux, overdetermined by the economy's lust for self-expansion. In this respect, the repressed negativity of the productive relation between capital and labor returns as the disavowed cause of the self-valorization process. While consumers gobble happiness pills from birth to grave, the system continues to feed off what it lacks. Profit, which one has never enough of, is homologous to surplus-value as the 'less than nothing' spawned by the valorization of labor-time.

As anticipated, Lacan grapples with the dual nature of capitalism as an *objective* dynamism whose functioning depends on *subjective* interpellation (ideology). On the one hand, capitalism promises paradise on earth, lifting all prohibitions as typical of traditional power structures based on symbolic authority; but, on the other hand, it stealthily administers commodified enjoyment as a disavowed form of superego authority or categorical imperative: "you must enjoy (consume)!" In fact, it is by relying on this overlapping of avowed freedom and disavowed command that the capitalist discourse attempts to revolutionize the logic of Lacan's four discourses (Master, Hysteric, University, and Analyst). It does so by establishing a radically new form of mastery.

The four discourses are presented by Lacan through quasi-algebraic configurations of four terms whose permutations (anticlockwise quarter-turn rotations) engender four signifying chains (modes of communication, social bonds). The main feature of these discourses is the *production of a structural impasse* that cannot be absorbed fully within signification, and that therefore antagonizes the discourse in different ways. With his theory of the four discourses Lacan proposes that any social bond, as such based in linguistic alienation, is decentered by the unconscious disturbance it generates. Just like the psychoanalytic subject, the social link is self-split, divided against its own logic, direction, and mode of appearance. This self-division is what threatens to undermine it, thus making it unstable and changeable. In my understanding, the subject's immersion in a given discourse reproduces, broadly speaking, the Hegelian dialectic of subject and substance, for in both cases the two entities are held together by their shared inconsistency.

Against the dialectical logic of the four discourses, capitalism for Lacan aspires to being a 'discourse without discourse,' thus setting up a worldless world, a disalienated space where dispersed, atomized human beings share only their common obligation to work and consume.[11] What characterizes this scenario is less the actual satisfaction of the drives than the generalized conviction that the human animal is selfish, narcissistic, and hedonistic,[12] or else characterized by that "blasé attitude" of indifference to others about which wrote Georg Simmel, which is testament to "the fading of all values into a mere mediating value."[13] Although the egotistic ideology informing capitalist utopia may be more readily associated, today, with the hegemony of neoliberalism and financial capitalism,[14] where self-discipline is assumed as the illusion of personal freedom, there is little doubt that it had already inspired the ideas of classical economists like Adam Smith, whose notorious metaphor of the invisible hand of the market aimed precisely at affirming self-interest.

While discussions of Lacan's critique of capitalism tend to emphasize the totalizing manner in which its discourse seeks to impose a noncastrated narrative, I argue that the significance of this critique is profoundly dialectical, as it concerns not only the subject but also capitalism's objective, structural self-destructiveness. Although the capitalist discourse lends itself to be read as a diabolical contraption for subjective capture,[15] it seems to me more auspicious to reflect on Lacan's warnings that the capitalist project is destined to fail by succeeding. Today, when the triumphant march of the economy has annihilated all antagonists, and the enjoyment of the value-fetish has acquired global traction, we are presented with the exceptional situation where the capitalist genie has found its way out of the bottle and is faced *only by itself*—by the libidinal core of a restless dynamism spinning around its own central emptiness.

In this scenario, the economy is free to visit all its structural violence upon societies that in many parts of the world are already on the verge of collapse. However, in doing so it also reveals its own impotence, which should energize us into planning a different architecture for our social bond. The structural impotence radiating from globalization should neither be negated nor overcome, but actively integrated within a new political project that prioritizes our collective destiny—not in the name of a utopian future, but of our radical finitude. Our feeble postpolitical imagination, however, seems unable to seize on this opportunity.

The premises of politics' capitulation to the dogma of economic rationality, which is increasingly experienced as fate, are seldom investigated. This is because the prohibition to engage with hidden causes is inscribed in the DNA of a social discourse founded upon the ubiquitous measurability and valorization of life. Starting with surplus-value, nothing counts unless it can be counted. Enjoyment itself is conceived as a matter of metrics, and an economy increasingly ruled by algorithms owes its strength to its ability to capitalize on selling consumer happiness, no matter how depressing life becomes. But while capitalist ideology mobilizes the Freudian pleasure principle, capital continues to be defined by its 'beyond' (the death-drive). This was clear to Lacan, whose idiosyncratic critique of value engaged directly with value's hidden (unconscious) cause.

In a similar vein, although inspired by René Girard's theory of the sacred, Jean-Pierre Dupuy has recently summarized the reasons for the economy's triumph as follows: "Once held in check by religion, and then by politics, it has today become both our religion *and* our politics. No longer subject to any higher authority, it cannot decide our future, or make us a world in which to live: it has become our future *and* our world."[16] For Dupuy, political economy has not only replaced but resignified the function of the sacred, disavowing its crucial role in providing a limit to human experience. The economy's hubris now translates as self-destruction:

> More and more openly today [. . .] Economy buys politicians, without for a moment making a secret of the pride it takes in doing this. [. . .] Economy takes great pleasure in inspiring fear in them [politicians], and in being feared by them in turn. Nothing delights it more than to see these puny creatures creeping around, terrified of making the slightest misstep or doing anything that might anger it in any way. But Economy makes a grave mistake. In degrading and neutering politics, it deprives itself of the means by which it might lift itself out of the swamp of managerialism into which it has now sunk, without even noticing it. Condemned to the pointless immanence of corporate housekeeping, it retreats into itself, unconcerned to give the young any reason to live, unmoved by the spectacle of whole populations reduced to hunger and misery. No longer able to contain violence, it confidently takes the world by the hand and leads it into the future—a still more horrifying future than the last.[17]

If we think of the enduring political debate between neo-Keynesian and neoliberal approaches to the economy and its crisis (stimulus vs. austerity), we can only be stricken by how hopelessly inconsequential our political narratives have grown. This is because both approaches share the same assumption that capital is an inexhaustible wellspring whose point of origin is *metaphysical*. In today's politics, questioning the finitude of such wellspring is akin to questioning the existence of God for a believer. Yet, while this debate continues to excite our political elites and their followers worldwide, its real function would best be sought in its (fetishistic) disavowal of the truly cardinal question that may save our future: how are we to overcome our chronically debilitated mode of production? The capitalist drive is already beyond any possible containment or repair, which is why we must politicize the urge for an exit strategy.

The New Master

My argument centers on the capitalist *mastering* of labor-power: the way in which capital in money-form turns the negative (uncountable) materiality of human praxis into a positive construct. The monetization of labor-time enacts the mortification of time as it is homologated into abstract units. In this context, surplus labor-time, the source of surplus-value, can be thought of as a *cut* that animates a deadened body: since labor-time is already dead time, or time subsumed by the capitalist matrix, its surplus is nothing but a rupture, a point of loss whose aim is to trigger the movement of capital as automatic subject. Put differently, surplus-value is the *meaningless remainder* produced by the capitalist signifier the moment it begins to master labor-time.

It is no surprise, then, that Lacan referred to capitalism as a new master. He exposed the capitalist ruse in no uncertain terms:

> [M]ake no mistake: the Master discourse still holds up, and how! I think you can put your finger sufficiently on it for me not to need to indicate to you what I could have done if it had amused me, namely, if I was seeking popularity. Show you the little turning point somewhere which makes of it the discourse of the Capitalist. It is exactly the same thing, simply it works better, it functions better, you are all the better screwed![18]

The specific cunning of capitalist ideology, according to Lacan,[19] lies in the way traditional mastery is relinquished but simultaneously reasserted *precisely in its relinquished form*, that is to say, as an objective, anonymous, and neutral knowledge. Lacan's point is that while the traditional master could rely on its symbolic authority, the new capitalist master functions by disavowing such authority, silently delegating it to the impersonal objectivity of its modus operandi, which in its deepest configuration concerns the semantic signification of time as labor-time. In this context, as claimed by Gorz, power has "an essentially *functional* legitimacy. It does not belong to an individual subject but to a function."[20] Nobody, then, can be said to hold power:

> Instead, all that can be found—from the bottom right up to the top of an industrial or administrative hierarchy—are agents obeying the categorical imperatives and inertias of the material system they serve. The personal power of capitalists, directors and managers of every kind is an optical illusion. It is a power that exists only in the eyes of those lower down the hierarchy who receive orders from "those above" and are personally at their mercy. [. . .] Marx described capitalists as functionaries of capital: at once oppressors and alienated, they have to submit to and uphold what appears to be a law beyond their power. They administer the workings of capital; they do not control them. They do not possess power; rather, they are possessed by it.[21]

Cornelius Castoriadis made a similar point when he claimed that:

> In the capitalist economy, individuals, whether proletarians or capitalists, are actually and wholly transformed into things, i.e. reified; they are submitted to the action of economic laws that differ in no way from natural laws, except that they use the "conscious" actions of individuals as the *unconscious* instrument of their realization.[22]

Against this background, Lacan's crucial insight, developed throughout Seminars 16 and 17, is that labor-power is not merely the expenditure of a certain amount of human energy predated upon by capital, but rather the unconscious know-how (*savoir-faire*) possessed by the slave/artisan/worker of precapitalist times—an opaque knowledge the traditional master knew nothing (and could not care less) about. By conceiving work as originating in a 'knowledge that does not know itself,' and that therefore does not know time either (the work of the unconscious), Lacan sought to reveal the ruse of the capitalist master.

This is why *savoir-faire* is not to be thought of as a set of pedagogical skills. Rather, it has to do with the awareness that "getting to know something always happens in a flash";[23] which means, essentially, that knowledge is inseparable from (and, ultimately, resides in) its unconscious roots. It could not be otherwise for Lacan: insofar as it is supported by the signifier, knowledge strikes against the wall of its negative substance, thereby yielding an entropic surplus, a meaningless leftover, a surplus-*jouissance* (*plus-de-jouir*) that, as such, cannot be counted. By saying that knowledge is a means of *jouissance*, then, Lacan suggested that, when at work, knowledge generates a *point of loss* that is irreducible to valorization.[24] It is therefore the unconscious opacity of knowledge (*savoir*) that is scientifically fictionalized (quantified) by capitalism in order to be invested in the accumulation cycle.

The distortion of *savoir-faire* (the work of the unconscious) into labor as a universally computable entity exchangeable against money (the labor-commodity), is the elementary ideological template upon which capitalist modernity is founded. This narrative abolishes the worker's *creative alienation* (as in Hegel's understanding), replacing it with surplus-value as meaningless leftover of the labor-time narrative, which, precisely as *meaningless*, vivifies the deadened body of the capitalist discourse. While capital enjoys its endless quest for ineffable surplus-value, labor subjectivities languish in muted acquiescence, unable to locate the cause of their numbing. All that is left is alienation pure and simple:

> [E]ighteenth-century bosses and present-day scientific management have been applying the same recipe: they organised the work process in such a way as to make it impossible for the worker to experience work as a potentially creative activity. The fragmentation of work, Taylorism, scientific management and, finally, automation have succeeded in abolishing the trades and the skilled workers whose pride in a job well done was indicative of a certain consciousness of their practical sovereignty.[25]

This ingenious social narrative, which puts valorized labor-power in the driving seat, undermines traditional mastery by replacing it with the quiet and indisputable assertiveness of the value-fetish, whose role is dual: it embodies the new objective spirit of modern scientific rationality while also providing a temporary sensory solution (commodity fetishism) for the anxiety of modern 'subjects of value.' Let us recall that in traditional societies work only mattered insofar as it got done, and social value resided elsewhere, in forms of symbolic authority related to prestige, blood, class, and religion. As argued by Hannah Arendt,[26] any laboring activity was regarded as unworthy and undignified because an expression of natural necessity, and therefore left for "inferior" human beings to undertake. In Gorz's words:

> Indeed, labour, that is, work carried out in order to ensure survival, was never a factor of social integration. It was rather a criterion for exclusion: in all pre-modern societies, those who performed it were considered inferior. They belonged to the realm of Nature, not the human realm. They were slaves to necessity and therefore incapable of the high-mindedness and disinterestedness which would have rendered them capable of taking charge of the affairs of the city-state.[27]

And again: "Far from being a source of 'social identity,' 'labour' defined private existence and excluded those who were enslaved by it from the public sphere."[28] With the advent of manufacturing capitalism, however, work emerged from exclusion and began to play a central role in the public sphere. As the basis for economic valorization, paid work—labor-power deprived of its sovereign *savoir-faire*—was gradually installed as *the only value* that mattered. It was objectified, counted, packaged (as in Lacan's university discourse of modern science), and turned into that unique commodity upon which the reproducibility of modern societies is based. In order to establish this new paradigm, the bourgeoisie had to break down old habits and forms of resistance by force. Eventually, it managed to accomplish its revolution by resignifying human relations in terms of valorized labor-time:

> The economic rationalization of labour did not, therefore, consist merely in making pre-existent productive activities more methodical and better adapted to their object. It was a revolution, a subversion of the way of life, the values, the social relations and relation to Nature, the *invention* in the full sense of the word of something which had never existed before. Productive activity was cut off from its meaning, its motivations and its object and became simply a *means* of earning a wage.[29]

Colonization of the Productive Mind

This new signification of work produced not only the possibility of profit-making, but also, with it, the *necessity* of wage work in connection with the *necessity* of commodity consumption. Thus, the precapitalist figure of the worker-producer morphed into that of the worker-consumer, which became the *conditio sine qua non* for socialization. Participation in paid work became indispensable for participation in the public sphere—an unheard-of conditionality in the history of humankind. In Lacan's words:

> Work has never been given such credit ever since humanity has existed. It is even out of the question that one not work. This is surely an accomplishment of what I am calling the master's discourse. [. . .] I am speaking of this capital mutation, also, which gives the master's discourse its capitalist style.[30]

Lacan's key intuition was to highlight how the ascendancy and triumph of valorized wage work resulted from a shift in the social link's relation to the *entropy* it generates. This new relation started to impose itself with the arrival of modern science, and it was based on the silent assumption that (unconscious) knowledge at work could be objectively known and exchanged for money. It is through this intangible but crucial *fictional construct* that the capitalist mode of production began to foist its unassailable mastery on human communities. Jean Baudrillard came to a similar conclusion in his 1973 book *The Mirror of Production*, where he lambasted the "unbridled romanticism of productivity" that qualifies the "revolutionary discourse" of his time: "From the liberation of productive forces in the 'unlimited productivity' of *Tel Quel* to Deleuze's factory-machine productivity of the unconscious, no revolution can place itself under any other sign."[31] For Baudrillard, "this aberrant sanctification of work has been the secret vice of Marxist political and economic strategy from the beginning."[32] More precisely:

> Marx shattered the fiction of *homo economicus*, the myth which sums up the whole process of the naturalization of the system of exchange-value, the market, and surplus-value and its forms. But he did so in the name of labor-power's emergence in action, of man's own power to give rise to value by his labor (*pro-ducere*). Isn't this a similar fiction, a similar naturalization—another wholly arbitrary convention, a simulation model bound to *code* all human material and every contingency of desire and exchange in terms of value, finality and production?[33]

Here Baudrillard relies on Lacan's theory of the mirror stage (hence the title of his book) to define the imaginary capture of the valorization dogma: "At the level of political economy there is something of what Lacan describes in the mirror stage: through this scheme of production, this *mirror* of production, the human species comes to consciousness in the imaginary."[34]

As described by Marx in *Capital*, the process of value-creation is the expression of a social relation of exploitation where the metabolism between humanity and nature is subsumed under the hyperproductive logic of accumulation. The centrality accorded to wage labor is at the heart of the paradigm-shift that sets up capital as a socially binding category.[35] In his reading of Marx's labor theory of value, Lacan agrees on the social character of labor exploitation. However, as anticipated, he argues that at the dawn of the capitalist revolution workers are not merely spoliated of surplus labor-time, but, more importantly, they are robbed of *savoir-faire*: "The proletariat is not simply exploited, he has been stripped of his function of knowledge."[36]

The historical novelty highlighted here is capitalism's ambition to transform uncountable *savoir-faire* into commodified knowledge, a measurable amount of work that feeds into the narrative of surplus-value production as its necessary form of appearance. The *forcing* of this *valorization programme* constitutes, for Lacan, the particular form of social alienation introduced by capitalism. Marx himself wrote that the medieval guild system was a "limited and as yet inadequate form of the relationship between capital and wage-labour," where the master, who owns "the conditions of production," is nevertheless "not as capitalist that he is *master*. He is an *artisan* in the first instance and is supposed to be a master of his craft."[37] However, Marx overlooked the extent to which capitalist mastery hinges on the redefinition of productive knowledge within the labor-capital dialectic. In Gorz's words:

> It is not the work of the peasant ploughing his field, the craftsman fashioning his piece, the writer crafting his text or the musician working at his instrument. The work which is disappearing is "abstract labour," labour that is measurable, quantifiable and detachable from the person who "provides" it; work which can be bought and sold in the "labour market." It is, in short, the monetarily exchangeable work or commodity labour which was invented and forcibly imposed by manufacturing capitalism from the end of the eighteenth century onwards.[38]

In Seminar 16 Lacan argues that capital's glorious course begins with the imperceptible conversion of surplus-*jouissance* into a countable value, which destabilizes the until then solid foundations of the discourse of the Master: "[T]he important point is that on a certain day surplus jouissance became calculable, could be counted, totalized. This is where what is called the accumulation of capital begins."[39] We are therefore referring to a momentous structural shift affecting the configuration of the big Other. In short, work started to be *colonized* by the mathematical *ratio* that coordinates the relationship between labor and capital. When we denounce colonialism as a historical phenomenon with evil political connotations (European empires subjugating non-European territories and populations) we should not lose sight of this original paradigm shift, namely, *the economic colonization of the modern mind*. It is this unprecedented epistemological alteration that lends colonialism its specific wickedness. From the first *conquistadores* of Mexico and South America in the sixteenth century to today's neocolonialist plundering of the African continent, capitalism systematically converts life into political economy.

Clouds of Impotence

Lacan's basic dialectical point about language is that the process of linguistic signification (symbolic castration) generates its own inconsistency. The effect of language is its own stumbling, which retroactively causes and sustains all communication. It is because language misfires that we continue to communicate. Any symbolization of the world, then, simultaneously generates the world's inconsistency, which the symbol is unable to illuminate. And Lacan's radical dialectical claim is that the impossibility of signification ultimately defines the subject of the unconscious, the divided subject whose impossible consistency is synonymous with freedom—the freedom radically to resignify its own relationship to the world.

Capitalism's fundamental hubris, however, lies in attempting to overcome the impasse of linguistic alienation, thus concealing the truth about the subject's rootedness in the unconscious. Here it is crucial to continue to emphasize *how* the capitalist narrative affirms itself. The "esoteric Marx" of value-critique provides more than a few clues about this *how*,[40] which are underscored by Lacan. In fact, Lacan goes beyond Marx by emphasizing that capitalism liquidates the opacity of knowledge-at-work (*savoir-faire*) by turning it into exchange-value, a signifying operation through which capital gestates surplus-value as its *lacking* (negativized) substance, or "pure differential."[41] All of a sudden, "we are in the field of values," and from that moment on, by virtue of the fact that the clouds of impotence have been aired, the master signifier only appears even more unassailable [. . .]. Where is it? How can it be named? How can it be located?—other than through its murderous effects, of course. Denounce imperialism? But how can this little mechanism be stopped?[42]

Capital is the new impersonal, depsychologized master whose discourse has internalized the symbolic authority (and violence) of traditional mastery. Fundamentally, the capitalist master delegates its power (and violence) to the structure it sets up. Thus, the "clouds of impotence" disappear as traditional mastery morphs into the pseudo-efficiency of the valorization dogma, which imposes itself as modernity's second nature. The reason why Lacanian psychoanalysis is intrinsically anti-capitalist is that its most urgent goal is to reveal the foundational impotence of the social bond. By contrast, capitalist accumulation totalizes life by colonizing impotence in an entirely new way: not by exorcising it, as earlier discourses did, but by foreclosing the empty cause (surplus-value) and redeploying it as commodified object of desire (profit). In capitalism, the nonexistence of surplus-value as cause is positivized into the existence of profit as effect.

Insofar as the traditional master coincided with the phallic function, its inconsistency and vulnerability were always available, since for Lacan the symbolic phallus is, ultimately, the signifier of lack, which pertains to the human being qua effect of language.[43] While it is precisely by turning its meaninglessness into symbolic authority that phallic mastery functions (providing an anchoring point to the endless sliding of the signifying chain), the veil of such authority can be lifted at any moment, thus exposing the master's imposture. What becomes invisible and therefore virtually unassailable with capitalism is precisely the *impotence* of the master qua phallic power.

Let us recall that the locus of the master's impotence, in Lacan's discourse, is fantasy as the impossibility for the subject of the unconscious to reach its cause qua object of desire (*objet a*).[44] With capitalism, on the other hand, every desired object (commodity) is in principle obtainable, since the impossible object-cause turns into a fetish-object, whose attainment is realized contractually. The discursive closure imposed by capitalism therefore depends on *objet a* morphing into a valorized object: the cause as impossibility is replaced by the commodified object. Lacan understood that this structural shift had a colossal impact on the social bond, as it changed the composition of the big Other, the virtual network of signifiers that, unbeknownst to us, provides us with a minimum of cognitive mapping.

Lacan conceived the social bond as affecting the *totality* of signifying operations available to the human being at a given historical time and place. Every subjective identity depends on the symbolic relationship it strikes with this alterity (big Other). The implication is that with the advent of the capitalist discourse the possibility of signification itself—the elementary human capacity to interact with the external world by symbolizing it—increasingly emerged in connection with the subject's fetishistic attachment to the value-form. This type of structural alienation is fundamentally *perverse*, for the subject disavows the 'crack' (lack, inconsistency) in the Other, obtaining in return the illusion of plenitude. As Lacan put it in 1971, in capitalism *castration is foreclosed*, and the subject is constantly promised the restitution of *jouissance*.[45] This promise of restitution is the fundamental lure at work in capitalist ideology: *jouissance* as impossible object is recycled into ersatz enjoyment, the restitution of something one pays for, or invests in. The recalcitrant surplus incarnated by *jouissance* is valorized, reined in by the value-fiction.

This results in the reification of our libidinal economy, in the precise sense that libido ossifies into an object whose destiny is to fall under the jurisdiction of what Adorno and Horkheimer named instrumental reason: "Enjoyment becomes the object of manipulation, until, ultimately, it is entirely extinguished in fixed entertainments. The process has developed from the primitive festival to the modern vacation."[46] However, on this point we should correct Adorno and Horkheimer's critique: the reign of instrumental rationality is not coterminous with Western civilization since time immemorial (since the myth of Odysseus, as they claim in *Dialectic of the Enlightenment*), but it is rooted in historically specific way in which capital and labor determine each other through their passionate dialectical embrace.

The outcome of that dialectic is a radically different type of mastery. The transcendental act (religious, political, or otherwise) through which *jouissance* was mastered in precapitalist times is replaced by the immanent process of valorization, where mastery becomes invisible. However, as claimed by Lacan, surplus-value is not a value but, in truth, surplus-*jouissance*, the point of entropy that drives the discourse. This is how it works as cause. And yet, it is only perceived in its effects as profit, its positivized phenomenon. Capitalism as camouflaged power requires the a priori submission of the subject to the dynamics of (self-)valorization: the subject enters reality only through the prism of economic value. As Sohn-Rethel put it succinctly, in capitalism money is the a priori in cash.[47] We should take this statement literally. If in precapitalist times the discursive density of the big Other was structured around a *symbolic* act of mastery, in capitalist times it coincides with a *real*, empirical act of exchange, which operates behind our backs and is naturalized into everyday life as *performance*—making us all believe, like the philanthropist of which Marx wrote, that "the mode of production is an eternal necessity ordained by nature."[48]

Labor as Vanishing Presupposition

Having psychoanalyzed Marx's critique of value, we can now address our central claim with renewed confidence. In this section, Lacan and Hegel join forces to subject the crucial Marxian *locus* of the 'labor presupposition' to further scrutiny.

In *Capital* volume 1, Marx reveals how the abstraction of the exchange relation (the buying and selling of commodities) requires the disavowal of the operation that takes place underground, in the hidden abode of production. The spellbinding character of the commodity-form is famously captured in the fourth and final section of the first chapter of *Capital* volume 1, aptly entitled "The Fetishism of the Commodity and Its Secret." Here Marx argues that the commodity is "a very strange thing, abounding in metaphysical subtleties and theological niceties"; he discusses "the mystical character" of commodities that makes them "sensuous things which are at the same time suprasensible or social"; and, most importantly, he claims that "this fetishism of the world of commodities arises from the peculiar social character of the labour which produces them."[49]

The metaphysical lure of the fetish-commodity as encountered in the sphere of circulation, in other words, has to do with its specific *social form*. It is this form that Marx reveals to be created in the sphere of production through a particular declension of the social character of labor. Thus, if the realm of circulation is the "very Eden of the innate rights of man," or more explicitly "the exclusive realm of Freedom, Equality, Property and Bentham" ("Bentham, because each looks only to his own advantage"),[50] Marx invites his readers to "leave this noisy sphere, where everything takes place on the surface and in full view of everyone," and follow him "into the hidden abode of production, on whose threshold there hangs the notice

'No admittance except on business.' Here we shall see, not only how capital produces, but how capital is itself produced. The secret of profit-making must at last be laid bare."[51]

In Marx, then, the negation of immediacy (the self-sufficiency of circulation) leads us straight into production as its dialectical other. This results in a processual loop whereby production and circulation constantly posit and presuppose each other. However, Marx's materialist theory neglects the decisive passage in Hegel's dialectic, namely, the question of the *groundlessness* of the labor-substance in its *grounding function*. In other words, if abstract (wage) labor provides the substantial ground for exchange-values and profits, the key Hegelian point is not only that production itself is mediated by circulation, but that, in becoming labor through its relationship with circulation, *labor shows its essence to be groundless*. What escapes Marx (and especially the Marxists movements that reified his Janus-faced value theory into a materialistic science) is that labor constitutes not only a negation (contradiction) of capital, but especially *a negation of itself as negation of capital*.

Precisely as negation of the negation of what takes place in the market, labor is subsumed under the capitalist-form of value as *socially substantial*. The point to emphasize is that wage labor is already form-determined by capital, preconfigured according to the specific logic of forms installed by the valorization process. In Gorz's succinct formulation:

> Capitalism has called into being a working class (or, more loosely, a mass of wage earners) whose interests, capacities and skills are functional to the existing productive forces, which themselves are functional solely to the rationality of capital.[52]

In capitalism, then, labor exercises its grounding/substantial role by vanishing as *insubstantial* ground, and from there by incarnating the abstract/fictional determinacy of value.

Here it is worth considering Lacan's remark that Marx "founded capitalism" by missing the insubstantial status of surplus-value, which for Lacan is fundamentally a semantic distortion of *jouissance*. From this angle, the valorization of surplus labor-time is actually testament to a *loss*. Surplus-value as surplus-*jouissance* means, essentially, that when capital employs work as its use-value, what it extracts from it is not a surplus qua added value, but a radically *devalued* leftover, an entropic residue that prompts the self-valorization drive of profit-making. Here is the crucial passage from Seminar 17:

We are not dealing with a transgression, an irruption into some forbidden field through the wearing away of vital regulatory apparatuses. In fact, it is only through this effect of entropy, through this wasting, that *jouissance* acquires a status and shows itself. This is why I initially introduced it by the term "*Mehrlust*," surplus *jouissance*. It is precisely through being perceived in the dimension of loss—something necessitates compensation, if I can put it like this, for what is initially a negative number—that this something that has come and struck, resonated on the walls of the bell, has created *jouissance, jouissance* that is to be repeated. Only the dimension of entropy gives body to the fact that there is surplus *jouissance* there to be recovered. And this is the dimension in which work, knowledge at work, becomes necessary, insofar as, whether it knows it or not, it initially stems from the unary trait and, in its wake, from everything that can possibly be articulated as signifier.[53]

It is in Seminar 17 that we find Lacan's decisive turn in his structuralist theory of subjectivity, when he claims that the signifier does not merely represent the human being, but rather *marks* the body, directly causing the irruption of *jouissance*. Therefore, the signifier now appears to be "an apparatus of *jouissance*":

When the signifier is introduced as an apparatus of *jouissance*, we should thus not be surprised to see something related to entropy appear, since entropy is defined precisely once one has started to lay this apparatus of signifiers over the physical world.[54]

Here we encounter a major change in Lacan's theory of the subject caught within the ever-sliding articulation of signifiers, for Lacan argues that the signifier, later renamed *lalangue*, produces a cut that *coincides with* the irruption of *jouissance*. What he asserts is "the equivalence of the gesture of making a mark and the body, object of *jouissance*."[55] We are, then, "at the level of *Beyond the Pleasure Principle*," where "the apparatus of the ego" is given "its real support, its consistency, [. . .] by this lost object [. . .] by which *jouissance* is introduced into the dimension of the subject's being."[56]

Given this new correspondence of language and *jouissance*, the symptom itself is now characterized as a modality of *jouissance* that comes to occupy the place of the trauma (lack), repeating itself beyond the individual's awareness of its role: "Repetition is [. . .] being identical with the unary trait, with the little stick, with the element of writing, the element of a trait insofar as it is the commemoration of an irruption of *jouissance*."[57] But what is the exact role of the symptom? As a nugget of senseless enjoyment, the Lacanian symptom remains ambiguous: it functions both as a protection against the underlying trauma of the subject, and, by embodying the trauma itself, it simultaneously speaks for what is lost in repetition, thus becoming a signifier of lack.

Let us stress it again: what Marx defines as surplus-value is, for Lacan, a memorial to surplus-*jouissance*, since it coincides with the intervention of a new master-signifier (or unary trait), which *marks the worker's body as valorized labor-time*. With his notion of surplus-value, Marx reduces labor to a countable entity to be accumulated, without realizing that the capitalist signification of work produces a point of entropy, which functions as capital's lacking substance and therefore as the engine of its reproductive drive. Furthermore, in line with the aforementioned Althusserian concept of aleatory materialism, Lacan claims that such signifying intervention, while arriving from the big Other, "comes into play by chance, an initial contingency, an accident."[58]

In the *Grundrisse* Marx came close to grasping this structural ruse, for instance when he wrote, at the end of Notebook II, that capital "can posit itself only by positing labour as not-capital, as pure use value," adding that the wage worker's "*valuelessness* and *devaluation* is the presupposition of capital and the precondition of free labour in general."[59] Or when he defined labor as "not as object, but as an activity; not as itself value, but as the living source of value"; or "the mere possibility of value-positing activity, which exists only as a capacity, as a resource in the bodilyness of the worker."[60] These remarks resonate with what we read at the start of *Capital* volume 1: "Human labour-power, in its fluid state, or human labour, creates value, but is not itself value. It becomes value in its coagulated state, in objective form."[61]

The crucial deduction, however, eluded Marx: surplus-value can only be created as the meaningless splinter of the symbolic/formal operation through which capital computes the intrinsic *valuelessness* of work. And my point is that Marx missed this passage because, for him, labor as such, labor as not-capital, remains a positive entity as producer of use-values. For him, labor enjoys ontological status as an affirmative potentiality that is consubstantial with being human:

Labour, then, as the creator of use-values, as useful labour, is a condition of human existence which is independent of all forms of society; it is an eternal natural necessity which mediates the metabolism between man and nature, and therefore human life itself.[62]

In Lacan's assessment, Marx's position on value-producing labor did not prevent him from designating "the function of surplus value [. . .] with complete pertinence in its devastating consequences." And yet, it also meant that his critique of political economy was framed by the ontological presuppositions of capital's economic rationality:

If, by means of this relentlessness to castrate himself that he had, he hadn't computed this surplus *jouissance*, if he hadn't converted it into surplus value, in other words if he hadn't founded capitalism, Marx would have realized that surplus value is surplus *jouissance*.[63]

Lacan was right: by endorsing the substantiality of labor-power as material presupposition of capitalist abstraction, Marx also authorized the foundational ruse through which capitalism asserts its social ontology. For this reason, his philosophy of history is premised on the teleological development of the productive forces. When in the *Communist Manifesto* Marx and Engels declare that in capitalism "[a]ll that is solid melts into air, and all that is holy is profaned," they are not merely criticizing. They are also affirming the necessity of economic rationality that, in their view, will eventually lead humankind to communism. Economic rationality here means that "man is at last compelled to face with sober senses, his real conditions of life, and his relations with his kind."[64]

Marx's Teleology

But before elaborating on the above "sober senses," let us briefly hark back to the teleological character of Marx's dialectical materialism. Marx was perfectly aware that, if in precapitalist times the connection between production and circulation was *causal* (from production to the market), with capitalism it becomes *dialectical*, since both spheres come to posit and presuppose each other. The influence of Hegel's *Logic* on this issue is particularly noticeable in some passages of the *Grundrisse* like the following ones:

> While, originally, the act of social production appeared as the positing of exchange values and this, in its later development, as circulation [. . .] now, circulation itself returns back into the activity which posits or produces exchange values. It returns into it as into its ground. [. . .] We have therefore reached the point of departure again, *production* which posits, creates exchange values; but this time, production which *presupposes circulation as a developed moment* and which appears as a constant process, which posits circulation and constantly returns from it into itself in order to posit it anew.[65]

Consequently:

> Production itself is here no longer present in advance of its products, i.e. presupposed; it rather appears as simultaneously bringing forth these results; but it does not bring them forth, as in the first stage, as merely leading into circulation but as simultaneously presupposing circulation, the developed process of circulation.[66]

For clarification, Marx uses the example of commercial relations between England and the Netherlands in the sixteenth century, where the import of Dutch commodities in exchange for wool forced England to produce a surplus:

> In order then to produce more wool, cultivated land was transformed into sheep-walks, the system of small tenant-farmers was broken up etc., clearing of estates took place etc. Agriculture thus lost the character of labour for use value, and the exchange of its overflow lost the character of relative indifference in respect to the inner construction of production. At certain points, agriculture itself became purely determined by circulation, transformed into production for exchange value. Not only was the mode of production altered thereby, but also all the old relations of population and of production, the economic relations which corresponded to it, were dissolved. Thus, here was a circulation

which presupposed a production in which only the overflow was created as exchange value; but it turned into a production which took place only in connection with circulation, a production which posited exchange values as its exclusive content.[67]

As Marx argues against classical political economy, capital is not simply money exchanged for labor. It is, rather, a social relation, and as such constitutes itself dialectically. This means that if to comprehend capital we have to start with money, money in its "abstract generality"[68] must first be negated. Money exchanged for labor is not the same as money in circulation, where it appears as "a simple positing of equivalents."[69] Instead, when it returns to itself as capital, money is a process, a self-valorizing capacity, which Marx calls *Vervielfältigen seiner selbst*, self-reproduction. The dialectical relationship entertained with labor is thus the magical point where money, from a rigid and tangible thing that aims to become immortal by withdrawing from circulation, begins to circulate as capital.

In respect of this dialectical liaison, Marx is very clear on the reciprocal alienness of labor and capital in its money-form:

> Let us analyse first the simple aspects contained in the relation of capital and labour [. . .]. The first presupposition is that capital stands on one side and labour on the other, both as independent forms relative to each other; both hence also alien to one another.[70]

It soon becomes clear, however, that his mutual alienness is not mere indifference. Rather, it turns into dialectical opposition (*Gegensatz*), since capital and labor are different only insofar as they relate to each other. They are two characters sharing the same narrative and destiny, coming to constitute a unit through the interaction of their specific contradictions. Delving further into this opposition, Marx discusses two types of labor: objectified labor and nonobjectified labor. The first exists *in space*, that is, as the congealed amount of labor contained in the commodity equivalent to a given amount of money. The second exists *in time*, that is, as the vital substance of the worker:

> If it is to be present in time, alive, then it can be present only as the *living subject*, in which it exists as capacity, as possibility; hence as *worker*. [. . .] Labour as mere performance of services

for the satisfaction of immediate needs has nothing whatever to do with capital, since that is not capital's concern.[71]

Marx here wants to distinguish between buying a service (e.g., hiring "a woodcutter to chop wood to roast his mutton over"),[72] and buying living labor as that which *animates* capital. The latter is labor as subjective capacity, as not-capital, which is appropriated and turned into objectified (abstract) labor: "Capital exchanges itself, or exists in this role, only in connection with *not-capital*, the negation of capital, without which it is not capital; the real *not-capital* is *labour*."[73]

Read through Hegel's spectacles, this passage suggests that capital in money-form posits living labor (not-capital) as its external presupposition. Marx therefore argues that labor as external substance is subsumed by capital as its own leavening agent: "Their [workers] co-operation begins only with the labour process, but by then they have ceased to belong to themselves. On entering that process, they are incorporated into capital. [. . .] they merely form a particular mode of existence of capital."[74] And yet, for all its dialectical acuity, such reading misses the properly speculative dimension of Hegel's thought, since Marx's positing of labor as external presupposition relies on labor as a *positive* living substance whose existence is independent of capital (such that, on the strength of that independence, it can antagonize and overthrow capitalism). For Hegel, on the contrary, any external opposition is a case of *self-othering*, in the specific sense that what one externalizes in the other is one's own irredeemable self-difference, and thus also one's positing capacity.

The positing of the presupposition, for Hegel, always takes place against a background of (mutual) impossibility, or ontological insubstantiality. What then connects capital and labor as incongruous entities is their inherent, universal inconsistency. That is to say: the difference between the two oppositional entities in question is, ultimately, their own self-difference in dialectical motion—their own impossibility to be, autonomously, *capital* and *labor*. Each contains within itself its nonbeing, its irredeemable contradiction, and what brings them together as the two poles of a self-valorizing dynamism is the specific mediation (fictionalization) of this intrinsic negativity. However, in Marx's dialectical narrative things work differently: labor as not-capital is conceived of as *pure capacity*, the Aristotelian potential to work that is already there prior to its capitalist mediation. Simply stated: for Marx labor is a plus that, when appropriated by capital, creates a surplus for the capitalist. In Hegelian (and Lacanian) terms, on the other hand, labor is a minus, a negative (impossible, uncountable, unconscious) substance, that, precisely as minus, triggers capital's self-valorization.

Among other things, this means that the conflict between capital and labor is always-already *the conflict of labor with itself*, which is speculatively identical to the conflict of capital with itself, the 'insufficiency principle' that constitutes capital as automatic subject, as well as competition between different capitals. The implication is that the self-valorizing logic of capital coincides with the development of a social fiction where capital and labor play two oppositional roles, each rendered consistent by their respective attachment to the value-fetish.[75] This fiction, anchored in the social character of labor as producer of value, is the means through which capital turns self-relating into a movement of self-expansion. By so doing, capital creates its formal matrix of self-reproduction out of the posited contradiction between itself and labor. In this specific sense, capitalism is a *retroactively self-grounding dialectic*: it subsumes the negativity of labor under the *form* of self-othering value. Herbert Marcuse hinted at this when he claimed that "the burdensome character of labor expresses nothing other than a negativity rooted in the very essence of human existence: man can achieve his own self only by passing through otherness: by passing through 'externalization' and 'alienation.'"[76] Marcuse's claim is both Hegelian and Lacanian, for it defines the human condition as "tarrying with the negative" (Hegel), which makes the process of alienation unavoidable—for what would the essence of the human being be prior to its alienation?

But Marx is unable to follow the Hegelian dialectic to the end, namely, to the self-relating negativity of the cause. In Žižek's words:

> [T]he problem is how to think together the Hegelian circulation of capital and its decentered cause, the labor force, that is, how to think the causality of a productive subject external to the circulation of capital without resorting to the Aristotelian positivity of workers' productive potential? For Marx, the starting point is precisely such a positivity: the productive force of human labor; and he accepts this starting point as unsurpassable, rejecting the logic of the dialectical process which, as Hegel put it, progresses "from nothing through nothing to nothing."[77]

It is because Marx's horizon is defined by the teleologically affirmative character of labor that, as Žižek notes, "Marx's reference to Hegel's dialectics in his 'critique of political economy' is ambiguous, oscillating between taking it as a mystified expression of the logic of capital and taking it as a model for the revolutionary process of emancipation."[78] The limit of Marx's labor theory of value, steeped as it is in the positivistic empiricism of his time, lies in its failure fully to accomplish the step from *value as positive ground* to *value as the grounding inconsistency* that triggers the dialectical self-deployment of the capitalist dynamic. As a concept, economic value is not only the abstract screen that socializes humanity in capitalist terms. It is also a negative substance: it functions by vanishing as insubstantial intermediary between capital and labor, thus establishing their socially synthetic antagonism.

Marx's ontology of labor-power allowed him to articulate his politico-revolutionary view of history's hidden teleology. As he put it unambiguously in the preface to the first edition of *Capital* volume 1, socioeconomic developments should be seen as "a process of natural history."[79] For Marx, the evolution of human society included its passing through the capitalist stage, intended as the last phase of human prehistory after which humanity would achieve real emancipation. The modes of production based on ancient slavery and feudal serfdom constituted a line of societal development that led to the first Hegelian negation: land expropriation and the organization of capitals in connection with 'freely available' wage labor. Subsequently, with the formidable development of the productive forces in conjunction with scientific progress, labor would become increasingly socialized by overcoming the initial division between manual and intellectual work, while the capitalists, weakened by ruthless competition, would progressively disconnect from the production process. Until, finally, the conditions would be objectively ready for the second Hegelian negation: the revolutionary expropriation of the expropriators, and the advent of communism.

In short, Marx believed that the exploited substance of work would turn into the emancipatory force of the proletariat. He never told us how this would happen, just that it would happen. It is apparent that this briefly summarized teleological narrative—the ultimate rags to riches story—is deeply reliant on a specific understanding of productive human praxis. Had Marx not conceptualized labor-power as the *primum movens* and Aristotelian dynamo of history, perhaps he would have endorsed the *speculative* constitution of the capitalist relation as the *groundless* opposition of two terms—capital and labor—whose substantial status depends on their positing and presupposing of each other, through which they aim to disavow their fundamental inconsistency.

The Transcendental Schema of Capitalist Time

The centerpiece of *Capital* volume 1 is the claim that labor is the value-forming substance of capital in general, measured as an average quantity of socially necessary labor-time. Starting from the abstraction of exchange-values, Marx wants to reveal the substantial materiality of labor-power insofar as it is constrained within the amount of exploited labor-time necessary for the reproduction of the capitalist social relation. But how does Marx define this substance? In chapter 6, "The Sale and Purchase of Labour-Power," he states:

> This peculiar commodity, labour-power, must now be examined more closely. Like all other commodities it has a value. How is that value determined? The value of labour-power is determined, as in the case of every other commodity, by the labour-time necessary for the production, and consequently also the reproduction, of this specific article. [. . .] the value of labour-power is the value of the means of subsistence necessary for the maintenance of its owner.

More precisely, "in a given country at a given period, the average amount of the means of subsistence necessary for the worker is a known *datum*." And, finally:

> The value of labour-power can be resolved into the value of a definite quantity of the means of subsistence. It therefore varies with the value of the means of subsistence, i.e. with the quantity of labour-time required to produce them.[80]

The tautological character of this reasoning cannot be missed, for the value of labor-power is defined as the quantity of labor-power employed during the labor-time necessary for the reproduction of labor-power itself. What we encounter here is the blind spot of Marx's notion of abstract labor as substance of value, a contradiction disavowed by his ambiguous reference to *socially necessary labor-time*. At the start of chapter 3 of *Capital* volume 1, we read that "[m]oney as a measure of value is the necessary form of appearance of the measure of value which is immanent in commodities, namely labour-time."[81] So money is the *necessary* mediator of the abstract human labor (substance of value) contained in commodities, which also implies that the money-form of value conceals social relations conditioned by the exploitation of labor. And this is no doubt correct. However, *money as a measure of value* should be understood as *money as a measure of labour*, though not in the naive sense that money can directly represent labor-time (as in the labor voucher theory proposed by Robert Owen and criticized by Marx), but as the *founding metaphor* of capitalism: money is the object-fetish that makes the computation of (surplus) labor-time possible.

From a certain historical point onward, money is equalized to a unit of labor-time, which is what allows capitalists to squeeze surplus-value out of surplus-labor. Strictly speaking, surplus-value is rooted not simply in (the exploitation of) labor, but in the labor-fiction created by money as its mirror-image. This means that abstract labor is labor-time reified in monetary terms, and as such the specific *mythology* through which precapitalist iterations of work become capitalist labor-power. Labor as substance of value, in other words, is a *consequence* of the act through which money redefines the social character of work.

It is worth reiterating that money is not merely the necessary measure of an amount of socially necessary labor *already* contained in the commodity, as Marx thought. Rather, in the first instance money is the fetish that makes the above measuring possible. The labor-as-substance-of-value narrative was established by the violent imposition of the spurious monetary equivalence through which labor-time was mortified into a calculable entity. From this inaugural act of labor reification, which yields the negative substantiality of surplus-value, the new temporality of capitalist productivity began to inform every social activity. Since then, *time has become capitalist time*, a capitalist category through and through. Whatever does not conform to capitalist temporality is simply a waste of time. In capitalism, all social entities and relations are validated ex ante by the temporality of capitalist production, which frames the present as much as redefines the past and preformats the future. The truth of the capitalist motto 'time is money,' then, is '*labour-time is money.*'

On this issue, Kant's notion of transcendental imagination, from the *Critique of Pure Reason*,[82] is enlightening, for it concerns how the mind establishes *a priori* the conditions for its representations. For Kant, our concrete experience of reality is always enabled by an unfathomable and yet spontaneous act of transcendental imagination that defines in advance the spatiotemporal framework of what is meaningful for us, allowing for the cognitive synthesis of the sensuous manifold, stabilizing social relations and regulating both memories of the past and expectations about the future.

However, as argued by Žižek,[83] the transcendental role of the imagination hinges on the negativity of the human being well beyond Kant's own readiness to confront or admit it. The mystery of what Kant calls the transcendental power of the imagination, its capacity to preformat sensible experience in order to prepare it for categorial synthesis, entails the intervention of the mind's disruptive propensity, an intrinsically violent act of tearing apart. That is to say, the capacity for rational activity cannot be separated from its obverse, the idiosyncratic *unruliness* of the human mind, which, as such, opens the space for the evolutionary step into the realm of culture by delivering the human animal from its immersion in nature:

> The key point is thus that the passage from "nature" to "culture" is not direct, that one cannot account for it within a continuous evolutionary narrative: something has to intervene between the two, a kind of "vanishing mediator," which is neither Nature not Culture—this In-between is silently presupposed in all evolutionary narratives. We are not idealists: this In-between is not the spark of *logos* magically conferred on *Homo sapiens*, enabling him to form his supplementary virtual symbolic surroundings, but precisely something that, although it is also no longer nature, is not yet *logos*, and has to be "repressed" *logos*—the Freudian name for this In-between, of course, is the death drive.[84]

We are able to experience reality only because, unconsciously, we have already created its conditions of possibility out of the chaotic material at our disposal. For instance, the empirical correspondence between the work we do and the salary we receive is a real and undisputable fact of life not because it really is so, but because our mind is preformatted in advance so that we perceive it as real and undisputable, to the extent that we organize our lives around it. Put differently, the work society is validated, as a symbolic order of sense, by our unconscious belief in its objective existence within a temporal horizon that binds together past, present, and future, thus generating the wondrous experience of homogenous time out of time's prediscursive confusion. And, as argued above, the specific homogeneity of capitalist time emerged with the coerced equivalence between money and labor, which created the *groundless ground* of capitalism, its ontological (in)consistency. This was the event that set up the relationship between capital and labor as a socially synthetic dialectic, engendering the familiar temporality that totalizes our lives.

Labor-time is thus the specific capitalist answer to *the trauma of atemporality*, the way in which the capitalist Other is called into existence to shield the subject from the trauma of its unconscious truth. However, this ontological process produces its own disturbing entropy (in Lacan's terms, surplus-*jouissance*, *plus-de-jouir*), which is both its cause and its self-destructive drive, a compulsive urge to repeat itself beyond the pleasure principle. Precisely because it is beyond the pleasure principle, capital needs to be tamed into capitalism as social bond. The traces of the original trauma do not disappear and must be neutralized into a system of rational choices. No wonder, then, that mainstream economic assumptions are based on rational choice theory, according to which individuals participating in an economy make sensible calculations depending on available information, seeking to actively maximize their advantage while minimizing their losses. Rationalizing the traumatic core of capital is the specific way in which modernity establishes itself as a social link anchored in the narrative of labor-time, which institutes a civilization whose reproduction depends on profit-making. It is the capitalist pleasure principle attempting to curb capital's death-drive. The retroactive obfuscation of capital's drive is ideological, inasmuch as every ideology is the necessary form of repressive alienation that shores up the fragile balance of the pleasure principle, which brings gratification by reducing the incidence of conflicts and traumas.

It is crucial to stress that the unprompted transcendental operation (Kant) through which we socialize capital is rooted in the original event that violently disconnects sociality from its previous (feudal) presuppositions. This means, essentially, that negativity remains operative in the background against which social transformation, and a new schematization of time, takes place. While capital as drive feeds off this persistent negativity, it also embodies the breaking point where the new emerges, literally, ex nihilo. The schematized temporality of capital, then, can only be genuinely disrupted by an experience of time that cannot be accounted for by the labor presupposition. My wager, rather, is that capital itself, by drastically curtailing its own labor-substance, is clearing the ground for a new type of socialization (a new form of life) that will be based on a different schematization of time.

Beyond Exploitation

We are now in a position to return to our initial critique of Marx and claim that what is missing in his labor theory of value is the speculative trigger point. Marx's theory, in other words, disavows the negative core of the dialectic of labor-time and capitalist value. It disavows the fact that the two terms are internally inconsistent, which is precisely the secret of their dialectical success. The notion of abstract labor is therefore only partially unraveled by Marx, arguably because his most pressing concern is to show how surplus-value results from its exploitation.[85] To Marx's political point about exploitation, which describes how the capitalist who buys labor-power pays for its full value (socially necessary labor-time) while also extracting from it a given amount of surplus labor-time that feeds into surplus-value,[86] we should add the crucial observation that the monetary computability of labor is *an invention pure and simple*, the creationist act that founds the capitalist narrative. By emphasizing exploitation, however, Marx's labor theory of value has to rely on a *substantialist* concept of labor, which is also the precondition of capitalist socialization.

At the same time, the value of labor-power cannot be deduced from its exploitation. Rather, the necessary condition for the exploitation of labor is the reified abstraction of its temporal quantification, which intervenes to make sense of labor's insubstantiality. Marx, then, stopped too soon in his dialectical exploration of the value of labor-power. He did so in order to press home the political relevance of his theory of surplus-value, which, however, fails to problematize the inherently capitalist fantasy that labor is *naturally* productive. This is why the burning issue of the worker's exploitation, at the heart of all labor movements, fails to intercept the disavowed cause of the capitalist mode of production. Capitalism consolidates itself as a predatory social bond not merely through the surreptitious exploitation of the workforce that offers itself up as exchange-value on the market. This is a secondary, though crucial, passage. The key question concerns the paradigm-changing transformation of the negative substantiality of work into a positive and quantifiable temporal measure of economic value. It is this new *signification* of time that generates surplus-value as *negativized* trigger of the accumulation cycle.

This signifying operation enjoys ontological priority over exploitation. The original ruse resides in the formalization of the liaison between money and labor, which elevates labor to a universal and indisputable value. This ruse runs the show by establishing labor as a productive category in relation to which the capitalist is a functionary: he/she works for the impersonal mechanism of value-extraction and profit-making, whose pillar is labor-power as substance of value. While Marx understood that the capitalist works for capital as its "functionary,"[87] he did not deduce the original point: the exploitation of labor relies on a creationist act that overdetermines the entire labor-capital dialectic. For labor is the substance of capital only because capital in money-form is the substance of labor.

Let us recall that chapter 6 of *Capital* volume 1 starts with the following statement: "We mean by labour-power, or labour capacity, the aggregate of those mental and physical capabilities existing in the physical form, the living personality, of a human being, capabilities which he sets in motion whenever he produces a use-value of any kind."[88] This is an iteration of the previously cited claim that, in itself, labor-power is a fluid and indeterminate potentiality. The notion of labor as a *generic* capacity to produce is Marx's starting point. However, when we endorse his explanation of how surplus-value is extracted from surplus labor-time (in part 3 of *Capital* volume 1), we cannot miss his tautological exposition of labor, which reflects his eagerness to conceive it as (to put it in Hegelese) external determination: a *positive* ground that will successfully antagonize capital. Herein lies the distortion, or disavowal, around which everything moves, *both* in Marx(ism) and in capitalism: the positivist illusion of the original productivity of human labor.

As an attempt to measure the quantity of labor contained in the commodity, Marx's labor theory of value is marred by a fundamental aporia, which, when turned into a political program, does more to corroborate than debunk the elementary logic of the capitalist mode of production. By positing labor-power as that exceptional commodity whose "process of consumption"[89] creates surplus-value, Marx effectively uncovers the enigma of capital, except for its foundational act of mystification. While he is right in identifying in the exploitation of labor-power the hidden cause of capital's self-reproduction, at the same time he fails to ascertain that this cause is not only hidden, but properly *lacking*, since at the heart of the capitalist dialectic we find nothing other than the truly seismic event of the creationist conversion of uncountable *savoir-faire* into countable labor-time.

Marx is therefore unable to conceptualize work as the negative ground that, on account of its negativity, holds within itself the potential for its reconfiguration into a noncapitalist social form. Through its cultic character, capitalism negates this negativity by fetishizing labor-time into a value-generating turbine. By itself, however, labor does not yield value. Rather, it entails a correlation between signifiers that produces an entropy, a lack of meaning that, precisely as lacking, is functional to the economy of desire and its drive. Knowledge-at-work generates a point of *loss*, which in capitalism is called surplus-value. It is a surplus, an added value, only because it is lacking. As a compulsive disorder, capital is interested only in repeating its movement around this negativized object, while representing it as a surplus in its social narrative. For this reason, capitalism is a substantial lie, a mystification of our consciousness. The Marxist theorization of labor as a productive substance with revolutionary potential therefore misses the target, for it installs a system of beliefs that, paradoxically, obscures the cause of the capitalist discourse, namely, the overlap of surplus and lack; or, in Hegelian terms, the impossibility of work as concretely universal. As Michel Henry put it:

> In the night of subjectivity where force is deployed, there is no object or measure, no light can clarify the relation of labor to the goods—there is nothing that can be measured. The power of living labor is never revealed in any other way than in the pathos of its effort. But this pathos is no more measurable than the "taste" in one's mouth or the intensity of love.[90]

Chapter 4

Dialectical Short Circuits

The Catastrophe of Liberation

Marx knew that the productive capacity of labor-power is validated from the future, since only exchange-values can tell us if labor is productive. Labor, in other words, is always contingent on the future realization of value; its productivity is decided *après-coup*, when commodities are sold. This dialectical point, however, needs to be radicalized. Reading Marx through Hegel and Lacan allows us to see that capital established its autotelic discourse not merely through the exploitation of labor-power as source of surplus-value. If we stop at this claim, we risk missing the *missing* cause of the whole process. Radically understood, labor-power as substance of capital is *labor-powerlessness*, its own immanent self-contradiction. It becomes a positive (valorized) substance only the moment capital signifies it retroactively as producer of value.

Lacanian psychoanalysis provides us with a dialectical *theory of the gap* that neither Hegel nor Marx were able to mobilize,[1] for it defines the gap between ontological indeterminacy (the *jouissance* of the Real, the symptom) and abstract determinacy (symbolic signification) in connection with libidinal attachments that elevate the subject of the unconscious to the central agent (indeed, the *secret* agent) of any form of life. If one wants to understand how certain presuppositions are posited rather than others, then, one should interrogate the unconscious attachments around which conscious existence is organized.

Let me summarize my critique of Marx's critique of political economy so far. Essentially, the pumping out of surplus-value from surplus-labor—within the processes of formal and real subsumption described by Marx—is rooted in the monetary *signification* of the unconscious roots of work. As neatly summarized by Baudrillard, "[t]he truth of labor is its capitalist definition."[2] The capitalist symbolization of labor produces a surplus that, however, coincides with a meaningless splinter of the signification process, an entropic *plus-de-jouir* around which capital constitutes itself as self-valorizing drive. The very fact that capital *is* its own frantic movement, since in a stagnant state it would perish, is proof that its ontology of self-reproduction is, literally, built upon *nothing*—or, rather, on the negativized remainder secreted by its labor semantics. Capital's restlessness, its boisterous hyperactivity, signals above all its *fear of introspection*.

In respect of this systemic anxiety, labor works as capital's decisive partner in crime: as the retroactively validated source of wealth, it is the fictional character that allowed capitalism to establish itself as a social narrative. Historically, we are now at a point where the labor-fiction qua self-othering of capital is untenable, and will not be given a second chance. What is evaporating is not just labor as wealth redeemed by money, but labor as the crucial *fantasy formation* that constitutes the essence of modernity. In Lacanese, labor is dissolving as a "fundamental fantasy,"[3] the deepest unconscious attachment shielding the modern subject from its inconsistency, which is at the same time the inconsistency of capital. As a fundamental fantasy, the very painfulness of "exploited labor" provides the primary mode of identification through which, unconsciously, we define ourselves as subjects in the capitalist universe. The implication here is that any political endeavor to move beyond capitalism must factor in the workers' profound existential attachment to the very cause of their suffering.

At the same time, however, we should also keep in mind that the capitalist subsumption of labor does not signal successful reconciliation with it, but the endless failure of reconciliation, which is the contradiction upon which capital founds its exploitative logic. Paradoxically, the power of capitalism hinges on its inability to actualize itself fully. This is why capitalist progress is not teleological. What is retroactively called into existence (the substantial character of labor) was already there prior to the arrival of capitalism. The laboring capacity as form-giving activity, interaction with nature and substance of wealth was already at the heart of feudal societies. The effect of the capitalist revolution was to gradually resignify labor by granting it a specific social agency through its commodification. Thus, the dividing line between capitalist and precapitalist rationality was progressively obfuscated, and the precapitalist past suddenly appeared within the telos of capitalist relations. Yet capitalism remains based on (the disavowal of) its impotence.

How, then, did capital subsume labor? In the course of modernity, the radical inconsistency of labor was sublated by the positing subject (capital) in the precise sense that such inconsistency was 'erased and preserved' (*Aufheben*) within the self-development of the notion (capitalism). This genuine act of sorcery should not prevent us from recognizing—to paraphrase Hegel—'the cross in the rose,' for the self-relating negativity of substance (labor) remains speculatively identical with the self-relating negativity of subject (capital). Labor as substance of capital needs to be recognized as a deeply inconsistent cause, and it is by tarrying with such inconsistency that the new might emerge—in Lacanian terms, a new social link based in a *qualitatively* new relation with the surplus-*jouissance* of our symptoms, our unconscious attachments to the world. As Lacan put it in Seminar 24, the condition for change is that the subject becomes free of the Other and its language:

> In any case, what I am saying is that the invention of a signifier is something different from memory. It is not that the child invents—he receives the signifier [. . .]. Our signifiers are always received. Why shouldn't we invent a new signifier? For instance, a signifier that would have no sense at all, just like the Real?[4]

From this perspective, the importance of the passage through labor as symptom cannot be emphasized enough. As Gorz put it, Marxism cannot help us here, since its eschatological promise rests on the positivistic framing of the proletariat:

> [I]f there is to be a rupture, then the working class must act as a force refusing, along with its class being, to accept the matrix of capitalist relations of production of which this being bears its imprint. But how will it acquire the capacity to undertake this negation of itself? This is a question which marxism as a "positive science" cannot possibly answer.[5]

Paraphrasing Cioran, we would say that labor must find the strength to benefit from its own *unreality*:

> Those who cannot benefit from their possibilities of nonexistence are strangers to themselves: puppets, objects "furnished"

> with a self, numbed by a neutral time that is neither duration nor eternity. To exist is to profit by our share of unreality, to be quickened by each contact with the void that is within. To this void the puppet remains insensible, abandons it, permits it to decay, to die out.

Labor must confront the dizziness of its own death, which was always at its roots: "A kind of germinative regression, a return to our roots, death destroys our identity only to permit us a surer access to it—a reconstitution; for death has no meaning unless we accord it all the attributes of life."[6]

Herbert Marcuse arrived at a similar conclusion in the final chapter of his *One-Dimensional Man*, which bears the wonderful title "The Catastrophe of Liberation." Reflecting on technological-scientific transformation as an eminently dialectical problem—which involves scientific rationality reaching its "determinate negation,"[7] thus opening up the redefinition of its ends—Marcuse was not afraid to confront the traumatic dimension of freedom. Against any romantic plea for the abolition of labor/work, he argued that the potential prospect of a fully automated, postcapitalist society would promote a qualitative change in our lives where the repoliticization of science as the basis for a new social bond would be experienced not only as liberating but also as painful:

> To take an (unfortunately fantastic) example: the mere absence of all advertising and of all indoctrinating media of information and entertainment would plunge the individual into a traumatic void where he would have the chance to wonder and to think, to know himself (or rather the negative of himself) and his society. Deprived of his false fathers, leaders, friends, and representatives, he would have to learn his ABC's again. But the words and sentences which he would form might come out very differently, and so might his aspirations and fears. To be sure, such a situation would be an unbearable nightmare. While the people can support the continuous creation of nuclear weapons, radioactive fallout, and questionable food-stuffs, they cannot (for this very reason!) tolerate being deprived of the entertainment and education which make them capable of reproducing the arrangements for their defense and/or destruction. [. . .] The creation of repressive needs has long since become part of

socially necessary labor—necessary in the sense that without it, the established mode of production could not be sustained.⁸

Here Marcuse hits the proverbial nail right on the head: the prospect of being deprived of our *repressive forms of alienation*, to which we grow accustomed and we cherish much more than we are prepared to admit, is what stops us from reconfiguring our needs, even when we rationally acknowledge the desperate urgency of the task. This is the crucial dialectical passage that the construction of a new language will need to take care of.

Blindness of the Automatic Subject

The collapse of socialism and the economic reorganization that followed (globalization) suggest that both *reformism* (distributive struggles gradually preparing the ground for change) and *revolution* (direct transformative interventions) have progressively lost their impetus. While this may seem lamentable, the historical fizzling out of leftist narratives allows for a major repositioning of our critical perspective. Most importantly, what these narratives show by disappearing is that capitalism as a social relation is founded upon the illusion that, within its productive relations, there is such a thing as a transformative subjectivity, whether gradually reformist or aggressively revolutionary. By continuing to invest our energy and beliefs in narratives evoking phantom-like laws of transition, effectively we continue to grant capital the reproductive capacity it is losing. Those who still believe that the capitalist dynamic is *explosive* in bringing together the exploited masses of workers, may well be saving their conscience but have definitely lost touch with reality. No objective process unifies the exploited, and this is particularly true for the supremely edifying fantasy of the international proletariat.

While capitalist relations continue to be based on labor exploitation, this does not by itself generate conditions for collective insubordination, or even any generic desire for the kind of transformation that may actually overcome its inevitably idealistic character. Rather, it is theoretically more coherent and practically more astute to acknowledge that, from the start, labor subjectivities occupied a position that is structurally consistent with the affirmation of capital as a "boundless drive for enrichment."⁹ All labor subjectivities, including the capitalist's, work for capital as anonymous master, and can therefore be regarded as *functionaries* of capital, to repeat Marx's expression from his *Notes on Adolph Wagner*.[10] Today, when the claim that the working class (or the collective worker) can alter the course of history has finally been exposed in all its emptiness, we should focus instead on the internal contradiction of our mode of social reproduction. In respect of this task, psychoanalysis offers uniquely significant critical tools.

In the early 1970s, Lacan argued that, despite being very clever, the well-lubricated, ever-accelerating capitalist machine was heading for self-destruction. The French word he used to indicate the coming implosion of capitalism was *crevaison* (puncture), which aptly conveys the image of a mechanism breaking down. But why should the frictionless *discours du capitaliste* suffer a lethal accident? Lacan began by endorsing Marx's following claim that capital is an "automatic subject" (*automatisches Subjekt*):

> On the other hand, in the circulation M-C-M both the money and the commodity function only as different modes of existence of value itself, the money as its general mode of existence, the commodity as its particular or, so to speak, disguised model. It is constantly changing from one form into the other, without becoming lost in this movement; it thus becomes transformed into an automatic subject.[11]

As an impersonal compulsion to generate value, the accumulation dynamic is in a state of continuous overexcitement, or *overdrive*, in that it tends toward infinite self-expansion. This condition is one of *necessity*: the movement of capital emerges out of capital's logical necessity to escape the void of its own contingency, the fact that its telos is ultimately groundless.

In his 1915 essay "Instincts and their Vicissitudes" Freud had already noted that the *aim* of any drive is not its *object* (in our case, profit-making) but rather the endless circuital gravitation *around* the object, which brings satisfaction not by obtaining but by missing the target. Lacan endorsed Freud's observation in Seminar 11, when he stated that "no object of any [. . .] need, can satisfy the drive [. . .]. This is what Freud tells us [. . .]. As far as the object in the drive is concerned, let it be clear that it is strictly speaking of no importance. It is a matter of total indifference."[12]

In capitalism, then, satisfaction is properly *beyond the pleasure principle*, for it comes from the Sisyphean task of endlessly circuiting around surplus-value qua negativized substance, and thus from never realizing enough profit: the more profit one makes, the more one becomes aware of not having (enough of) *it*, of *lacking* it, which triggers the compulsive repetition of the same sovereign gesture of accumulation. As with any addiction, the satisfaction of the drive coincides with its missing the target. The paradox is that the moment 'we get some of it,' we are immediately overwhelmed by the awareness that we lack *it*, and this is why we want more. As with any pathological dependence, we are addicted to the object as lack, an object embodying the lacking substance.

The splitting of the drive between object and aim is of fundamental relevance if we are to grasp the contradictory nature of capitalist accumulation from a Lacanian perspective. While capitalists consciously crave profit, what they really want is *not having enough of it*, so that they can continue to crave it. It goes without saying that this unconscious elevation of lack to centerpiece of the accumulation logic clashes with the conscious targeting of profit, in the precise sense that *it makes capitalism blind to its own cause*. The result of this blindness is signaled in the lower part of Lacan's discourse of the capitalist, where surplus-value qua surplus-*jouissance* (*a*) is unable to connect with the master-signifier as driver of the discourse (S1).

The main implication here is that capital, which cares only about its own self-reproduction, remains ignorant as to how surplus-value functions as its lacking substance. Instead of nothing, the capitalist sees profits everywhere, thus extending the law of value over the entire world. Put differently, capital needs to objectivize its own nonexistence into concrete forms of value like profit, interest, and rent. Because capital is fundamentally *not there*, then, Lacan renames surplus-value (Marx's *mehrwert*) *mehrlust* (surplus-*jouissance*), a libidinal object whose pulsating presence dissimulates its own real absence—a kind of equivalent of the proverbial empty eye of the hurricane; or, as Lacan put it poetically in his short essay "On Freud's *Trieb*," "the colour of emptiness, suspended in the light of a gap."[13] As discussed in chapter 3, Lacan's critical point was that Marx, by conceding that labor is, ultimately, a quantifiable economic value subsumable in temporal terms, stopped too soon in his critique of surplus-value, neglecting "the initial stage of its articulation,"[14] thereby endorsing the scientific premises of modern economic thought in general.

Lacan was aware that Marx's critique of political economy came about in relation to two distinct methodological pressures: the idealist philosophical model asserted by Hegel, and the positivist approach to scientific knowledge that became overwhelmingly dominant in the second half of the nineteenth century. In many ways, Marx's thought can be regarded as a syncretism of these methodologies, with the addition of Christian teleology. Let us recall that in his theory of the three stages of human development, Auguste Comte, the father of positivism, argued that religion (the theological stage) is for children, philosophy (the metaphysical stage, extension of the former) for adolescents, and that only the scientific method (positivism) is for adults. His conviction that scientific observation, measurement, and comparison represented the highest developmental stage for humanity was, by the time Comte put ink to paper, the dominant discourse of his epoch. The fact that Comte went on to found a secular religion based on strict principles and organized in a liturgical structure replete with a panoply of beliefs, sacraments, and rituals is highly symptomatic of the fundamentally *hysterical* character of the positivist revolution, whose urge to eliminate the philosophical search for hidden causes generated the very anxiety it sought to abolish.

If we consider how Marx's mature thought was turned into a teleological vision of history (historical materialism), we should seek the cause for this development in the dogma of Marx's time, which is already at work in his critique: the injunction to analyze the object (the capitalist mode of production) like a physicist who "either observes natural processes where they occur in their most significant form, and are least affected by disturbing influences, or, wherever possible, he makes experiments under conditions which ensure that the process will occur in its pure state."[15] Marx could not be free from the pressure of positivism, and yet he did not give in to its requirements completely. Arguably, from around 1845 (*The German Ideology*) he felt increasingly obliged to incorporate into his philosophy the analytical method of positivism, which allowed him to provide an empirical basis for his critique of capital, as well as to imbue his thinking with the same faith in historical progress and finality that pertained to the bourgeois declension of scientific objectivity. In this respect, he followed the positivistic anthropology of his time, which is why, to use Castoriadis's pungent remark, positivism ultimately represents "the profoundly persistent hold of Marx's contemporary capitalist world on his thought."[16]

Simultaneously, however, Marx's critique continued to implement a dialectical understanding of social relations that was not limited to the study of the observable, but also sought to probe entities and magnitudes that were not directly measurable.[17] From this viewpoint, the tragic dimension of Marxism is to have discovered the exploitative engine of capitalism while also peddling the illusion of its dialectical overcoming by the proletariat. What Lacan's critique underlines is that, within the capitalist relation, there are no antagonistic subjectivities that might be able to overthrow capitalism; no Aristotelian potentiality that might trigger a revolutionary act. Quite differently, capital socializes itself precisely by *producing* an antagonistic bond with labor-power. The proletariat and its productive potential are *internal* to the logic of capital, metaphysically overdetermined and alienated by the cunning of capitalist reason.

This would seem to confirm that what is missing in Marx's labor theory of value is none other than *the cause* insofar as it is *lacking*: the cause as *the negative substantiality of human knowledge-at-work*, the unconscious substance that informs the relation between knowledge, work, and matter, and from there the spurious economic magnitude captured as surplus-value. Adorno neatly summed up this point in the introduction to *Negative Dialectics*: "Thought as such, before all particular contents, is an act of negation, of resistance to that which is forced upon it; this is what thought has inherited from its archetype, the relation between labor and material."[18]

In his reading of Marx, Lacan urges Marxists to probe further into the nature of surplus-value. If they do, he contends, they will realize that the value-fetish is a fictional construct whose role is to conceal not only the exploitation of labor-power, but especially the epochal transformation affecting the unconscious roots of knowledge, and thus the very meaning of labor. In the reign of the value-form, commodity fetishism, like all perversions, functions as the minimal instance of disavowal that sets up our socio-ontological horizon of sense. Within this paradigm, our inability to confront and assume the disavowed cause of the global capitalist disorder translates into our inability to tackle its terminal crisis at its roots. And Lacan insists that the exploitation denounced by Marx obscures this *lacking* truth, the self-relating negativity of labor-power insofar as it is rooted in "the gap-like structure that is the structure of the unconscious."[19]

Hegel: Being as Self-mediated Groundlessness

Let us now confront head-on the theoretical hard core of the argument. As already noted, in *Capital* Marx provides us with a clear account of dialectical retroactivity: he begins from capital at first glance—the sphere of commodity circulation—and proceeds backward to show us how circulation is mediated by production. Already in the *Grundrisse* he had claimed that "the simple movement of exchange values, such as is present in pure circulation, can never realize capital." Or, in more explicit Hegelian terms:

> *Circulation therefore does not carry within itself the principle of self-renewal.* [. . .] Circulation [. . .], which appears as that which is immediately present on the surface of bourgeois society, exists only in so far as it is constantly mediated. [. . .] Its immediate being is therefore pure semblance. *It is the phenomenon of a process taking place behind it.*[20]

Both *Grundrisse* and *Capital* indicate that Marx derived his concept of circulation from Hegel's "immediate being," the starting point of the *Logic*. The sphere of market exchange is described by Marx as form without content, ruled as it is by the abstract principle of exchangeability. Let us recall how, in the *Logic*, being appears initially as an abstract and unmediated form, and as such it is "the unity of being and nothing."[21] Subsequently, this simple, abstract immediacy is mediated by reflection, which negates being by relating it to its essence. The immediacy of Hegel's initial conceptualization of being corresponds to the immediacy of Marx's capitalist system as it appears on the surface, in circulation. Insofar as they seem purely formal configurations, they share an absolute indifference to any content.

The initial task for both Hegel and Marx is to reveal the mediated nature of what appears as simple immediacy. Hegel's dialectical logic is retroactive and circular, for it shows how being, in its simple appearance, had from the start constituted itself via an in-built act of self-mediation. Thus, the move backwards from being, through which being finds itself first as *essence* and then, crucially, as *concept*, coincides uncannily, in Hegel's treatment, with a movement forward, a conceptual progression of self-discovery. In my reading, this movement ultimately reveals the ontological inconsistency at the heart of being. I situate contemporary capitalism precisely at this point of radical inconsistency, where the system's driving presuppositions have stopped working, while the question of systemic reconfiguration continues to be evaded through the reassertion of the very logic that produces the system's implosion.

In Hegelian terms, what is missing is the contraction from dialectical opposition (reflection as the power of negativity) to the self-sublation of opposition/negativity (reflective determination). This is arguably the leitmotif and highest point in Hegel's *Logic*, capturing the speculative coincidence of a positive whole and its inconsistency.[22] Hegel already states this paradox of 'advancing by retreating,' or of 'creation through loss,' at the start of book 1 of the *Logic* ("The Doctrine of Being"), where he argues that

> it is an important consideration [. . .] that the advance is a *retreat into the ground*, to what is *primary* and *true* [. . .]. Thus consciousness on its onward path from the immediacy with which it began is led back to absolute knowledge as its innermost *truth*. This last, the ground, is then also that from which the first proceeds, that which at first appeared as an immediacy.

For Hegel, then, as he writes in the first paragraph of book 2 of the *Logic* ("The Doctrine of Essence"), "knowledge [. . .] does not stop at the immediate and its determinations, but penetrates it on the supposition that at the back of this being there is something else, something other than being itself, and that this background constitutes the truth of being."[23] This is the same supposition that guides Marx's enquiry in his 'forward move backward' from the sphere of circulation to that of production: circulation, like Hegel's being, cannot be self-sufficient; to *be*, it must come about as the result of a series of antecedent mediations. But what is there, for Marx, behind the curtain of appearances? What is the secret of exchange values? As we shall see, on answering these questions Marx parts ways with Hegel.

In the *Science of Logic*, Hegel shows how the mediation of being leads to essence as an inward reflection whose triadic movement repeats, at a deeper level, precisely the topos of 'creation by self-contraction' that, for Hegel, characterizes dialectical thinking. Although the decisive part of Hegel's argument is developed in the 'subjective logic' (the third sphere of the concept), where determinations show themselves to be self-determining, let us briefly focus on reflection as it appears in the sphere of essence. First, reflection is qualified by its positing capacity, the ability to assert a given identity in its simple ontological immediacy (*positing* reflection); in a second move (*external* reflection), it teases out the epistemological presuppositions of its positing, namely, the underlying premises to what was initially asserted, thereby establishing with it a differential relation of mutual dependency; finally, by uniting the first two movements, reflection discovers itself to be radically out of joint. As Hegel puts it, it "has bent back its reflection-into-other into reflection-into-self," thus showing that the differential relation between what was posited and what was presupposed was actually self-referential, a self-relation: "[T]he determinateness of reflection is its *relation to its otherness within itself*."[24] External reflection was always the self-othering of positing reflection.

In this third movement, then, the determination of reflection is not a positing or a presupposing, but "reflectedness-into-itself"; it is *"positedness*, negation, which however bends back into itself."[25] This notion of *determining reflection* captures the crucial relevance of self-withdrawal as inherent contradiction. It is important to emphasize that with this third dialectical movement we get a second negation (*Aufhebung* as negation of negation), rather than a synthesis of the previous two movements: while external reflection negates its positing activity, determining reflection brings that negation within externality proper, making it deeply inconsistent. Thus, external reflection now finds *within* itself the negativity it employed to gain a distance from the posited content of being. In this way, essence discovers that negativity (lack, inconsistency) is self-relating, inherent to its own essentiality. The key speculative moment in Hegel, however, implies a redoubling of determining reflection into reflective determination: the inherent inconsistency of reflection (thought) functions as a *productive* and *affirmative* notional apparatus. This productiveness is asserted by Hegel, for instance, toward the end of the second book of the *Logic*, in the section called "The Absolute Idea," when he repeatedly conjectures that "the term counted as *third* can also be counted as *fourth*."[26] The reason why the three movements of the dialectic should be regarded as *four* is that the self-relating negativity asserted by the third (determining) reflection ultimately coincides or overlaps with its own self-sublation into a new speculatively reconciled whole.

The role of this fourth movement (reflective determination, *Reflexionbestimmung*) is what Theodor Adorno's "negative dialectics" fails to grasp, for it remains stuck at the level of *determining reflection*, engendering from there a negatively transcendental search for what it rejects as strictly speaking impossible reconciliation.[27] The crucial difference between Hegel and Adorno is the difference between three and four, between negative dialectics and its speculative redoubling: for Hegel, reality is always-already the redoubling of the negative into a condition of possibility that, far from eliminating the negative, it 'includes it out' as its own ontological and thus inerasable inconsistent ground. What Adorno (and, more generally, critical theory since its inception) cannot fathom is that *three is always-already four*, since self-relating negativity—the inherent tension or impossibility of reflection—is *the silent, invisible presupposition of the dialectical self-deployment of knowledge*. In more simple terms: while the dialectic eventually unravels the inherently self-contradictory character of any notion, the proper speculative breakthrough consists in acknowledging how the negative ground, the groundlessness of essence, is the flipside of the affirmative dimension of knowledge. Through a reflective inversion, what is perceived as an abyssal kernel of negativity acquires ontological status: the inherent impasse (limit, obstacle) of cognition is cognition's own condition of possibility.

Furthermore, this speculative coincidence of opposites is predicated upon the intervention of the subject as mediator of the self-relating negativity of substance, and by the same token of its own impossibility/void. At this final stage of the dialectic, the Hegelian Absolute itself is nothing but (the repetition of) the failed self-sublation that qualifies the subjective work of reflection. And in this failure of the Absolute, subject and substance coincide as the expression of the True.

So far, then, we have noticed how, in Hegel's dialectical reversal, knowledge finds itself not only as the negation of the immediacy of being (qua illusory being, or *Schein*),[28] but especially as self-relating negativity: "[E]ssence as it has here come to be, is what it is through a negativity which is not alien to it but is its very own, the infinite movement of being."[29] The dialectic of being and essence, in other words, leads back to being as radically inconsistent essence; or, differently put, to essence as ontologically ruptured being. This is why, immediately after discussing determining reflection, Hegel claims: "Reflection is *the showing of the illusory being of essence within essence itself*. Essence, as infinite return-into-self, is [. . .] absolute self-mediation."[30]

If we look at the bigger picture, it should now be clear that Hegel proceeds from the negativity of immediate being, to the negativity of essence as external reflection, and to the concept as double negation of essence qua self-mediated truth of being. Once again, it is crucial to underline that double negation does not produce the positivity of being as the final truth of knowing. Rather, it delivers *what was already there from the beginning*, namely, the negativity of being as self-mediated substance. The difference between the beginning and the conclusion of the dialectical sequence consists in the *speculative* awareness that *being qua appearance is always-already the self-mediation of its inherent inconsistency*. Therefore, being is constituted by "the negation of a nothing," which, however, does not constitute a positive, but is rather "the movement from nothing to nothing, and as such it is essence."[31] This self-mediation of being's negativity takes place via that necessary retro-performative movement that involves positing the presuppositions and presupposing the capacity to posit them.

This logic is further asserted when Hegel defines the properties of essence ("essentialities") as identity, difference, and contradiction: "Essence is at first, simple self-relation, pure *identity*"; secondly, however, it discovers *difference* in the form of its external opposition to being, which becomes illusory being; then, crucially, this external opposition is reflected back into the very ground of essence, as the self-fracture within essence itself: "[t]hirdly, as *contradiction*, the opposition is reflected into itself and withdraws into its *ground*."[32] In its positing or mediating activity, then, essence discovers itself to be constitutively antagonized, which means that external opposition is always-already *essential*, inward looking, immanent to essence itself. It is in this sense that we should think the Hegelian complex logic of positing/presupposing: what is posited by essence is, ultimately, its own presupposition as a contradiction that *withdraws into its ground*. Positing/mediating difference with an other is in fact positing/mediating self-difference as ontological presupposition. What is initially perceived as difference, or more explicitly as an external obstacle that thwarts the development of essence, falls back upon itself as the dynamic core of essence, and essence is the result of this act of self-mediation. In relation to capital, this confirms our hypothesis: capital posits labor as its own (capital's) dynamic core.

Another way of looking at this figure of dialectical productiveness through retroactive self-mediation is by observing how the contradiction that allows for the self-development of a particular notion is always-already inscribed in the totality of the relations between that particular notion and the external conditions. In the chapter on "Ground," which follows that on the essentialities, Hegel applies his usual dialectical insight according to which the difference between two opposites is reflected back into self-difference. In this case, the difference between ground (foundation) and its conditions (whatever it is that this ground 'grounds,' i.e., contains and supports) is inherent to ground, inasmuch as the latter, in its grounding function, coincides with a particular relation to its conditions. This is exactly what 'complete ground' (the final stage of the dialectical development of ground into 'formal' and 'real' ground) stands for: not a higher or more complete synthesis of ground and conditions, but the identity between ground and a part of the grounded content, *insofar as only through such identity can ground exercise its grounding function*. What is asserted here is the dialectical correlation between abstract and concrete universality as developed in the subjective logic (concept): in order for abstract university to break out of its aloofness, it must include itself among its concrete particulars.

Thus, far from representing an all-comprehensive whole, ground is grounding *because* it is inherently contradictory: to exercise its foundational role, it must emerge as a *distortion* of ground as substrate. Because of this final determination of ground, the thing or fact that emerges from it is both *unconditioned* and *groundless*, as Hegel puts it at the end of the chapter:

> Ground, therefore, does not remain behind as something distinct from the grounded, but the truth of grounding is that in it ground is united with itself, so that its reflection into another is its reflection into itself. Consequently, the fact is not only the *unconditioned* but also the *groundless*, and it emerges from ground only in so far as ground has "*fallen to the ground*" and ceased to be ground: it emerges from the groundless, that is, from its own essential negativity or pure form.[33]

Through the dialectical process of mediation, then, the fact posits its own preconditions and emerges as unconditioned, that is to say, as something seemingly immediate and self-identical. But, crucially, it also emerges as *groundless*, since the ground has sublated itself, "*fallen to the ground*"; it has collapsed into its inherent distortion. Simply put, the emergence of reality in its essential immediacy (being) is strictly correlative to the vanishing of ground qua external support: all there is, is the appearance of being in its illusory form, but now (after the intervention of *Vernunft*, speculative reason) this form is shown to be mediated by the groundlessness of ground; or, in different terms, *by the impossibility of substance to exert its foundational role*. This paradox has to be taken literally: ground does its job of grounding reality—thus bestowing upon reality the appearance of consistency—by vanishing (or morphing) into a particular relation with its conditions. Ground and conditions mediate themselves to the extent that, as Hegel put it concisely, "[t]he emergence into Existence is therefore immediate in such a manner that it is mediated only by the vanishing of mediation."[34] What confers consistency upon life is an invisible and tautological gesture of grounding whereby ground posits itself as a particular relation to its conditions.[35]

The Speculative Breakthrough

In narrative cinema, editing provides a perfect exemplification of the Hegelian logic of grounding. While embodying the impossibility of representation (the void undermining signification in cinematic images), editing succeeds in conferring consistency upon a given filmic representation the moment it vanishes (or morphs) into a relationship of continuity between two shots.

The more this dialectical relationship strengthens continuity (as in classical narrative cinema), the more editing succeeds in mediating two shots by disappearing and generating the illusion of realism. Alternatively, editing can also problematize continuity by calling attention upon itself. At its most elementary level, however, any filmic narration is enabled by the speculative coincidence of opposites of which Hegel speaks: negativity (the gap between two shots) is the inherent condition of possibility of filmic representation.

In this regard, the use of the long take is particularly interesting because it displaces the formal tension implicit in the editing process onto the filmed content. This logic of displacement is clearly exemplified in the experimental use of the long take that we find in a film like Alexander Sokurov's *Russian Ark* (2002), a ninety-six minute single shot taken inside the Hermitage Museum in Saint Petersburg: here the effect of narrative continuity normally created through editing in post-production is fully *externalized* onto the filmed reality, a real stage of thirty-three museum rooms that reproduce, in condensed format, different epochs in Russian history (though not necessarily in chronological order). This way, editing is shown to be already operative *within* the filmed reality—which is why, incidentally, the experience of visiting a museum is always implicitly cinematic, being based on a flow of moving images that are both separated and connected in spatiotemporal terms.[36]

The speculative mechanism that triggers the constitution of narrative meaning in filmic fictions is exactly the same mechanism that secures a minimum of signification to our subjective experience of reality. Our mind, in other words, is constantly engaged in an editing process, without which reality for us would be meaningless and therefore unbearable. Our reality is always the result of a scene-selection process, whereby certain parts are eliminated while others are spliced together to create meanings. While technological evolution allows for increasingly sophisticated filmmaking techniques, the fundamental rationality involved in any form of representation remains unchanged. As I will discuss in the final sections of the book, the very possibility of representation, which alone allows us to access reality, is what the advent of virtuality threatens to abolish.

Ultimately, then, the Hegelian logic of grounding hinges on this *necessary* passage through the *insubstantial* core of substance: essence creates its own conditions of possibility by acknowledging the failure of being in its grounding function. This is why Kant's antinomies of reason are not merely the expression of an epistemological limitation or deadlock (the gap between the mind and the thing-in-itself), but are instead *ontological*, constitutive of reality as such. What Kant theorized as epistemological limitation becomes for Hegel the ontological proof of reality's inherent contradictoriness.[37] For Hegel, it is precisely on account of its ruptured substance that reality comes into being. There are no external presuppositions to hold on to, only the split within substance. Insofar as reality can be construed and conceptualized, its actual empirical existence depends on the inherent tension at its core. Let us exemplify this through Marx's own conceptualization of capital: Marx's lifelong struggle to capture the essence of the capitalist mode of production, his approximations to the elusive capital-thing, is not just a symptom of his unfinished, failed, or epistemologically incomplete effort. Rather, it marks the very impossibility of capital itself as an ontological formation. Thus, Marx's epistemological limitations (e.g., the antinomies of his labor theory of value) are intrinsic to the object of his analysis.

Lamenting the self-contradictory limit of (any) knowledge implies missing how knowledge by necessity takes into account its own inherent limitation. To put it in the immortal line from Leonard Cohen's song *Anthem*, "there is a crack in everything, that's how the light gets in." In Hegel, the crack within the concept (the fact that reflection is constitutively self-split and inconsistent) is not just the humbling ratification of the epistemological weakness of reason; it is, instead, the ontological condition of possibility of cognition as such. In speculative terms: the light of reason (the affirmative, self-identical dimension of the concept) coincides with its opposite, the crack whose negativity is constantly sublated (mediated, but also preserved) into cognition. This crucial act of self-mediation, always-already inscribed into cognition and its determinations, marks the intervention of the Hegelian subject, whose role is, strictly speaking, that of an unwitting illusionist: its job is to perform the magical trick that converts *contingency* (the groundlessness of the concept) into *necessity* (a specific affirmative self-mediation of groundlessness).

And Hegel's central philosophical argument is that this purely formal act of self-mediation of the negative essence of being is the very condition of reflection, of thinking as such and therefore of consciousness. Against the Kantian-Fichtean subject, who is still capable of transforming the world directly, the Hegelian subject is *absolute* in the specific sense that it assumes responsibility for an act of purely formal conversion. In other words, it presupposes its own capacity to establish its own conditions of possibility, which implies a passage through its own inconsistency. This is why the speculative wisdom we acquire at the end of the dialectical journey depends on a minimal but decisive shift in the way we perceive the appearance of being. While the immediacy of being is all there is, we now realize that this 'being there' is the result of the cognitive sublation of being's impossibility, of the fact that there is *nothing* (literally) behind the appearance of being.

Paradoxically, the failure to accomplish the inversion from *dialectical* to *speculative* reason risks turning into a very sophisticated way of endorsing the power of whatever we oppose or criticize, since this powerful other is conceived as an imposter rather than as a fully mediated entity. The danger implicit in any type of morality, for instance, is that the moralizing subject lends legitimacy to the unmediated content of what it chastises. The limit of morality lies in its failure to perform the dialectical step *from two to four*: from *external reflection* (step 2) to a *determining reflection* (step 3) which is coupled with its *reflective determination* (step 4). For this reason, the moralizing subject ends up deadlocked within a stance of external reflection *whose very existence depends on that which it opposes*. More generally, the disavowed content of the struggle between Good and Evil is the very *groundlessness* of its conditions, which alone is capable of mobilizing authentic antagonism.

This is why, as Hegel argues, the moralizing subject ends up occupying the position of the Beautiful Soul,[38] complaining about the other's evil-doing from a privileged and safe place of externality. Put differently, the moralistic subject fails to discern not only how his/her own position is dialectically mediated by the other—that is to say, how he/she shares with the other the same social substance. More importantly, the Beautiful Soul misses how this substance itself is groundless, insofar as the gap between him/her and the other is reflected back into the missing, nonexistent presuppositions of the struggle. And the political point here would be that only the awareness of such 'common groundlessness' can trigger a real struggle for emancipation.

However, with the disintegration of the capitalist big Other firmly under way, and the tsunami of mass anxiety that comes with it, the moral majority is instinctively prone to safeguard the illusion that there is such a thing as a solid common ground, which is normally evoked by blaming external enemies for its erosion. This fallacy, as thematized by Freud,[39] is constitutive of what we call culture. Ultimately, it is the illusion of freedom, which hinges on the disavowal of the knowledge that there is no stable ground, and that therefore we are in fact caught within a largely deterministic mechanism. Choice, Freud once wrote, operates through a "wishful reversal," which makes it appear "in the place of necessity, destiny."⁴⁰ A degree of disavowal is therefore existentially necessary. In Cioran's enlightening words:

> *Life is possible only by the deficiencies of our imagination and our memory.* We derive our power from our forgetting and from our incapacity to conceive of the plurality of simultaneous fates. No one could survive the instantaneous comprehension of universal grief, each heart being stirred only for a certain quantity of sufferings.⁴¹

The Labor Decoy

The above understanding of Hegel's dialectic is at the heart of my critique of Marx's reading of Hegel. I argue that Marx grasped the dialectical dynamism of capital constituted in circulation (value-form) as *posited* content, and in production (labor) as *external* presupposition, but ended up 1) intuiting but fundamentally neglecting determining reflection as the self-relating negativity of labor qua external presupposition of exchange-value; and consequently 2) missing the speculative passage from determining reflection to reflective determination, which captures the Hegelian theme of the speculative coincidence of opposites. This theoretical shortfall proved decisive in limiting the potential of Marx's critique, for it forced labor into a fundamentally unspeculative dialectical constellation. If conceived 'merely' as external presupposition of value, labor remains caught in the vicious circle of mutual dialectical interrelations. In turn, this prevents labor from realizing how its antagonistic potential vis-à-vis capital can only emerge *after* reflecting back onto itself—after endorsing its negative status. Put differently, as simple negation of its posited content (the capitalist form of value), labor cannot act as vanishing mediator of a postcapitalist social substance, for it remains defined, dialectically, by its relation to what it opposes.

That is to say: labor is not only the negation of its posited capitalist content, but it also harbors such antagonistic potential *within itself.* In-itself, then, labor is, strictly speaking, the impossibility to labor 'for an other'; for-itself, it is a moment of capital's own impossibility qua self-valorizing value; finally, in-and-for-itself, it is the self-mediation of this impossibility, which contains the potential for a formal choice that could convert it into a different relation with its conditions. Thus, only by assuming its own negativity would labor be open to the possibility of reflective determination, the fourth step in which the truth of dialectical opposition turns into its speculative doppelganger, which in our case would coincide with the redefinition of the substantiality of labor.

So far, within the history of capitalist relations, labor has been unable to accomplish the above reconfiguration of its social role. While its relation to capital has remained fundamentally the same, the current science and technology acceleration offers labor the chance to accomplish a thorough redefinition of its essence by endorsing its increasingly redundant status. Today, labor is virtually free from its dialectical struggle with capital and, at least in principle, has a chance to elect a different relation to its conditions *by redefining them radically*, a move that would inevitably generate new sets of systemic contradictions.

This is the speculative power of reflection applied to the key Marxian category of labor-power. Reflective determination is only a step away from its determinate reflection, and yet this is no doubt the hardest step to take. If the capitalist drive has developed labor to the limit of its notional capacity, the trap to avoid is to continue to believe that, if only the political conditions are right, we can reinstate the familiar narrative. What is required is a reflective step into the unknown of a new relation; a thought-act with political traction that, just as it takes that step, simultaneously creates its own conditions. Libertarian theorizations of postwork society invariably fail to take into account how human work is a negative substance that travels through history in search of a home. *Work needs to be told what it is working for.* It needs a politics to coordinate its restlessness and intractability, which in its deepest configuration corresponds to the laboring of the unconscious, the surplus-*jouissance* attached to whatever we do or think.

If Lacan was right, then, labor-power is truly a vanishing mediator, in the precise sense that *it was never there in the first place.* Labor-power can be regarded as the capitalist MacGuffin, the empty cause around which the capitalist narrative turns. Alfred Hitchcock repeatedly told the same story about the MacGuffin:

> It might be a Scottish name, taken from a story about two men on a train. One man says, "What's that package up there in the baggage rack?" And the other answers, "Oh, that's a MacGuffin." The first one asks, "What's a MacGuffin?" "Well," the other man says, "it's an apparatus for trapping lions in the Scottish

Highlands." The first man says, "But there are no lions in the Scottish Highlands," and the other one answers, "Well then, that's no MacGuffin!" So you see that a MacGuffin is actually nothing at all.[42]

In Marx's formula for capital, M-C-M', the mediator C (labor-power as the exceptional commodity that produces surplus-value) is the 'capitalist apparatus' whose role is to conceal the groundlessness of the act through which M magically becomes M'. In short, the truth of M-C-M' is M-M', and not vice versa.[43]

Strictly speaking, labor-power is employed as a *decoy* to conceal the fundamental sleight of hand, the extraordinary act of sorcery, that marks the advent of capitalism and sustains its dialectic of forms, the self-valorization of value.[44] More precisely, labor-power occupies the structural inconsistency of the value-form (*Wertform*). Insofar as it becomes a measurable entity, labor bolsters the illusion that the realm of value is ontologically consistent, defined by discrete and autonomous parts (M and M') that can be productively connected. And the more Marx insisted that labor-power is the substance of value, the more he missed the role of labor-power as decoy. By identifying in the extraction of surplus labor-time the source of surplus-value, Marx effectively discovered, without fully drawing the consequences, how capitalism *anthropomorphizes* its own substance. Or, to put it in Hegelese, how, as truth, capitalism is *not only Substance, but also Subject*. As Žižek put it:[45]

> The subject is the distance of value from itself—also at the level of political economy, where the subject (labor-power) is not only a commodity with a value but also the source of value, i.e., that which, through its use, enriches value by adding surplus-value to it. It is crucial to locate the subject at this "abstract" level of value, not simply at the level of use value—if we do the latter, we reduce the subject to an empirical entity.

From this, Žižek draws the correct conclusion:

> What this means with regard to capitalism is that the basic illusion of the capitalist universe is not that it appears to itself as a speculative circle of self-propagation detached from reality (M-M'), but rather the opposite: not too much speculative

fiction, but too rooted in reality—the reference of the capitalist process of self-reproduction has to remain the fiction that this entire process is grounded in concrete human needs, that it is a complex way in which actual individuals satisfy their actual needs.

If, as Žižek argues, the problem resides in how capitalism claims to satisfy real needs, we should insist that such claim is corroborated by labor and its use-value as determinations of exchange-value. There is no use-value outside the anthropological horizon of exchange-value. As pointed out by Baudrillard, use-value is the *alibi* of the abstract logic of exchange-value; the latter "foments the concrete as its ideological ectoplasm, its phantasm of origin and transcendence."[46] In a similar vein, the universal value of human labor's productivity as upheld by Marx needs to be seen as a retroactive projection of the capitalist dialectic of forms anchored in the alibi of valorized human productivity. When Marx writes of labor and its intrinsic generative power (*Arbeitsvermögen*), he remains caught within the net of the capitalist Other, which, as it were, speaks through him. However, it is not simply, as Baudrillard argued, that the materialist thesis of productive labor as universal human value and categorical imperative is intrinsically idealistic, as it simulates bourgeois ideology. Rather, the materiality of labor is the necessary condition for the capitalist dialectic to unfold. It is the ballast that allows the capitalist aerostat to glide across the stratosphere without being sucked up into space, which is where it is currently heading.

For all its brilliance, Baudrillard's critique of labor shares with other (much less insightful) accounts what Mark Poster described as the "false assumption" of an "ontology of centered presence,"[47] as if beyond the alienating veil of dialectical mediations, one could unearth original symbolic exchanges that would speak for the primeval authenticity of human life. In Cioran's apodictic summation: "Masquerade rules all the living, from the troglodyte to the skeptic."[48] It is because Baudrillard refuses dialectical mediation as the necessary condition of human existence that he flirts with primitivism and "an empty invocation for a spontaneous overthrow of the code à la May, 1968."[49] Thus, his notion of symbolic exchange as alternative to economic productivity remains disappointingly elusive and underdeveloped for the simple reason that it stands for a theoretically weak ontology of presence. Baudrillard's injunction to abandon "the terrorism of value" in order to "rethink discharge and symbolic exchange"[50] can only be translated into a dialectical rearrangement of the sociosymbolic link currently sustained by capitalist alienation, one which would necessarily preserve the dialectical form while reconfiguring the symptom.

Big Data and the Fanaticism of Breathing

By ontologizing the relationship between labor and value-production, most variants of the Marxist labor movements of the twentieth century remained defined by the same narrative that framed the historical evolution of the capitalist mode of production since its inception. In Kurz's words: "[I]n Marxism the aporia of Marx's concept of labour was dissolved one-sidedly into the positive ontology of labour."[51] So-called orthodox Marxism has largely operated within a definition of political economy that resembles capitalism's own. Thus, dialectical materialism ended up playing the socialist game on the ontological turf of capital, which explains why socialist work societies embraced the dogma of productivity.

Here, again, it is useful to quote Baudrillard: "By presupposing the axiom of the economic, the Marxist critique perhaps deciphers the *functioning* of the *system* of political economy; but at the same time it reproduces it as a model."[52] Identifying in labor-power the lever by which to overturn the order of capital only results in affirming "the most subtle ideological phantasm [i.e., fantasy] that capital itself has elaborated."[53] As full-blown work societies, socialist regimes were effectively state capitalist societies, and as such they were worthy of Engels's famous characterization of the State as *der ideelle Gesammtkapitalist* (the ideal total capitalist). Socialism shares with capitalism the grounding deception that labor *is* economic value, exchangeable against value. The mistake, therefore, lies in considering socialism as a process of systemic overcoming of the capitalist mode of production. While 'actually existing socialism' also stood for working-class solidarity in the face of capitalist exploitation, socialist ideology was affected by a considerable degree of dialectical naivety. What a postcapitalist society requires, then, cannot be defined in traditional socialist terms.

Similarly, the proponents of workers' autonomy, based on the *general intellect* to usher in a ready-made postcapitalist society without work, tend to forget the basics: that capitalism is a powerful *social* relation where antagonistic forces are posited as *necessary* to its reproduction. For this reason, a world where full automation replaces human labor is more likely to resemble an obscene, dystopian carnival than luxury communism. The central problem with postwork utopias is their disavowal of the causal connection between wealth and the capital-labor dialectic. Once the latter is abolished, wealth as we know it also vanishes. As brilliantly summed up by Wassily Leontief a few decades ago, "everyone would starve in Paradise."[54]

The key Hegelian and psychoanalytic lesson is that the painful liberation from the symbolic narratives that make us who we are can only be tolerated for the time it takes us to assume a new symbolic mandate. Such freedom must therefore be endorsed as the driving force that leads us from a decaying world like ours, to the formation of a new network of social mediations. The latter could well redeploy a range of normative principles including democratic deliberation and decentralized administration.

In respect of a hypothetical transition, the feedback infrastructure of contemporary information technology is likely to play a crucial role in determining new ecologies of noncapitalist social coordination.[55] It would therefore be unwise to reject Big Data on the basis of its current misuse. Rather, we ought to note that the digital feedback infrastructure at the heart of the ongoing high-tech revolution reflects the elementary feedback loop that qualifies the dialectic. Think of Amazon's patent on anticipatory shipping. This is a system of predictive analytics through which Amazon delivers products to consumers in a specific area *before* they actually place an order, i.e., before they know they want them. Its logic is retroactive: by collecting troves of data about customer preference and habits, the info-savvy company knows what our shopping list 'will have looked like.' While this is horribly dystopian, it is worth considering how its logic actually reproduces the retroactive loop of the dialectic, whereby subjective identities are always taken care of *in advance* by a backward mechanism of grounding.

Jacques Lacan devised a similar model of structural grounding with his post-Saussurean theory of language, where the big Other works similarly to Big Data in holding advance information about what we 'will have been.' Interestingly, in her book *The Age of Surveillance Capitalism*, Shoshana Zuboff, arguably unaware of Lacan, uses the term big Other to capture the monstrous, totalitarian digital apparatus through which surveillance capitalism works by "replacing the engineering of souls with the engineering of behaviour":[56]

> Big Other does not care what we think, feel, or do as long as its millions, billions, and trillions of sensate, actuating, computational eyes and ears can observe, render, datafy, and instrumentalize the vast reservoirs of behavioral surplus that are generated in the galactic uproar of connection and communication.[57]

A technologically upgraded version of Bentham's panopticon, big Other here is what numbs us into obeying the "capitalist Leviathan," as our democratic values and freedom of choice crumble worldwide. While this point is objectively true, it is also articulated around a nondialectical vision whose logic is suspect, for it fails to consider how the (Lacanian) big Other is *the very condition of possibility of our subjectivity*. The dialectical point to highlight—which is missed by Zuboff and others who lament the unethical, antidemocratic character of surveillance capitalism, rather than addressing the capitalist mode of production as such—is that our alienation in the big Other is the ontological precondition for (what we regard as) subjective freedom. The paradox is that the only way for us to exercise any kind of free choice is to give up on freedom in the first place: our identities are strictly speaking predetermined through our necessary immersion in, and unconscious internalization of, the sociosymbolic substance into which we are born. At a basic human level, we are all puppets or automata, and it is only against this deterministic background that the possibility of actual freedom arises.

While the deterministic preformatting of our identities by definition fails, since it generates a nonsymbolizable remainder that escapes its own logic, it is nevertheless undeniable that any substantial content we acquire as subjects requires our compulsory immersion in the alienating Other, a symbolic narrative whose power over us predates our capacity to comprehend it critically. This is the theme that Žižek has popularized with the motto "belief before belief":[58] in order to exercise my freedom of choice as a rational human being, I must have already accepted, unconsciously, the elementary ideological coordinates of my world. In Cioran's words: "[E]ven a trifle of existence presupposes an unavowed faith; a simple step—even toward a mock-up of reality—is an apostasy with regard to nothingness; breathing itself proceeds from an implicit fanaticism, like any participation in movement."[59]

My philosophical wager here is that Big Data is, in its most profound signification, the market's current mode of exploiting the ontological architecture of subjectivity, which explains why the world's largest financial banks are investing extraordinary amounts of money in research on data and information technology.[60] In Evgeny Morozov's words, "the possibilities opened up by latest innovations make even the most pragmatic and down-to-earth venture capitalists reach for their wallets."[61] While this forward-escaping mechanism into data-driven high tech must be subjected to ruthless criticism, since it perpetuates the moribund logic of value accumulation, its form should not be jettisoned a priori. Rather, we ought to be bold enough to see in its feedback logic the dialectical matrix of the social constellation to come, *beyond* the Silicon Valley model.

Whether in the form of a Green New Deal,[62] or of a New Deal on Data, our relationship with technology will do precious little to prevent the erosion of the capitalist ice sheet, with its attendant ethical, ecological and sociopolitical values. Information technology will neither reinvent capitalism nor save it from implosion, especially if we continue to confuse capitalism with market efficiency. The recent flurry of publications on the impact of Big Data, for instance, reflects the above shortsightedness. Despite their differences, the authors of such books as *Reinventing Capitalism in the Age of Big Data*, *Capitalism without Capital*, *The Age of Surveillance Capitalism*, and *World after Capital* all miss the fundamental insight that surplus-value is a social category. This is why it is worth reiterating that the target of Marx's critique is capitalism as a social mode of production: it concerns the production of social (including political and cultural) relations, from which it derives ontological plasticity.[63] As I discuss in the following chapter, failing to grasp capitalist ontology means retreating into nondialectical nostalgia, which is politically conservative despite its good intentions.

Chapter 5

The Financial Demon

Shackled by Nostalgia

The near-ubiquitous critique of financial capitalism is one of the most fascinating events of our time. Arguably, in recent years it has risen to the dignity of what in psychoanalysis is known as a symptom. What does the financial symptom relate to? What traumatic truth does it intercept? After the 2008 meltdown, we have all been made aware of how intrinsically corrupt our financial system is. I am referring to the regime of accumulation that has progressively become dominant after the fall of the Berlin wall: the so-called "new economy," with neoliberalism as its politico-ideological counterpart (insofar as neoliberalism is, to paraphrase Clausewitz's famous aphorism, "the continuation of politics by other means"). It was then that we entered the golden age of what Marx called "fictitious capitalism." Friedrich Hayek, Ludwig von Mises, Milton Friedman, and their disciples were saluted across the world as prophets of a new socioeconomic gospel that was going to free the developed world from the diabolical stagflation of the 1970s. To retrigger growth after the demise of Fordism and its Keynesian policies, they told us, it would be enough to eliminate all (juridical, political, cultural, etc.) obstacles to the free proliferation of the markets, while cultivating the potentiation of an old weapon in the capitalist arsenal: finance.

Indeed, deregulated financial productivity has been the bread and butter of capitalism ever since, to the extent that, as argued by Michael Hudson,[1] contemporary politics is effectively controlled by the finance, insurance, and real estate (FIRE) sector, and its neorentier economies. Against the rationale of industrial capitalism, FIRE seek wealth primarily through the extraction of economic rent, which is capitalized by the financial industry into bank loans, stocks, and bonds. In the meantime, the exploitation of labor is increasingly mediated by debt (credit-card debt, student debt, etc.), while housing and other prices are inflated on credit. This results in deflation, as less income can be spent on goods and services.

More generally, financial productivity has equipped the system with the decisive tool to exit the cul-de-sac of postwar state (welfare) capitalism, while offering everyone the irresistible prospect of investments with immense profitability (and loss) margins. At the same time, post-Fordism has managed to obfuscate the political scene of the antagonism between labor and capital, inaugurating a new and more insidious type of subjugation. In Gorz's words: "The conflictual dynamics of Fordist relations of production tended towards ever greater limitation of the space-time available to capital for exploiting labour and of the scope of that exploitation. It is this dynamic which was first halted, then reversed, in post-Fordism."[2]

While the systematic bursting of financial bubbles since the 1990s should have alerted us to the illusory nature of financial growth, this awareness seems to have materialized only in 2008, with the subprime mortgage crisis and consequent credit crunch, which threatened the collapse of the world economy—were it not, of course, for the swift intervention of state-sponsored bail-out packages that, by drawing on public liquidity, jumpstarted the financial markets and restored the illusion of sustainability. Yet, despite 2008, financial transactions, which now take place at the speed of algorithmic light, continue to constitute the core of our economy. The finance industry is constantly refining its art of creating capital through buying and selling various forms of money, especially debt, making its decoupling from the real economy ever more palpable. This means that economic wealth, and annexed social reproduction, increasingly takes the form of hypertrophic speculations on future gains rather than on value that has already been obtained. As Hyman Minsky famously put it, our economy looks increasingly like an "inverted pyramid," where the "point upon which it rests, that which carries the largest load, consists of business profits."[3]

Despite the painful lesson of 2008, then, we continue to count our chickens before they hatch: the titles that make up the greatest mass of value today only count as a priority claim over future production and realization of value in the real economy, a prospect increasingly dependent upon the spiritual category known as 'blind faith.' Furthermore, the global propagation of deregulated spaces for speculative trading has had the dubious merit of displacing exploitation from recognizable social groups to an invisible financial virus that suffocates the whole of society. We are borrowing from a future that does not exist and will never come, for it is made of speculative iterations—literally, mirror reflections (*speculum* = mirror)—of fictitious value disengaged from human labor. Like Pinocchio, we believe that by planting it, money will naturally grow on trees. Or, as Marx put it:

> As in the case of labour-power, the use-value of money here is its capacity of creating value—a value greater than it contains. Money as money is potentially self-expanding value and is loaned out as such—which is the form of sale for this singular commodity. It becomes a property of money to generate value and yield interest, much as it is an attribute of pear-trees to bear pears. And the money-lender sells his money as just such an interest-bearing thing.[4]

Yet, when the financial mirror cracks it reflects a broken society.

Here, however, we should pause and cool down our rage against the financial popcorn industry. The dominant view among those who decry the abnormity of the economy's financial dilation is that, at one point in its long history, capitalism took the wrong turn, falling victim to the greed of the usual suspects, the Bernie Madoffs in our midst—a familiar narrative in a meritocratic world that loves to personalize guilt. This view is fundamentally flawed. It presumes the healthy nature of earlier forms of capitalism and fails to take into account how today's speculative appetite has always fueled the engine of the capitalist machine. The reason why the financial sector has become so dominant is that the labor narrative has grown impotent. The foundations of the world we live in no longer reside in the labor contained in commodities like cars, phones, or toothpaste. Instead, it increasingly consists of debt-leveraged speculations on future returns of financial titles like bonds, stocks, options, and annuities, whose value is securitized potentially ad infinitum. It is true that only a religious belief that the huge mass of these titles will yield value keeps us from staring into the gaping abyss beneath our feet (like the Walt Disney cartoon character suspended in midair after running over the edge of a cliff). However, to believe that the scene of the labor-capital dialectic can be resuscitated only means that we are willing to be fooled twice.

With artificial intelligence looming large on our posthuman horizon, labor will be further marginalized in absolute terms, and growth prospects will increasingly depend on the acrobatics performed in the magical world of finance. In more mundane terms: there is no turning back. The global volume of financial products exchanged every day on the world's financial markets is already incongruent with the mass of value produced in the real economy, and this alone ought to make us think long and hard about our nostalgia for a world built upon 'concrete' capitalist wealth. It is now estimated that three major index fund managers (BlackRock, Vanguard, and State Street Global Advisors), which together employ around 35,000 workers, will soon control a financial mass equal to half of the GDP produced globally.[5]

As repeatedly underlined by the late Robert Kurz (and, more recently, by Ernst Lohoff and Norbert Trenkle),[6] when we discuss real and financial capital today, we are referring to two separate entities with no common ground. The market value of both Apple and Google (Alphabet) has now breached the astronomical threshold of $1 trillion, while the number of workers they each employ is estimated at around 135,000 (in 2020). The disproportion between market value and labor productivity is so staggering that no sane person would believe for a moment that there is a causal connection between the value generated by the sweat of one's brow and the value of financial capitalization.

Consequently, it really makes little sense to continue to indulge in the illusory (but morally edifying) tale that, due to its immoderate and parasitic voraciousness, casino capitalism has perverted healthy economic dynamism. This is probably the most shackling nostalgic narrative we could fall for. As always with nostalgia, it tends to distort the object it longingly evokes. Suffice it to recall how the great Fordist boom itself was in large part financed by state debt, as fiscal revenues alone were already insufficient to cover the costs of social spending and infrastructures. At that point, most of a state's internal expenditure did not emerge from labor, but from debt, the interest on which began to be paid back via the issuing of state credit as marketable government bonds. As states found it increasingly difficult to finance public services through revenues originating in surplus-values, they were forced to rely on the financial composition of credit.

Simulated growth, then, was already inscribed in the model of economic expansion that characterized the postwar period, which is often wistfully conjured up as a still viable alternative to financial degeneration. By the same token, it is equally pointless to believe that industrial capitalism will, if only managed correctly, catch up with its financial overgrowth. This rationale drives austerity policies, which cause further impoverishment and the structural disintegration of societies that had to indebt themselves up to their ears to step in line with the requirements of speculative accumulation. The financial services sector represents capital's self-styled, implicitly desperate attempt to escape the internal contradiction of its mode of production. In concrete terms, our economic system sustains itself against the impossible promise to repay a monstrous amount of global debt (approximately $300 trillion, i.e., 300 plus 12 zeros, growing as you read this).[7]

We should therefore insist that the financial demon does not constitute a malicious deviation from a healthy economy, but is instead a necessary *surrogate* of the original mode of (industrial) production. The financial demon is an expression of the inner demons of capitalism as such. More explicitly stated: the monetary capital that cannot be reinvested profitably in the real economy has no choice but to head for the financial markets, where it inflates bubbles. Over the last quarter century, leading macroeconomists and policymakers have invariably implemented monetary programs that they have proudly considered to be safe (as Gordon Brown did from 1997 to 2007, when he repeatedly declared the end of boom and bust).[8] Yet, it was precisely the period from the 1980s to 2007 that saw the quickest, wildest, and most corrosive increase in real estate, stocks, and bonds investments since 1945. The great majority of these speculations were debt-leveraged investment strategies (based on borrowed money). While this means that credit ended up fueling financial investment, which inevitably depressed wages, it is wrong to assume that it is simply a matter of greed or shortsightedness—as if capitalism were not *by definition* greedy and shortsighted. Rather, if banks and investment funds began backing speculations on property and financial assets, this ought to have been seen as a clear warning that the traditional option was becoming increasingly unrealistic, as less and less value could be wrung out of labor.

What we tend to disavow when we blame financial capitalism for the fragility of our condition, is that the real economy is already dead, although its *specter* is still circulating. Such is the strength of the capitalist symptom: it enjoins us to stick with a socioeconomic narrative that has passed its use-by date. The contemporary dominance of the financial industry confronts us with the nakedness of the capitalist symptom, which is no longer clouded in the modern architecture of liberal-democratic values that were installed to safeguard the work society. Finance, in other words, embodies our symptomatic attachment to the capitalist regime. It is not a tumor of such regime, but its essence. How, then, should we confront it?

Starting from the claim that the derivative (an asset whose value depends on the value of another asset, including another derivative) is a purely linguistic phenomenon that sums up the semantics of financial speculation, Arjun Appadurai has recently suggested that a retro-performative redefinition of sociality through the creative democratization of the risk-taking logic of financial capitalism could mean "beating global finance at its own game," since it would point to a way out of self-cannibalizing finance by destroying its foundations in the modern social contract.[9] The merit of Appadurai's proposal is that it avoids any nostalgic pining for the work society and its value system. However, it also fails to tackle both commodity fetishism as the elementary form of capitalist ideology, and, consequently, the crucial issue of wealth-creation in a future society that would no longer be based on labor-power. In short, any attempt to redefine the social bond from the vantage point of the volatile financial sector cannot evade the critique of the tectonic processes of value-formation.

Capitalist Bulimia

As a rule, capitalists invest in the financial industry when experiencing a fall in the rate of profit, which drives up the price of the assets they buy. While the expansion of speculative capital allows enterprises to keep up the appearance of prosperity, in truth this prosperity depends on debt—a paradoxical situation turned endemic over the last three decades. During this period, the massive increase in global liquidity in the form of bank loans, securitized debt, and especially derivatives (from 150 percent, in 1990, to 350 percent of global GDP in 2011), produced four credit bubbles.[10] The destructive bursting of the last bubble (2008) forced governments to bail out their banking systems. How? Essentially, by increasing their borrowing. The economic system's major contradiction, visible to the naked eye (private debt to GDP ratio), was absorbed by the public sector, which ran to the rescue of corporate meltdown to prevent social collapse. The result of this maneuver was a major escalation in sovereign (public) debt. (It is worth recalling that the unprecedented rise in private sector debt had already started in the 1970s, when, for the first time in the twentieth century, it became larger than sovereign debt.)[11]

As reported by the McKinsey Global Institute in February 2015 and August 2018, despite the post-2008 deleveraging of private debt at the expense of sovereign debt (which also had to finance widening budget deficits), the ratio of global debt (private and public) to global GDP has continued to increase: "As the Great Recession receded, many expected to see a wave of deleveraging. But it never came. Confounding expectations, the combined global debt of governments, nonfinancial corporations, and households has grown by $72 trillion since the end of 2007."[12] Thus, the 2008 crisis, which set off the first global recession since World War II, not only planted the seeds for a sovereign debt crisis, especially in the Eurozone; it also failed to remedy the debt hemorrhage in the corporate sector, which continued to rise worldwide. The predictable result is that, today, advanced economies "appear to run on ever-larger amounts of debt."[13]

In light of this debt-addiction, current economic debates continue to focus on the "austerity vs stimulus" alternative, where growth is either determined by cutting sovereign debt through austerity policies (which effectively shift the weight of debt from capital to labor) or by neglecting debt and attempting to boost the economy through investments that are expected to stimulate demand. The contemporary neoliberal versus neo-/post-Keynesian debate, however, reproduces the same form of disavowal: it ignores the simple yet crucial insight that what determines the economy's dependency on debt and finance is a growing and unstoppable contraction in profitability. Since the 1980s we have been faced with warning signs of gigantic proportions: masses of unproductive capitals seeking profitability through credit and financial speculation rather than investments in the real economy. This is because financial gains, primarily by debt leverage, started to outstrip profits made by hiring labor. The capacity to create wealth through traditional channels was eroded dramatically by the unprecedented rise in the organic composition of capital, which Marx defined as the ratio between investment in *constant* capital (machinery, raw materials, energy, etc.) and in *variable* capital (wage labor).

The (in)famous law of the "tendency of the rate of profit to fall," expounded in chapter 13 of *Capital* volume 3, is still, in this sense, Marx's most significant "law of motion," and a useful theoretical tool to measure the aging process of our economy. Let us briefly summarize it. Counterintuitively, Marx claims that raising profitability through investment in new machines and technology impacts negatively on the rate of profit. This means that, as capitalism grows, its very process of expansion undermines its conditions of possibility. But what is the rate of profit? Marx calculates it as the ratio between surplus-value (the added value extracted from labor-power and not covered by the salary) and the totality of capital invested in production (the organic composition of capital, i.e., *constant* plus *variable* capital). If we call the value of constant capital c, the value of variable capital v, and surplus-value s, the rate of profit is $s/(c + v)$.

For this rate to grow, surplus-value (the rate of exploitation of labor-power) has to increase progressively in relation to the organic composition of capital. So, why does this rate decline instead of growing? Essentially, because the extraction of surplus-value from labor-power is undermined by the rise in c/v, that is, by growing technological investment in constant capital (machines), which drives production costs down. To put it in more profane terms: by investing in labor-shedding technologies, the capitalist loses sight of the causal link between labor-power and surplus-value; he 'forgets' that only living labor creates new surplus-value. Thus, the rise in the organic composition of capital and the concurrent displacement of labor-power trigger a crisis of profitability. As summarized by Jeremy Rifkin:

> Marx believed that the ongoing effort by producers to continue to replace human labor with machines would prove self-defeating in the end. By directly eliminating human labor from the production process and by creating a reserve army of unemployed workers whose wages could be bid down lower and lower, the capitalists were inadvertently digging their own grave, as there would be fewer and fewer consumers with sufficient purchasing power to buy their products.[14]

While Marx was right in observing that technological innovation has long-time adverse consequences for the rate of profit, he also highlighted how, in the short or medium term, a number of countervailing forces are able to offset the decline of the rate of profit. For instance, constant capital can become cheaper through either technological progress or destructive economic crises; or the rate of surplus-value can be increased by more intense exploitation of the workforce by various means. Irrespective of these and other forces, however, Marx believed that the tendency of profits to fall was intrinsic to the capitalist mode of production, thus providing a reliable instrument to measure the latter's historical decline.[15]

What Marx could not foresee, however, was the magnitude of the current impact of automation. What is at stake today, then, is not only a tendency that, as such, still allowed capital to resort to several counter-balancing strategies. Rather, the current rate of automation of work, and consequent drastic reduction of investment in living labor in all sectors of the economy, causes a calamitous fall in the *absolute mass of profit*, as Marx had intuited in the often-cited "fragment on the machine" in the *Grundrisse*. Here, Marx gives a precise definition of capital as a "moving contradiction": "Capital itself is the moving contradiction, [in] that it presses to reduce labour time to a minimum, while it posits labour time, on the other side, as sole measure and source of wealth."[16] Such contradiction now affects the profitability of capital as a social totality. Robert Kurz expressed this point with clarity back in 1999:

> What happens in a crisis is not primarily an intensified fall in the rate of profit, but above all a fall in the absolute mass of profit, which means that the compensating expansionary movement and hence production itself comes to a halt on a large, social scale. [. . .] The absolute mass of profit falls without limit, and the majority of people are put out of the running. This is because at a certain stage of the scientification of production (which includes a degree of substitution of technical units for workers) the underlying production of the "substance of value" is not feasible anymore on a socially substantial scale. At this point the degeneration of the substance of value is transformed from a relative (fall in the rate of profit) into an absolute (fall in the mass of profit) status, which becomes apparent by a broad shut-down of production and persistent large-scale unemployment.[17]

The difference between an absolute fall in the mass of profits and a tendential fall in the rate of profit is decisive. If we consider computer technology, which is at the heart of the above revolution, we only need to recall Moore's law and its core principle that computational power roughly doubles every two years. While the speed of this acceleration might tickle our futuristic imagination, it also spells doom for the economy, for it generates structural mass unemployment, a category that includes underemployment, wage dumping, social welfare (e.g., basic income), socioeconomic exclusion, and all forms of destitution and immiseration. As noted by Gorz in 1997, these features bring to mind "social conditions which prevailed at the beginning of the nineteenth century for a growing proportion of the workforce":

> Since 1993, permanent, full-time employees have made up only 10 per cent of the workforces of the 500 largest American companies. In Europe, particularly in Great Britain and France, that particular form of insecure employment known as "contract

work" has developed. These contract workers, found in the public services and elsewhere, do the same work as the regular staff, but have neither the same status, nor the same benefit entitlements, nor the same levels of pay. They are at the beck and call of the employer, who (in the French education system or postal services, for example) guarantees them what is often a derisory minimum of hours per month or per year, without, however, fixing the date and times of their service beforehand: they are informed of these only a day in advance, or even—as in the British "zero-hours contract"—on the actual day.[18]

The above constellation, which Keynes in 1930 had explicitly called "technological unemployment,"[19] suggests that "the compensating historical expansionary movement of capital has come to a standstill."[20] And it is precisely at this point that investment in fictitious capital comes into the equation. For it is not accidental that, since the early 1970s, all advanced economies have squeezed their capital investment in labor while compensating with higher investment in financial and property speculation. Put differently, the share of national income going to labor is falling dramatically if compared to that going to capital. What we have witnessed in recent decades is the radical *decoupling* of productivity and employment: while the former continues to grow, the latter sags. If some mainstream economists still argue that technological progress, overall, creates more jobs than it destroys, this is because they elect to ignore the causal connection between labor and profit, preferring instead to look at the economy through quantitative spectacles.[21] But even then, the situation appears dire. Suffice it to consider that, in the US, the first decade of the twenty-first century saw a "zero net job creation"[22]—against 27 percent in the 1970s, a decade normally associated with stagflation and crisis—to get an idea of how delusional the optimistic views are.

Incidentally, it is in this context that we should place the link between Malthusianism and capitalism. With capitalism, overpopulation does not simply mean that there are areas of the world perceived as overcrowded, but that vast portions of humanity are superfluous in relation to the capitalist logic of accumulation. Specifically, this relates to unproductive categories such as the old and the permanently unemployed, who are not part of the "industrial reserve army" because they are no longer needed by capital. The neo-Malthusian idea that there is a surplus population consuming resources and polluting without being productive is inscribed in the exploitative DNA of capitalism, just as it was at the heart of Nazism.

Going back to the main argument, let us reiterate that the object of Marx's critique is not a particular empirical capital, but capital as a social totality, an entity comparable to Hegel's *Geist*. This means that if a potential increase in productivity through technological automation can be beneficial to individual companies, it nevertheless reduces the total mass of value realized. In the past, this immanent contradiction only had a minimal impact on capitalism's ability to produce wealth and sustain its self-expansion, for market extensions have always allowed capital to engage more human labor than the amount it made superfluous. Not long ago, however, we have passed the point of no return, reaching an absolute historical limit where the compulsive pursuit of profit becomes fatally counterproductive. Bulimia is not just one of the so-called new symptoms of the contemporary subject. It is also the brutal manifestation of the objective impotence of capitalist dynamism, for the more accumulation continues, the more it results in a debilitated social body.

Contemporary crisis should not be regarded only as a matter of underaccumulation or overproduction, as often claimed by orthodox Marxist theory. Rather, it concerns a mode of production that has made financial accumulation necessary for its own survival. Contemporary capitalism is condemned to *borrow from an imaginary future*. Since this delusive aspiration demands ever-greater sacrifices, the simple question to pose is: why are our lives still dependent on the valorization fetish? Why are we complicit with the criminal demand that our societies reproduce themselves through the exhausted logic of accumulation, which causes widespread economic depression, socioeconomic apartheid, and an impending ecological catastrophe?

The Anatomy of Finance Is the Key to the Anatomy of the Real Economy

While today's financial engineering has assumed a life of its own, in order to understand its logic we must place it fully within the fold of the original mode of production. One of the reasons why Marx's theory of value is still relevant is that it allows us to grasp how—to paraphrase Marx's claim from the *Grundrisse*—[23] the anatomy of today's 'casino capitalism' is the key to the anatomy of capital's self-valorization, the original engine of its mode of production. What financial capitalism reveals is the elementary form through which political economy acquires social effectivity in the modern world. How? In its autotelic logic, M-M' lays bare the fundamental bluff of M-C-M', where the labor commodity is employed as the precondition for capitalist accumulation, the *quantified human factor* that turns capitalism into a *social* ontology. In other words, M-M' reveals the truth of capital insofar as it is already at work in M-C-M', although here obscured by the signifier *labor*.

Marx clearly understood what is widely neglected by mainstream economics, namely, that only living labor creates capitalist value, as commodities need to possess a certain amount of congealed human labor if they are to yield profits when they are sold. This fundamental negligence leads Nobel-prized, world-leading economists to give bizarre explanations for global disasters like the 2008 credit crunch. Take Alan Greenspan (chairman of the US Federal Reserve until 2006) and Henry Paulson (US Secretary of Treasury between 2006 and 2009, who only in April 2007 had claimed that the economy was healthy): they both agreed that the crisis was a 'perfect storm,' a once-in-a-lifetime event that could not have been predicted. The 'chance explanation' is indeed a common denominator in postcrisis assessments. Ben Bernanke, the world expert of 'depression economics,' and Fed chairman after Greenspan (2006–14), not only reassured everyone, in May 2007, on the solidity of the subprime mortgage market. He also explained 2008 and the ensuing recession as a classic case of "financial panic":[24] speculative investment gets out of control and, because financial institutions lack proper regulation and pile up risky assets, at some point panic sets in, triggering a fire sale. And if chance alone cannot explain crisis, then it must be bankers' greed. Or, alternatively, not enough greed (the liquidity trap, insufficient desire to buy or invest).

Whether of the neoclassical or the Keynesian persuasion, mainstream explanations remain largely tautological and descriptive, looking for causes in the financial market rather than in the big bang moment of value production. For the proponents of neoclassical economics, who believe in the natural efficiency of free markets, the culprit is excessive credit, originating in central banks and government intervention. For Keynesians, crises are caused by the opposite obsession with cutting government spending, which leads to a drop in demand that in turn affects what Keynes famously called *animal spirits*: all of a sudden, a general lack of confidence creeps in, the most harmful thing that could ever happen to an otherwise perfectly lubricated machine. For Keynes himself, as for neo- and post-Keynesians, there is nothing wrong with the capitalist locomotive. In the words of Paul

Krugman, the leading Keynesian economist and Nobel laureate, "the problem is not with the economic engine, which is as powerful as ever. Instead, we are talking about what is basically a technical problem, a problem of organization and coordination."[25]

While Keynesians like Krugman as a rule agree that excessive financial risk-taking is deleterious, they again and again offer the same alternative: less money hoarding and more spending (investment). In other words, they stop short of asking *why* our societies have been put on the drip of financial speculation, which Keynes himself had already tagged as "a by-product of the activities of a casino."[26] Even left Keynesians like Hyman Minsky opt to ignore the fundamental question. While the so-called "Minsky moment" is no doubt useful to describe how the expansion of the financial industry eventually collapses into debt deflation, Minsky's theory continues, like mainstream economics as a whole, to emphasize subjective variables like expectations about investments, thus neglecting the profitability issue. Something similar can be said for post-Keynesians like Thomas Piketty and his "inequality theory," or contemporary Marxist Keynesians like John Bellamy Foster and David Harvey, for whom capitalist crisis is, fundamentally, a problem of overaccumulation (surpluses that cannot be absorbed profitably in the economy).[27] In short, whether in favor or against stimulus, mainstream economics uniformly disavows the issue concerning the creation of surplus value out of living labor.

It is indeed remarkable how for mainstream economists across the board establishing the origin of profits is fundamentally irrelevant. What they miss is, in economic terms, a relation of profitability (the capitalist profits from the worker's labor power); in political terms, one of exploitation (the worker is expropriated of a given amount of labor power); and in philosophical terms, one of *dialectical autopoiesis* (the creation of our 'world' through the creation of its conditions of possibility). These dimensions are kept together by the third one, which constitutes the blind spot of capitalist modernity insofar as it informs our symptomatic attachment to conditions that are no longer working.

Genie out of the Capitalist Bottle

In Lacanian terms, a symptom (*sinthome*) is the kernel of unconscious *jouissance* (libidinal attachment) that glues us to a given lifeworld. As such, it constitutes the foundation of subjectivity inasmuch as it remains fundamentally removed from consciousness. Counterintuitively, this split at the heart of subjectivity is what makes a social bond possible, allowing our life to acquire the semblance of coherence and meaningfulness. All social bonds are ultimately held together by our unconscious enjoyment of specific aspects of their operating structure. What Marx termed "commodity fetishism," for instance, represents our blind, symptomatic attachment to the imploding work society. Will such implosion unlock the potential for a reconfiguration of the capitalist symptom?

Our condition remains ambivalent: if the labor narrative has reached the end of its historical line, we are nevertheless faced by the most difficult task of all, which is structurally identical with the task of the analysand vis-à-vis his/her symptom. That is to say, we need to recognize the *contingency* and *partiality* of our unconscious enjoyment of the capitalist symptom. The lesson of Lacanian psychoanalysis is that, while our unconscious attachments cannot be dissolved, we can nevertheless reconfigure their content, changing the way we signify the world through them. This change is what is required today, when our world is turning worldless, insofar as it is represented solely by the asocial *jouissance* of the capitalist drive. A postcapitalist social syntax can only emerge after a break from our unconscious attachment to our depressive existential horizon.

Let us remind ourselves that the capitalist drive is inherently self-revolutionary, constantly engaged in escaping its own contradiction, overcoming it whichever way it can. This explains why, in the 1980s, capitalism leaped into the enchanted world of growth simulation, to the extent that by 2005 global financial assets reached 316 percent of world output.[28] In its contemporary condition, however, capitalism finds it increasingly hard to self-revolutionize without revealing its ruse, addiction, and therefore impotence. Whether through new forms of political authoritarianism or disguised under ever-thinner varieties of liberal democracy, the financial industry pulls the strings in every corner of our world. And, as often claimed by (among others) Jean-Claude Michèa,[29] since the end of the 1970s the liberal "left" (from Helmut Schmidt to Francois Mitterrand, Tony Blair, Bill Clinton, Barack Obama, and now Joe Biden) has proved to be financial capital's more reliable ally in the fight to eliminate the last vestiges of implicit or explicit resistance to its proliferation.

The belief that capital is naturally predisposed to bear fruits remains today the central fetish in virtually all discussions of political economy. Sadly, the figure of the "vulgar economist" that Marx critiqued in the early 1860s is the *only* figure remaining:

> To the vulgar economist who desires to represent capital as an independent source of value, a source which creates value, this form [interest-bearing capital] is of course a godsend, a form in which the source of profit is no longer recognisable and the result of the capitalist process—separated from the process itself—acquires an independent existence. In M-C-M' an intermediate link is still retained. In M-M' we have the incomprehensible form of capital, the most extreme inversion and materialisation of production relations.[30]

Faced as we are by the naked contradiction of accumulation, expressed in its purest form by the autotelic logic of finance (M-M', money begetting money), it is nothing short of perverse to continue to deny the impasse of our mode of production.

What needs to be confronted urgently when assessing the financial symptom is unbridled capitalism's growing inability to hide its original bluff. The cause of this fallibility was already exposed in 1913 by Rosa Luxemburg, who identified it in capital's imperialist tendency:

> [T]he more violently, ruthlessly and thoroughly imperialism brings about the decline of non-capitalist civilisations, the more rapidly it cuts the very ground from under the feet of capitalist accumulation. Though imperialism is the historical method for prolonging the career of capitalism, it is also a sure means of bringing it to a swift conclusion. This is not to say that capitalist development must be actually driven to this extreme: the mere tendency towards imperialism of itself takes forms which make the final phase of capitalism a period of catastrophe.[31]

When exploring our "period of catastrophe," we should acknowledge that 'old and new' are traversed by the same ontological inconsistency. The irreconcilable difference between 'real economy' and 'new economy' is the ontological contradiction of both, and as such it accompanies the historical trajectory of capitalism as its ominous shadow. Today's financial imperialism throws into relief the contradiction of the capitalist relation as such.

Let us recall that, in Hegel, the positive totality of a notion—its power to mediate reality fully—is speculatively identical with a nonmediated, contingent remainder that, produced by the very vortex of the dialectical spiral, escapes its sublating activity. The most concise formulation of such speculative coincidence can be found in the "Phrenology" section of the *Phenomenology of Spirit*, where Hegel famously contends that "Spirit is a bone": Spirit, representing the totalizing power of dialectical mediation, is identical with an inert 'piece of reality' (the bone) that, as such, gives form to the latter's inconsistency or inherent contradiction.[32] The speculative twist here consists in the fact that the unfolding of the dialectic overlaps with the inconsistency it produces, which remains outside its grasp while representing its core. Hence the significance of Hegel's notion of *speculative* identity between subject and object: it is an identity predicated upon an instance of nonrecognition, whereby Spirit (subject, reason) ultimately coincides with that which cannot be caught or recognized in its own mediating activity, a particular element of contingent reality that eludes its grasp completely. The conclusion to draw is that the inconsistency of a notion does not merely represent its potential breaking point, but also its condition of possibility—exactly like the symptom in Lacan's theory.

Accordingly, in Marxian terms an economic crisis stands not only for a negative, inherently destructive moment in the cycle of capitalist accumulation, but also for what makes (the repetition of) that cycle possible, which is why we are entitled to claim that crisis is speculatively identical with capital, just like "bone" is with "Spirit." We should take this coincidence literally, beyond the familiar boom and bust truism: capitalism owes its existence to its being in a constant state of imbalance and turmoil, perpetually battling away with its constitutive limit, attempting to escape its own congenital impossibility. Crisis, then, captures the *symptomatic* excess of capitalism *qua* condition of possibility. As with Lacan's notion of symptom/*sinthome*, we are dealing with a *radically ambiguous determination*, which both sustains and threatens to destroy the dominant discourse. This means that what we often regard as the limit to capitalist expansion is also capital's conditions of possibility. In Peter Fleming's words: "These limits do not represent capitalism's 'breaking point' but play a proactive role in generating the endless social 'noise' that keeps a moribund economic paradigm alive . . . for now."[33]

The dialectical point to stress is that Spirit *does not recognize* itself as bone. In its long history, the 'spirit' of capitalism has consistently externalized its crisis onto an exception to what it regarded as its normal functioning. At the same time, capitalist spirit has sought 'ontological cover' in various noneconomic domains, especially in political and religious ideologies. We can put this, again, in Hegelian terms: insofar as capital's self-movement is always the movement of 'nothing,' it generates narrative meaning precisely through its vortex-like hyperactivity. It is only today that, having triumphed globally, the capitalist discourse is increasingly naked, coinciding with its self-expanding madness. Only today is the genie truly out of the bottle.

This exceptional situation can be observed by looking at the recent phenomenon of the monetary response to COVID-19. What tends to escape us when considering this response is the simple fact that the virus exposed a situation that was already with us before its arrival, namely, the obsolescence of a mode of production that is only able to sustain itself through *the socialization of its losses* (so much for the efficiency of free markets and their invisible hands). As we know, in 2008 a global economic breakdown was averted through the nationalization of junk credits and various policies of cheap money and state indebtedness. In the following years, supposedly provisional measures like quantitative easing (QE) became the norm, as the system grew dependent on the intervention of central banks.

As I have argued in a recent piece,[34] the pre-COVID-19 global economy was already on the verge of a colossal meltdown, particularly when the US repo market crashed on September 15, 2019, due to a sudden spike in interest rates. Repo is shorthand for 'repurchase agreement,' a contract where investment funds lend money against collateral assets (normally Treasury securities). Repos are, essentially, short-term collateralized loans. As such, they constitute the main source of funding for traders in most markets, especially the derivatives galaxy. This means that a liquidity trap in the repo market is likely to have a devastating domino effect on all major financial sectors. On September 17, 2019, the Federal Reserve started its extraordinary monetary program aimed at plugging the holes in the repo market, pumping hundreds of billions of dollars per week into Wall Street.

In my view, the coronavirus health emergency should be framed as a consequence of this event, rather than as its cause. With lockdowns came the suspension of many business transactions, which drained the demand for credit and stopped the contagion. In other words, restructuring the financial architecture through extraordinary monetary policy *was contingent on the economy's engine being turned off*. Had the enormous mass of liquidity injected into the financial sector reached transactions on the ground, a monetary tsunami of catastrophic consequence (hyperinflation) would have been unleashed. That is to say, only an *induced economic coma* would provide the Federal Reserve (and, later, other major central banks) with the necessary room to defuse the time bomb ticking away in the financial sector. Inevitably, this resulted in a socioeconomic deadlock: the condition for Wall Street to be inundated with computer-created central bank cash is the closure or controlled demolition of Main Street.

The prolonged coronavirus crisis further exacerbated this deadlock. Monumental operations of fiscal and wage compensation have been deployed in most advanced economies, including traditional large-scale purchase of government bonds (QE), long-term zero-interest loans, direct fiscal transfers and grants, and—last but not least on the list of creative monetary interventions—various forms of 'helicopter money,' as already entertained by right-wing neoliberal guru Milton Friedman. In what looked increasingly like 2008 on steroids, central banks responded to GDP losses through liquidity injections of exceptional magnitude. In short, enormous amounts of money were created out of thin air and pumped into the financial system to prevent it from going bust. Faced by the deployment of such monetary artillery, we ought to ask ourselves what this colossal recourse to money-printing is symptomatic of.

While expanding the monetary base of a major economy is not a new phenomenon, the response to both the repo crash and, later, COVID-19, has taken this remedial approach to a whole new level. Structural forms of compensation have been deployed regularly in recent years, not only in relation to natural disasters (floods, wildfires, earthquakes, etc.), but especially to rescue capitalism from what I have called its historical 'constipation'—its organic inability to create new value. Since 2008, in Anatole Kaletsky's words, "banks, insurance companies, and financial markets have received fiscal transfers in many countries amounting to far more than 25% of GDP."[35] Although Kaletsky was optimistic about stemming the coronavirus tide through expansive monetary policies, he (together with other leading Keynesian commentators like Adair Turner, Martin Wolf, Will Hutton, Larry Summers, Paul de Grauwe, etc.) tended to ignore the root question of the accelerating erosion of the basis of capitalist accumulation. Tackling the coronavirus crisis as yet another temporary aberration that can be rectified by doing, again, 'whatever is necessary' is supremely disingenuous, not only because of the deluge of (further) debt, unemployment, and immiseration it brought, but especially in light of the evidence that, in pre-COVID-19 times, the system was already powerless vis-à-vis its disabling contradiction. In short, the downward spiral of contemporary capitalism is unstoppable.

The first point to bear in mind when we look at monetary policies related to COVID-19 is that artificial money does not increase credit to the economy, but, at best, only partially replaces what was lost, while the economy continues to shrink regardless. The reason for this is that, in capitalism, money is not supposed to grow on trees, or in central banks. Rather, it exists as the expression of the economic value produced by investment in that special commodity called labor. This is what sets up the 'scene' of capitalist societies. The reason why money creation will not boost aggregate demand (investment and consumption), then, is that a capitalist economy works the other way around: not through money drops but through the perceived profitability of investment. As various QE programs have shown in recent times, expansionary monetary policies have little impact on job creation and consumption, since the appetite for investment in the real economy remains low.

A capitalist system that is increasingly unable to make productive use of labor-power is bound to implode, no matter how much money you throw at it, or how much richer the 0.1 percent gets. What artificial credit can achieve is limited to a temporary backstopping through low interest rates and improved balance sheets. Beyond that, it only generates a new spell of volatile financial asset speculation. The implication is that the process of "creative destruction" facilitated by COVID-19, no matter how protracted in time, will not cause the economy to bounce back. The inevitable increase in the debt multiplier will not lead to a mass of new investments in the real economy. Rather, a significant part of this new debt will continue to migrate to the financial sector, making social life hostage to money printing and the artificial inflation of financial assets.

In respect of this miserable outlook, the sheer magnitude of the coronavirus rescue operation is nevertheless emblematic of an epochal shift in the way capitalism relates to its own increasingly unworkable imbalance. If central banks bypass the markets to hoover up government bonds with such desperate voracity, and if hitherto taboo recipes like UBI (universal basic income) and MMT (modern monetary theory) are advocated across the board, this can only mean that the king is naked. Emergency measures of this magnitude are telling us that capitalism is running out of rabbits to pull out of its hat. Naturally, this does not mean that it will collapse overnight, or that an international anti-capitalist movement will emerge to antagonize our bankrupt power structure. More realistically, it suggests that in order to prolong its lifespan, capitalism is now forced to rely on increasingly explicit forms of political repression and censorship. This authoritarian turn involves the reengineering of our identities from consumer-centered to legally disenfranchised. The relentless pathologizing of life serves this precise purpose: to pulverize the last remnants of resistance to the installation of a tyrannical regime of accumulation.

Yet, we should not lose sight of how, while attempting to rescue itself through increasingly sophisticated forms of techno-domination, contemporary capitalism is simultaneously undermining its own conditions of possibility.

When money is created ex nihilo because the capital-labor relation cannot sustain the social body, the mask of the economy as a self-enhancing narrative falls, revealing the truth of its empty core.

Neoliberal Perversions

Since the 1980s (end of the Cold War and beginning of endemic financialization) a merciless type of mass conformity has imposed itself, passed off as the only way to achieve personal fulfillment. In colonizing the unconscious, global consumerism has become sovereign, weakening our social bonds with others and consigning us to a solipsistic relationship with capital. The virtualization of experience that came with the digital era has further bolstered consumer conformity. The basic problem with our enslavement to virtuality and its *Gestell* ("enframing," to use Heidegger's term),[36] is that it deprives us of our capacity to establish symbolic relations, thus paving the way for authoritarian capitalism. More and more we inhabit a flat ontology where the subject of the unconscious (the subject defined by a fundamental inconsistency, which triggers the search for meanings and connections) is abolished. The *asocial* model touted as the highest form of individual freedom can only be a depressive one. For the subject incapable of introspection—for whom connecting with others amounts to exhibitionistic rituals of virtualized self-promotion (from sexting to food selfies, through a heterogeneous typology of standardized miniperversions)—life contracts into a mechanical performance, whose other side is anomie and existential emptiness. Overwhelmed by the speed of information and numbed by simulated overstimulation, the contemporary subject gives in to "capitalist realism."[37]

By identifying with the object-commodity, contemporary subjects willingly abolish their own singularity. The Cartesian distance between *res cogitans* and *res extensa* collapses, since thinking subjects (*cogitans*) flatten into the empty objectuality (*extensa*) of commodities, from which they can no longer distinguish themselves. The cause of all this, however, is not to be found in epiphenomena like dystopian technology or political corruption and incompetence, but in a centuries-old process of socialization based on the dogma of capitalist productivism. Today, at the peak of this historical process, people find themselves increasingly *reified*, as well as immiserated and deprived of fundamental rights (home, food, health). Without collective symbolic ties, the mind collapses into the thingness of the object-commodity. The very meaning of rebellion is being erased from our vocabulary and collective memory. Since the late 1980s, we have been gradually convinced that rebelling is undemocratic and uncivilized, a practice for violent thugs who refuse 'dialogue.'

In our epoch, then, the world dominated by commodities institutes both a global governance dictated by an oligarchic conglomerate of billionaires, and a typically obtuse brand of neoliberal individualism that inhibits critical thinking while fomenting an intrinsically fragile delusion of omnipotence. Our virtual utopia lures us into a false sense of security, for it is built on the illusion of eternal time. Yet, predictably, the step from this atemporal illusion to anxiety and panic is very short: "There is no such thing as a time of virtuality, because time is only in life, decomposition, and the becoming-death of the living. Virtuality is the collapse of the living; it is panic taking power in temporal perception."[38]

With the onslaught of neoliberal ideology and the shift to financialization, a significant change occurred at the level of subjectivity, whose 'poverty' now concerns not only material wealth, but also sociality. The global capitalist subsumption of communication (so-called communicative capitalism) is the prime example of how the social bond is crumbling while still peddling the democratic illusion. Social networks are the *steroidal caricature* of a vanishing social discourse. If in the Fordist era accumulation triggered class solidarity, now it commands a monadic type of individualism, while the atomization of 'connected subjectivities' leads to depression.

The ideological regime forced on us as a political response to the coronavirus crisis had already conquered the psyche of the neoliberal subject, and is only its paroxysm. The techno-bio capitalism imposed by the global elites generates the illusion of social participation and solidarity while in fact shaping stubbornly asocial identities whose old interrelations have been torn apart alongside the dissolution of the labor-capital dialectic. In Byung-Chul Han's words: "Neoliberal psychopolitics is a technology of domination that stabilizes and perpetuates the prevailing system by means of psychological programming and steering" that enforces "the violence of consensus."[39] While the labor dialectic was premised on the production of symbolic identities supported by a shared vision of the world, the decline of the work-based society makes identification possible only in narcissistic terms. By circumventing the social relation, identity is reduced to the ephemeral plasticity of the self-image. This implies that individuals are unable to recognize their participation in a social bond where the meaning of one's life depends on the meaning ascribed to one's relations to others.

Here, however, we should again take a reflective pause. Rather than lamenting the loss of earlier forms of capitalist identification, which were always conditional on the accumulation paradigm, perhaps we ought to think the desertification of the sociosymbolic order as the *only chance* we have to establish new battle lines against the global dominance of capitalist power. Traditional working-class identities are not coming back, which means that the phoenix of social struggle can only be reborn from the ashes of labor and its various political iterations. What must shift now is our libidinal attachment to global capitalism and its increasingly totalitarian ideological pressures.

While the ongoing debacle of the work-society is characterized by the triumph of the (narcissistic) Imaginary over the (social) Symbolic, the specific psychic formation that continues to grant the system a sufficient degree of ideological purchase is, as anticipated, perversion. Replacing the good old days of neurotic resistance, perversion functions by commanding the individual to *enjoy* the dominant power relations. Rather than experiencing the Other as a threatening external agency, the contemporary subject readily submits to its demand *in a desperate bid to make it exist*. Contemporary perversion, then, is not necessarily the psychopathology we normally associate it with. Rather, it functions as the default mechanism through which we seek to maintain a degree of sanity in the face of the ongoing dissolution of the big Other. When the traditional horizon of sense recedes out of sight, the subject surrenders to the only reality that appears to subsist: economic valorization. This way, the law of value is artificially kept alive in spite of its vanishing. Gorz's analysis of the knowledge economy went in this direction when he claimed:

> The order to be "active subjects," but to be so in the service of an Other whose rights you will never contest, is in fact the accepted lot of all those creative individuals *with a real, but limited, subjugated sovereignty*, the jobbing producers of ideas, fantasies and messages.[40]

This perverse form of subjugation is now ubiquitous, a kind of spontaneous, 'creative' disposition toward prostitution where the greatest virtue of all is to know how to sell oneself.[41] This eagerness is exemplified in the curious behavior of neoliberal workers who transmute into their own bosses, assuming the command once held by the traditional master, whose "clouds of impotence" (to refer again to Lacan's statement from Seminar 16) are truly "aired." Thus, systemic discipline turns into self-discipline as individuals are co-opted into measuring their own productivity: "As a project deeming itself free of external and alien limitations, the *I* is now subjugating itself to internal limitations and self-constraints, which are taking the form of compulsive achievement and optimization."[42] The escalation of what Moore and Robinson call the "quantified self"[43]—the self-evaluation of productivity through online tools tracking everything from fitness activities to calories ingested or burnt and sleeping patterns—is the latest form taken by capital's founding act of valorization. When life itself (*bios*) turns into a relentless process of vigilant and aggressive self-measurement, capitalist ideology becomes total, and arguably reaches its tipping point.

We should therefore reject any defense of creativity as evidence that the contemporary worker can achieve mastery over the working process. The technological know-how of contemporary skilled workers is by no means a sign of their autonomy over their machines, tools, and practices. It is naive to argue that such workers, on account of either their cognitive skills or the liberation from dehumanizing factory work, can finally assume moral or political responsibility for what they do. Such a capacity presupposes the existence of a *whole culture* that is able to transcend the job society, which continues to demand the dependence of one's life on increasingly oppressive forms of salaried work and related institutional practices:

> *The intrinsic interest of a job does not guarantee its being meaningful, just as its humanization does not guarantee the humanization of the ultimate objectives it serves.* Humanizing a job can make even the most barbaric of enterprises attractive for the people who work in them. Work can develop individual abilities, including the capacity for autonomous action, but the individuals' professional autonomy does not necessarily lead to their moral autonomy, that is, their insistence that they will not work towards goals that have not been publicly debated and that they have not been able to examine and assume personally.[44]

Neoliberalism, then, has not altered the elementary capitalist matrix; it has 'merely' produced a perverse model of its intrinsically destructive aggressiveness.

The reason why thinkers like Michael Hardt and Toni Negri, among others, argue that cognitive labor has the power to self-valorize autonomously from capital is that they grant work an immediately productive potential it does not possess, while also failing to recognize how deeply the capitalist matrix is at work in its neoliberal variety. As argued by Gorz:

> In their haste to come up with an inherently revolutionary subject engendered by the production process, these authors resort to a kind of systemist Spinozism which evades the most difficult task, namely that of creating the cultural and political mediations through which the challenge to the mode and goals of production will emerge. In so doing, they merely throw into sharper relief the questions they sidestep.[45]

In short, "lean production itself produces the social and cultural conditions which enable capital to control the autonomy of living labour."[46] Any instance of self-valorization within a world colonized by capitalist relations is necessarily valorization for capitalist ends. Rather than opening up lines of flight from capital, the shift toward cognitive labor should be framed within the rise of the self-quantification society, which is revealing of the extent to which the valorization dogma continues to totalize our lives. Our perverse obsession with 'counting life' is the contemporary manifestation of the paradigm-changing ruse that centuries ago turned work into a measurable and profitable activity; they are basically the same thing.

In December 1969, Lacan warned the students of the autonomous, 'Marxist-Leninist' University of Vincennes (Paris 8) that the introduction of credit points in higher education was reducing knowledge to a numerical unit for marketing purposes, just like any other commodity.[47] Whether credit points or fitness tracker bracelets, what is at stake is the same epistemological operation through which the unknown roots of knowledge are translated into a quantifiable unit that, on the strength of its presumed self-transparency, must be valorized and accumulated. The new episteme forces one to count what does not count and cannot be counted. Already in Seminar 12 (1964–65), Lacan had claimed that capitalist accumulation was, in its deepest configuration, an accumulation of knowledge, insofar as the problem of the unconscious truth of the subject (*savoir insu*, knowledge that does not know itself) was being foreclosed:

> From Descartes on, knowledge, that of science, is constituted on the mode of the production of knowledge. Just as an essential stage of our structure which is called social, but which is in reality metaphysical and is called capitalism, is the accumulation of capital, so is the relationship of the Cartesian subject to that being which is affirmed in it, founded on the accumulation of knowledge. Knowledge from Descartes on is what can serve to

increase knowledge. And this is a completely different question to that of the truth.[48]

On the one hand, this quotation suggests that, far from being a liberating force, the shift toward cognitive capitalism leads us out of the frying pan into the fire, since what triggered the capitalist revolution was precisely the spurious computation of knowledge that has now colonized the knowledge economy. On the other hand, Lacan's critique throws into sharp relief the epistemological overlapping of capitalism and modern science, emphasizing how the birth of capitalist modernity coincided with the arrival on the scene of the new scientific method. The latter is best represented not only by Descartes, but especially by Isaac Newton and his depiction of the universe as a clockwork mechanism of watertight actions and reactions, causes and effects.

For Lacan, the novelty of modern science (since the seventeenth century) coincides with the systemic introduction of a signifying articulation attempting to foreclose the subject of the unconscious—the subject that reveals itself in the "stumblings" and "intervals" of discourse, where "a truth is announced to me where I do not protect myself from what comes in my word."[49] Modern science inaugurates a regime of knowledge accumulation that Lacan considers homologous to the regime of capitalist accumulation. However, Lacan is also keen to emphasize the inherent flaw of this operation. For instance, in his reading of the revolutionary scientific method introduced by Newtonian physics, through which all divine shadows are expelled from the heavens,[50] he notes that the subject, although foreclosed, is also secretly presupposed. That is to say, the Newtonian formula *hypotheses non fingo* (I do not need causes, for I only describe phenomena) "presupposes in itself a subject who maintains the action of the law," since "the operation of gravity does not appear to him [Newton] to be able to be supported except by this pure and supreme subject, this sort of acme of the ideal subject that the Newtonian God represents."[51] In other words, the epistemology of modern science was able to affirm itself only against the background of a disavowed belief in the Creator. Belief, then, remains central to scientific rationalism. The presupposition of a subject who *believes* rather than simply *knows* is the same presupposition that sustains the narrative of the capitalist computation of work. While the purpose of this belief is to install a sociosymbolic order, it simultaneously signals the fallibility of the signifying structure that supports modernity. Precisely because the historical development of modern science, in its 'copulation' with capitalism, is predicated on a belief that forecloses the fallibility of what it signifies, such fallibility continues to haunt us like a ghost.

Populist Symptoms

What are the chances of contemporary politics intercepting the *cause* of the implosion of capitalist civilization? Should the rise of populism be taken seriously as a political form that might problematize our perverse attachment to a mechanism of social reproduction in terminal crisis? Today we definitely live in a time of *postpolitical economic naturalization*. As demonstrated by the repeated fiascos of international climate negotiations, and the dramatic failure of health systems in the face of a resistible epidemic, all political decisions are framed in advance by the diktat of economic rationality, as they all stop short of asking serious questions about our moribund mode of production.

Perhaps the symptomatic dimension of populism should not be haughtily rejected. In Europe, the austerity measures imposed on potentially insolvent states are not to be supinely accepted as the inevitable consequence of the gap between productive and unproductive countries, that is to say between 'honest and industrious' and 'corrupt and lazy' people. This, unfortunately, is the racist justification used by those who continue to profit from the financial exploitation of countries who got indebted to their teeth in a desperate bid to sustain the required standards of development.

As extensively argued by, among others, Maurizio Lazzarato, debt today is imposed as infinite and essentially unpayable, thus expressing a political relation of subjection and enslavement. Debt disciplines populations, dictates structural reforms and austerity packages, and legitimizes the suspension of democracy in favor of technocratic governments serving the interests of global capitalism.[52] This is why, as summarized by Arjun Appadurai, the production of debt today is central to capitalist accumulation:

> All of us who live in a financialized economy generate debt in many forms: consumer debt, housing debt, health debt, and others related to these. Capitalist forms also operate through debt, since borrowing on the capital markets has become much more important than issuing stock or equity. From this point of view, the major form of labor today is not labor for wages but rather labor for the production of debt. Some of us today

are no doubt wage-laborers, in the classic sense. But many of us are in fact debt-laborers, whose main task is to produce debt that can then be further monetized for profit by financial entrepreneurs who control the means of the production of profit through monetizing debts.[53]

However, just as it is deplorable to personalize debt by racializing it (e.g., by blaming it on the backward or corrupt nature of southern Europeans), it is equally wrong to locate the cause of this tragic state of affairs in the exploitative greed of finance. The more populist movements insist on laying responsibility on discrete subjects or groups of people, the more they miss the target, hence postponing the confrontation with the *systemic* cause of failure.

If capital is increasingly financialized, this shift in its make-up is only superficially rooted in subjective greed and moral degeneration. Ontologically, it is the *necessary* outcome of capital's effort to overcome its internal barrier concerning the production of wealth. If the survival of capitalist societies today depends on their ability to *make money work*, this is because they are increasingly unable to *make labor work*, thus finally fulfilling capital's self-sabotaging vocation. The slow yet inevitable decomposition of our societies and their institutions—their *cupio dissolvi*—is the inevitable result of capitalism's implosion as a sociohistorical formation. Today the capitalist *Aufhebung* misfires, with devastating consequences. For structural reasons, the capitalist drive looks increasingly like a car accelerating against a wall: it has lost its wheels and the engine is melting, and yet it continues to accelerate. The risk is that, when we finally wake up from this nightmare, it will be too late.

Politically speaking, the bottom line is that the antagonism between nationalist populism and finance-driven globalization is *false*, since it fails to intercept the assumption upon which capitalist totality is built. If the populist rhetoric remains rooted, at best, in the critique of financial exploitation without problematizing the value-creation impasse, it is destined to fizzle out or, worse, develop into neofascist ideology. We should not forget that populisms rely on the identification of an exception, an external enemy, that is, the financier or the immigrant. It is the political construction of this enemy that supports the mythology of 'the people' as a coherent unit, whose stability depends precisely on the removal of the exception/enemy.[54] Populism, therefore, tends to displace social antagonism.

If there is a leftist concern with social rights in populism, it needs to politicize the structural obsolescence of the valorization fetish—a mission left unaccomplished by the historical left. Traditionally, left-wing workers' movements were unable to tackle head-on the central Marxian issue of value production, opting instead to place all their stakes on wealth distribution, as if the furnace of economic value were inexhaustible. This fatal misrecognition is responsible for the left's by-now consolidated blindness vis-à-vis the plea of ever-increasing masses of workers without work or political representation.

The metastatic growth of populism is a consequence of this debilitating political shortsightedness, characterized by an obstinate unwillingness to confront the inexorable deterioration of capitalist civilization. This type of fetishistic disavowal qualifies both the contemporary neoliberal version of the left, and its neo-Keynesian variant (often surreptitiously included in the former), which insists on prioritizing redistribution through state intervention. Populism, on the other hand, shares in this fetishistic attitude by externalizing guilt and responsibility onto the greed of financial operators or the figure of the immigrant, both of which are bearers of a particular type of corruption.

In respect of this degenerative tendency of populism, Robert Kurz has theorized a "political economy of antisemitism," which is meant to capture the transhistorical *form* of a reductionist critique of interest-bearing capital.[55] Kurz argues that the global triumph of the type of subjectivity linked to market economy, which disavows the processes of value-production, engenders two distinct types of discrimination: a racist and an anti-Semitic one. While racism identifies "genetically inferior individuals" (blacks, Arabs, migrants, Eastern and Southern Europeans, etc.), anti-Semitism targets "superior individuals" who are nevertheless regarded as "genetically dispensable." According to Kurz, the totalized bourgeois subjectivity of commodity-fetishistic societies perceives itself, on the one hand, as productive, consistent, and self-identical vis-à-vis the racialized fantasy image of the unproductive (lazy, inefficient, and oversexed) other; and, on the other hand, as "genetically healthy" in respect of the spectral apparition of the global conspiracy of financial capital. With economic collapse looming large on the horizon, it is likely that the increasingly frustrated "subjects of productivity and competition" will seek to vent their justified rage against the "unproductive" or "parasitic" masses, as well as against the "exploitative" global elites of the financial markets. In either case, resistance to capitalist collapse will continue to assume the *distorted* forms of nationalist chauvinism and xenophobia. If populist movements want to avoid falling into these predictable pitfalls, they must find the courage to antagonize the broken engine of the capitalist machine.

Viral Simulations

When he first introduced the notion of simulation in the early 1970s,[56] Baudrillard was acutely aware that modernity was being replaced by postmodernity.[57] For him, this shift meant that social relations were no longer grounded in *production* but in the serial *reproduction* of reality's signs. With the rise of postindustrial consumer capitalism, in other words, referents are gradually substituted by the potentially endless reduplication of their signs: "the annihilation of any goal as regards the contents of production allows the latter to function as a code" and therefore "to escape into infinite speculation, beyond all reference to a real of production, or even to a gold-standard."[58] In such a regime, society is organized around prearranged models where conflicts and contradictions are neutralized by indifference, modeling, and commutability ("of the beautiful and the ugly in fashion, of the left and the right in politics, of the true and the false in every media message").[59]

Simulation, then, denotes the intrinsically totalitarian transfiguration of the real into the virtual code, which, in dramatically accelerating the elimination of referentiality, consigns the social to its viral reproduction. What Baudrillard lamented was the abandonment of "the referential base of the sign, with its singularity and the opacity of its signified in the real, its very powerful affect and its minimal commutability." The "hot phase" of the sign, which was still attached to symbolically authoritative signifiers, was being replaced by its "cool phase," characterized by "the pure play of the values of discourse [. . .] the omnipotence of operational simulation."[60] In the new millennium, this epochal shift threatens "the glaciation of meaning,"[61] for the increasing fascination with hypermediatized signs is proportional to a growing disaffection with critical thinking, political struggle, and subversion.

Crucially, for Baudrillard the coding of reality takes the form of a *gift* that blackmails everyone into obedience. Contemporary capitalism retains the exclusivity of gift-giving, which it uses to exert real domination. Baudrillard developed a radicalized version of Marcel Mauss's theory of the gift by conceiving the latter not as a type of generous exchange that predates or exceeds political economy,[62] but as the ideological core of modern societies. Today, gift-giving is correlative to absolute power. As such, it materializes not only as the reward of wage labor, but especially as the ubiquitous network of media information, virtual interaction, and the normativity of "protection agency, security, gratification, and the solicitation of the social from which nothing is any longer permitted to escape."[63] In this respect, today's most refined form of gift-giving is what is often referred to as "philanthrocapitalism," the practice whereby the 0.01 percent—the winners of globalization, the most predatory class in the history of humankind (from Bill Gates to Warren Buffett, Bill Clinton, Mark Zuckerberg, George Soros)—commit to supporting noble causes such as global health, education, and the fight against hunger. Thanks to their large donations (most of which end up in tax-relieved private funds that they control) the philanthropic prophets of 'emergency capitalism' exercise an increasingly tyrannical influence over governments and their fragile institutions.[64] As capitalist philanthropy becomes unilateral, easily accessible, and immensely attractive for indebted economies and personal gain, all strategies of refusal—which Baudrillard invoked through the mobilization of "counter-gifts"—[65] seem increasingly unrealistic.

Baudrillard's theory of simulation does not merely amount to another version of Marshall McLuhan's well-known claim that real contents and referents are neutralized by the medium ("the medium is the message").[66] Rather, it implies that the medium itself, insofar as it becomes hegemonic through operational codes, generates its own "integral reality," which Baudrillard called *hyperreality*:

> The real is produced from miniaturized units, from matrices, memory banks and command models—and with these, it can be reproduced an indefinite number of times. It no longer has to be rational, since it is no longer measured against some ideal or negative instance. It is nothing more than operational. In fact, since it is no longer enveloped by an imaginary, it is no longer real at all. It is hyperreal, the product of an irradiating synthesis of combinatory models in a hyperspace without atmosphere.[67]

This "disappearance of reality" is akin to "a perfect crime,"[68] since the real evaporates before our eyes without leaving traces of its former configuration. All we are left with is a gigantic machinery of simulation, which signals the impossibility of critical intervention either through content or form. Every radical intervention is defused in advance, and vacuous transparency replaces the opacity of the real. Alienation itself can no longer be grasped, since ideological manipulation now comes in the form of "social control by means of prediction, simulation, programmed anticipation and indeterminate mutation," which takes us "[f]rom a capitalist productivist society to a neo-capitalist cybernetic order, aiming this time at absolute control."[69] As a consequence, our enslavement to the virtual matrix and its numbing utopia (a dimensionless, nonrepresentational space-time where countless intelligent agents meet to share and create their 'realities') drastically undermines our capacity to build relations based on symbolic exchange. Thus, society ends up buried beneath the simulation of the real, just as sexuality is buried beneath pornography:[70]

> This is really what we are seeing today: the disintegration of the whole idea of the social, the consumption and involution of the social, the breakdown of the social simulacrum, a genuine defiance of the constructive and productive approach to the social which dominates us. All quite suddenly, as if the social had never existed. A breakdown which has all the features of a catastrophe, not an evolution or revolution.[71]

The dissolution of the social bond is offset by the triumph of *simulated sociality*, which is assembled around "the lowest form of social energy: that of an environmental, behavioral utility."[72] While Baudrillard shared the Freudian postulate that any human community depends on a degree of repression, he argued that, with the advent of viral simulation, the possibility of perceiving the alienating substance of the social tends to vanish. The more we are denied the experience of the gap between the real and its organization into a sociosymbolic structure, the more alienation morphs into hyperreality. When the sign loses its symbolic anchoring in the real, it begins to free-float, proliferating in metastatic fashion, while meanings turn commutable and superfluous. The rational exercise of thought is thus interdicted, as reality is replaced by self-reproducing simulacra.

In Baudrillard's view, the endless flow of information, the entropic virulence of the media, has far more ideological traction than any kind of material surveillance, since the media behave like a genetic code that ceaselessly defuse any spark of critical awareness and political contestation: "Everywhere socialization is measured according to exposure through media messages. Those who are under-exposed to the media are virtually asocial or desocialized."[73] Media virality imposes itself with the force of a magnetic field made of largely insignificant diffractions and polarizations, whose only role is to reaffirm a code based on the universal principle of equivalence and exchangeability.

Mass manipulation and propaganda are strictly connected with the ever-growing power of coding and modeling. Search engines are perfect examples of what Baudrillard meant by the ideology of simulation. A Google search on a controversial topic, for instance, is likely to return the same piece of information under different headings, giving its users the confidence to believe it and share it. As argued by Robert Epstein, algorithms can select and rank information to create what he calls "the search engine manipulation effect" (SEME), which is so powerful that it can easily impact on the outcome of elections.[74] Self-proclaimed independent fact-checkers like Snopes, Factcheck.Org, and Politifact are neither independent nor factual, but rather reproduce the same ideology deployed by those who fund or host them. Wikipedia itself, owned by Wikimedia Foundation, depends on a long list of "major benefactors" including Apple, Microsoft, and Google, and others who prefer to remain anonymous. What began as an unbiased, open-source platform, is now weaponized by those who control it. For instance, it can easily smear single individuals with false information while locking them out from making changes.

Especially since the advent of digitality, we are dominated by a flat social ontology without breaks or ruptures, a spurious discourse of pure operationality where the subject is progressively obliterated—just as Lacan had predicted in his remarks on the capitalist discourse. Put differently, we are only free to slot into a prepackaged binary feedback system where "differential poles implode into each other."[75] Thus, "the cool universe of digitality," which "has absorbed the world of metaphor and metonymy,"[76] elevates ubiquitous communication and connectedness to repressive banality.

The above insights are nicely encapsulated in Baudrillard's early 1980s observations on New York's World Trade Center as the architectural embodiment of the binary code of hyperreality:

> Why are there *two* towers at New York's World Trade Center? All of Manhattan's great buildings were always happy enough to affront each other in a competitive verticality [. . .]. This new architecture incarnates a system that is no longer competitive, but compatible, and where competition has disappeared for the benefit of correlations. [. . . T]he two W. T. C. towers, perfect parallelepipeds a ¼-mile high on a square base, perfectly balanced and blind communicating vessels. The fact that there are two of them *signifies* the end of competition, the end of all original reference. [. . .] There is a particular fascination in this reduplication. As high as they are, higher than all the others, the two towers signify nevertheless the end of verticality.[77]

THE FINANCIAL DEMON   143

Essentially, the "end of verticality" informs a fake social bond where the subject is *foreclosed*. In the digital system, reality is hyperrealized and simultaneously derealized. No wonder that *The Matrix* (Wachowski brothers, 1999) was inspired by Baudrillard's notion of simulation—even though Baudrillard said that the film was too Platonic: "The Matrix is the kind of film about the matrix that the matrix would have been able to produce."[78]

With simulation, then, the irreducible ambivalence of the real is wiped out by the dogma of the infinite reproducibility of virtualized signs. In this context, the significance of Andy Warhol—for Baudrillard the last great modern artist—is that he *dramatized* the operational principle of seriality that lies at the heart of global capitalism, today exemplified by the speculative play of financial signifiers. An example of this simulation can be found in Warhol's famous grids of Marilyn Monroe, Campbell Soup, and many other of his replicas. What we witness there is the potentially infinite reproduction of the same image through minimal differences that are integral to the same code. With digitality, the capacity for serial simulation reaches its apex, for all reality can now be coded in a virtual reproductive flow. And all that matters is that it continues to flow, to feign some kind of existence. As anticipated, the financialization of the economy provides a perfect illustration of this logic. Our economies are increasingly replete with enormous masses of fictitious capital that, to avoid collapse, blindly continue to follow their generative flows, while condemning large parts of the world to closures, immiseration, and destruction. Contemporary capitalism increasingly resembles an enormous dump of rotting nominal values replicating themselves in a parallel orbit with respect to the human suffering on the ground—an insanity that the International Monetary Fund and the *Financial Times* today elegantly call "the Great Disconnect."[79] In 1988, Baudrillard had captured this criminal disconnection with the following provocation:

> But can we still speak of the "economy"? Or, indeed, of political economy (the logic of capital)? Certainly not. At the very least, the striking prominence of the economy at the moment has not at all the same meaning it had in the classical or Marxist analysis. For it is no longer in any sense driven by the infrastructure of material production, nor indeed by the superstructure. The engine of the economy is the destructuring of value, the destabilizing of markets and real economies [. . .]; it is the triumph of a virtual economy relieved of real economies (not

really, of course, but virtually: yet it is not reality which holds sway today but virtuality); *the triumph of a viral economy which connects up in this way with all the other viral processes*. It is as an arena of special effects, of unpredictable (almost meteorological) happenings—as the destruction and exacerbation of its own logic—that it is becoming once again a kind of exemplary theatre of current events.[80]

In partial disagreement with Baudrillard, I have argued that in an economy driven by the self-referential logic of finance, capital emerges in its purest form: a cold, impersonal, and merciless mechanism of self-reproduction. As sheer accumulation of self-cloning fetish-signs, contemporary capital dances to the rhythm of its virtual melody, turning into what it always-already was: a purely immanent phenomenon, indifferent to the human suffering it causes and destined to self-destruction.

Epilogue

*Emergency Capitalism and the
Exhaustion of a Form of Life*

Capitalist ideology is particularly effective in the context of a post-growth economy that is now desperately intent on denying its *structural* failure. When entire populations are damaged by fear, destruction, and immiseration, the hypnotic power of narratives of salvation works wonders, while the elites mop up the mess by laying claim to pretty much everything that can be owned and controlled. Emergency capitalism is the ideological front of an agonizing socioeconomic model that has no way of perpetuating itself other than by imposing its destructive reshaping as necessary and even desirable. The implementation of the Great Reset is not aimed at global sustainability and social justice,[1] but at reaffirming the systemic violence of capital at the time of its Great Disconnect, the gaping rift between the real economy (measured as GDP) and the nominal value of financial markets.

Hailed by World Economic Forum as a "golden opportunity"[2] offered by the coronavirus emergency, the Great Reset had already been announced at the 2014 WEF meeting in Davos, and since then its rebooting agenda was pushed with increasing determination.[3] Its program, which promotes the fourth industrial revolution as a sweeping revamping of economy and society through emerging technologies like AI, 5G, Blockchain, and increased levels of biometric surveillance, was escalated from 2018, when the WEF partnered with the Johns Hopkins Center for Health Security to simulate a fictitious pandemic named Clade X.[4] Finally, in October 2019 (two months prior to the COVID outbreak) the WEF teamed-up with Johns Hopkins and the Bill and Melinda Gates Foundation to stage the pandemic simulation called Event 201.[5] There can be little doubt that an all-encompassing plan for a new world order dictated by unelected elites has a much better chance of succeeding on the back of a global crisis.

The bottom line is that when GloboCap is increasingly threatened by its own incontinence, it has no choice but to gamble on the therapeutic power of emergencies,[6] upping the stakes on what was always a favorite weapon. How can we oppose this ideological ruse? When no head-on resistance seems to have any chance of succeeding; when integral virality infiltrates every nook and cranny of our lives; when all negativity is absorbed into systemic entropy; then, arguably, our only chance is to bet on the system's inconsistency, which alone countenances the possibility for new singularities to emerge. Baudrillard defined singularity as that "which doesn't resist, but constitutes itself as another universe with another set of rules, which may conceivably get exterminated, but which, at a particular moment, represent an insuperable obstacle for the system itself."[7] He also intimated that in any perfect crime, the crime is perfection: it coincides with the delusional attempt to set up a watertight social structure where all accidents are either deterred or defused and eliminated.[8] Today, this crime is instigated by the capitalist will to cleanse the world of what cannot be brought under total control. But a world propelled by the reduplication of its destructive effects can no longer hide its implosion. Domination, in other words, cannot totalize itself. It is in connection with this impossibility that the strength of our desire to oppose the ongoing descent into the Orwellian rabbit hole will be measured. If we fail, it will mean that we have compromised on our desire, and by implication that our will has also been done.

In a footnote of *Capital* volume 1, Marx quoted British trade unionist Thomas Dunning to highlight the cynical voracity of the profit-making machine:

> Capital eschews no profit, or very small profit, just as Nature was formerly said to abhor a vacuum. With adequate profit, capital is very bold. A certain 10 percent will ensure its employment anywhere; 20 percent certain will produce eagerness; 50 percent, positive audacity; 100 percent will make it ready to trample on all human laws; 300 percent, and there is not a crime at which it will scruple, nor a risk it will not run, even to the chance of its owner being hanged.

Dunning's conclusion perfectly captures our predicament: "If turbulence and strife will bring a profit, it will freely encourage both. Smuggling and the slave-trade have amply proved all that is here stated."[9] Yet, the criminal nature of global capitalism continues to be concealed by the ideological coding of reality into its hyperreal simulation. For any event that might disturb the apparatus of global governance is neutralized in advance, or exploited to propel its inner logic. The chances of an accident escaping this quasi-deterministic system are tied, in the first instance, to our popular will to oppose the descent into barbarism.

What our predicament is revealing is that capitalist implosion is not necessarily *explosive*: it does not automatically produce revolutionary dialectical contradictions. Rather, in its current phase implosion generates only its own despotic deterrence. The crisis we are experiencing, in other words, is perfectly in tune with the logic of contemporary capitalism. Within the context of financial restructuring, the creative destruction of large sectors of the real economy is integral to the insane rationality of capital, which by nature is indifferent to those who are crushed or left behind. As Marx had indicated, the capitalist mode of production is so blind in its lust for profit that it even destroys the very sources of value, that is, wage-earners on the one hand, and land or natural resources on the other. At best, then, the millions of losers in this violent process of social devastation will be compensated with the alms of some form or other of universal basic income. The latter, however, does not "point toward Communism," as Žižek naively intimates,[10] for it is one of the pillars of the neofeudal order currently in the making. The rolling out of social credit and a rent-only economy are other likely consequences of our inability to address the root causes of capitalist implosion.

Our brave new world begins with the stipulation of a new social contract in which the survival of entire populations depends on state protection coupled with the charitable intervention of supranational monetary institutions. The present emergency enjoins us to accept the protection/obedience correlation that typifies Hobbes's state, which offers security while requiring compliance and submission. Hobbes's state neutralizes fear by concentrating it on itself and making it visible, so that abiding by the will of the Leviathan may protect us from the unpredictability of violent death. In this sense, the capitalist state that is being resuscitated today is, as Max Weber put it, that "human community which (successfully) lays claim to the *monopoly of legitimate physical violence* within a certain territory."[11]

Subjectively, the result is widespread resignation and misology; objectively, "a generalised deterrence of every chance, of every accident, of every transversality, of every finality, of every contradiction, rupture or complexity in a sociality illuminated by the norm and doomed to the transparency of detail radiated by data-collecting mechanisms."[12]

This is why today's emergencies are capitalism's perfect alibi: "Capital, which is immoral and unscrupulous, can only function behind a moral superstructure, and whoever regenerates this public morality (by indignation, denunciation, etc.), spontaneously furthers the order of capital."[13] Our precarious social membership is shored up by 'ethical deficits,' whose role is to consolidate the misconception that capitalism is *morally grounded*. A global economic system that has reached saturation cannot stand on its own feet. With rampant technological automation and dwindling natural resources, capitalism 'knows' that work ethics and mass-consumerism can no longer function as the superglue of social life, while democracy itself needs to be radically redefined. Yet, the more it perseveres in liquidating anything that refuses to comply with its blind automatism, the more capitalism becomes hostage to its perversely authoritarian strategy of immunization.[14]

Within this context, the left is either opportunistically compliant or hopelessly in denial (or both). The vanishing of any meaningful left-wing opposition, already a key factor in the success of the neoliberal revolution, is now decisive for the deployment of the new phase of capitalist domination based on the demolition of the work society and its liberal-democratic superstructure. Bereft of political energy, the postmodern left was always prone to compromise, to the extent that 'capitalism with a human face' became its only slogan, now rebranded 'inclusive capitalism.' Choosing to invest in capital's social responsibility—that is, choosing to disavow the fact that "[c]apital doesn't give a damn about the [social] contract" since "it is a monstrous unprincipled undertaking, nothing more"—[15] proved to be the left's coup de grâce. By trading in social antagonism and critical thought for moral immunity, the left capitulated to the theater of postpolitical simulations, where the left/right binary is mostly exploited as perception management. Arguably, such political degeneration produces now the most formidable TINA (there is no alternative) moment ever experienced by humanity.

Given the populist dimension of today's postpolitics, the left's only chance to rehabilitate itself depends on its desire to "out-populist the populists."¹⁶ That is to say, in the willingness to repoliticize those social struggles (from endemic poverty to technological unemployment and ideological manipulation) that are symptomatic of capitalist implosion. Most crucially, it must redefine its own mandate to socialize the means of production in a future increasingly characterized by automation. The above task entails abandoning the nostalgia for *traditional* working-class struggles,¹⁷ or the naive misconception that, considering the magnitude of our global crisis, 'some form' of socialism must be around the corner. Reclaiming work *as it is* is nothing but a desperate move whose deeply delusional aim is to salvage capitalism from its own curse. Consequently, the only realistic strategy at present is twofold: while fighting, without hypocrisy, to retain a dignified place in our crumbling social (dis)order, we should have the courage to think in the modality of *as if*: as if this order were already dead; as if its self-fulfilling prophecies were not only empty but also increasingly catastrophic. Gorz grasped the significance of this dual approach when he claimed: "The task of politics here is to define intermediate strategic objectives, the pursuit of which meets the urgent needs of the present while at the same time prefiguring the alternative society that is asking to be born."¹⁸ Ultimately, if we persist in thinking of our life as defined by the labor-capital dialectic, nothing but further social butchery will come our way.¹⁹

At present, however, nothing can be more self-evident than the inertia of a form of life that has outgrown its conditions of possibility and yet persists—blindly, madly—in deploying them. The technocratic elite that puts the phasing out of wage labor (and its liberal-democratic superstructure) at the heart of its agenda is able to do so by turning fear and insecurity into a way of life. If it is accurate to claim that "the crisis of the industrial system heralds no new world," and that "no redeeming transformation" is in sight, since "the present does not receive any meaning from the future,"²⁰ the first step out of this objectively desolate condition is to consider it, in Hegelian terms, ontologically true. When a social narrative loses its symbolic moorings, what it reveals is its hollow core, no matter how stubbornly it attempts to conceal it. Any process of self-emptying sooner or later uncovers the nakedness of being, and, ultimately, the attendant human necessity of making 'new clothes to wear': new social narratives to identify with, new ideas through which to rebuild the preconditions of our shared existence. Difficult though it may be, our depressing stagnation must be seized as an opportunity to rethink the content of our social alienation. Today, however, when all deviations from the official agenda are demonized, the most urgent task of all is to reject the double bind of capitalist authoritarianism and its convenient emergency narratives. Much more than we are ready to acknowledge, any future struggle for emancipation depends on our capacity to antagonize the destructive course of emergency capitalism.

Notes

Prologue

1. I borrow this term from Chris Harman, *Zombie Capitalism: Global Crisis and the Relevance of Marx* (London: Bookmarks, 2009).

2. Georg Wilhelm Friedrich Hegel, *Outlines of the Philosophy of Right*, trans. T. M. Knox (Oxford: Oxford University Press, 2008), 16.

3. Emil Cioran, *A Short History of Decay*, trans. Richard Howard (New York: Arcade, 2012), 18.

4. Ibid., 21.

5. On fatalism and Hegel see Frank Ruda, *Abolishing Freedom: A Plea for a Contemporary Use of Fatalism* (Lincoln: University of Nebraska Press, 2016).

6. Emil Cioran, *The Temptation to Exist*, trans. Richard Howard (Chicago: University of Chicago Press, 1998), 59.

7. See Byung-Chul Han, *Psychopolitics: Neoliberalism and New Technologies of Power*, trans. Erik Butler (London and New York: Verso, 2017), 44–45.

8. Jacques Lacan, "RSI," Seminar, bk. 22, unpublished, 1974–75, lesson of February 18, 1975.

9. Karl Marx, *Grundrisse*, trans. Martin Nicolaus (London: Penguin, 1993), 296.

Chapter 1

1. See the discussion of this Marxian notion in Alfred Sohn-Rethel, *Intellectual and Manual Labour: A Critique of Epistemology*, trans. Martin Sohn-Rethel (London: Macmillan, 1978).

2. Marx gave this point a clear Hegelian spin in the *Grundrisse*: "While in the completed bourgeois system every economic relation presupposes every other in its bourgeois economic form, and everything posited is thus also a presupposition, this is the case with every organic system." Marx, *Grundrisse*, 278.

3. Domenico Losurdo, *Liberalism: A Counter-history*, trans. Gregory Elliott (London: Verso, 2014), 20.

4. The obvious reference here is Karl Polanyi, *The Great Transformation: The Political and Economic Origins of Our Time* (London: Beacon, 2002), first published in 1944.

5. Hegel, *Philosophy of Right*, 101.

6. "Were the state to be considered as exchangeable with civic society, and were its decisive features to be regarded as the security and protection of property and personal freedom, the interest of the individual as such becomes the ultimate purpose of the social union. It would also be at one's option to be a member of the state. But the state has a totally different relation to the individual. It is objective spirit, and he has his truth, real existence and ethical status only in being a member of it." Ibid., 133.

7. On this question see especially Chris Arthur, *The New Dialectic and Marx's Capital* (Leiden: Brill, 2002).

8. As Marx states in the preface to the 1844 Manuscripts, "I have deemed the concluding chapter of the present work—the settling of accounts with *Hegelian dialectic* and Hegelian philosophy as a whole—to be absolutely necessary, a task not yet performed." Karl Marx, *Economic and Philosophic Manuscripts of 1844*, trans. Martin Milligan (Radford, VA: Wilder, 2011), 17. As is well-known, Marx's critique of Hegelian philosophy as theology was deeply influenced by Ludwig Feuerbach. For a detailed analysis of Marx's complex reading of Hegel in the 1844 Manuscripts, see Chris Arthur, *Dialectics of Labour: Marx and His Relation to Hegel* (Oxford: Blackwell, 1986).

9. Chris Arthur, *The New Dialectic and Marx's Capital*, 102.

10. See Karl Marx, *Capital: A Critique of Political Economy*, vol. 1, trans. Ben Fowkes (London: Penguin, 1990), 253–54, 267.

11. Marx, *Grundrisse*, 270.

12. Gilles Deleuze and Felix Guattari, "Capitalism: A Very Special Delirium," in *Hatred of Capitalism: A Reader*, eds. Chris Kraus and Sylvère Lotringer (Los Angeles: Semiotext(e), 2001), 215.

13. Marx, *Capital*, 1: 290.

14. Herbert Marcuse, "On the Philosophical Foundations of the Concept of Labor in Economics," *Telos*, no. 16 (Summer 1973): 17.

15. Ibid., 875.

16. Ibid.

17. Ibid.

18. Marx, *Capital*, 1: 273.

19. As summarized by Marx, the new status quo was built on "the forcible creation of a class of free and rightless proletarians, the bloody discipline that turned them into wage-labourers, the disgraceful proceedings of the state which employed police methods to accelerate the accumulation of capital by increasing the degree of exploitation of labour." Ibid., 905. In his ground-breaking 1944

book *Capitalism and Slavery*, Eric Williams demonstrated how slavery, supposedly a precapitalist form of labor, was actually regenerated and expanded by capitalism not only as its foundational moment (primitive or original accumulation) but also as its fodder. See Eric Williams, *Capitalism and Slavery* (Chapel Hill: University of North Carolina Press, 1994).

20. Henry Heller, *The Birth of Capitalism: A 21st Century Perspective* (London: Pluto, 2011), 9.

21. Louis Althusser, *Philosophy of the Encounter: Later Writings, 1978–87* (London: Verso, 2006), 198.

22. Ibid., 197.

23. Ibid., 169.

24. Ibid., 198.

25. Ibid., 193.

26. On this point see also Gregor Moder, *Hegel and Spinoza: Substance and Negativity* (Evanston, IL: Northwestern University Press, 2017), 114–20.

27. Marx himself used this metaphor. See *Grundrisse*, 298.

28. Ibid., 715.

29. Karl Marx, *The Poverty of Philosophy*, in *Karl Marx and Friedrich Engels: Collected Works*, vol. 6 (New York: International Publishers, 1976), 127.

30. Marx, *Capital*, 1: 166–67.

31. See Mario Tronti, "I 'grilli' della merce," in *Figure del feticismo*, ed. Stefano Mistura (Turin: Einaudi, 2011), 103–22.

32. See André Gorz, *Critique of Economic Reason*, trans. Gillian Handyside and Chris Turner (London: Verso, 1989), 13–22.

33. André Gorz, *Farewell to the Working Class: An Essay on Post-industrial Socialism*, trans. Michael Sonenscher (London: Pluto, 1982), 39.

34. Michel Henry, *From Communism to Capitalism: Theory of a Catastrophe*, trans. Scott Davidson (London: Bloomsbury, 2014), 58.

35. Christopher Arthur, *The New Dialectic and Marx's Capital*, 54.

36. Marx, *Grundrisse*, 693. In Gorz's words: "The very meaning of the notion of work is changed. It is no longer the workers who work the machines and adjust their actions and movements to obtain the desired result; rather they are being worked on by the machinery. The result of their labour is already there, rigorously programmed, expecting to be produced; the machine is pre-set, requiring a progression of simple, regular motions. The mechanised system does the work; you merely lend your body, your brains and your time in order to get the work done." *Farewell to the Working Class*, 38.

37. Ibid., 40.

38. Ibid., 44.

39. Riccardo Bellofiore, "Marx after Hegel: Capital as Totality and the Centrality of Production," in *Crisis and Critique* 3, no. 3 (2016): 47. Bellofiore drives his main point home when he claims that "the abstraction of living labour" needs to be reconstructed "as a *process* opened by initial (bank-)finance as *monetary ante-validation*,

before production. As a consequence of the *monetary dimension* marking the buying and selling of labour power, living labour too earns a 'latent' sociality *in anticipation* of the final ex post–validation in exchange. [. . .] Money is not just a passive 'reflection' of value, *ex post*: it is actually essential to 'constitute' it, *ex ante*" (55).

40. Marx, *Grundrisse*, 305.

41. Marx uses the symptomatic term "transubstantiation" in the *Grundrisse* to undermine the argument that capital is merely a displacement [*verrückung*] of the productive force of labor, claiming instead that "capital itself is essentially this *displacement, this transposition*, and that wage labour as such presupposes capital, so that, from its standpoint as well, there is this *transubstantiation*, the necessary process of positing its own powers as *alien* to the worker. Therefore, the demand that wage labour be continued but capital suspended is self-contradictory, self-dissolving." Marx, *Grundrisse*, 308–9.

42. Marx, *Capital*, 1: 138–39.

43. Ibid., 128.

44. This understanding of Hegel's dialectical method is loosely shared by a number of authors who, in recent years, have developed a substantial body of work on the relationship between Hegel and Marx that generally goes under the name of the New Dialectic. These authors include Christopher Arthur, Tony Smith, Geert Reuten, Mark Meaney, Patrick Murray, Moishe Postone, and Roberto Finelli. Despite their differences, they share the view that Hegel's *Science of Logic* was a major influence on Marx's *Capital*, though not in determining Marx's theory of history, but in shaping his systematic critique of capital. See for instance Fred Moseley and Tony Smith, eds., *Marx's Capital and Hegel's Logic: A Reexamination* (Leiden: Brill, 2014).

45. As Marx put it in the preface to the second edition of *Capital* volume 1: "In so far as such a critique represents a class, it can only represent the class whose historical task is the overthrow of the capitalist mode of production and the final abolition of all classes—the proletariat" (98).

46. Although Marx never wrote a single line about the communist mode of production, and although his critique of political economy should also be regarded as a negative ontology (insofar as it tells us what communism is not—no commodities, no division of labor, no state power, and so on), such ontology is nevertheless characterized by the Promethean dynamism of the working class.

47. Karl Marx and Friedrich Engels, *Selected Correspondence* (Moscow: Progress Publishers, 1975), 93.

48. As well as by the previously mentioned authors of the New (or Systematic) Dialectic, this view is generally shared also by the revisionist critique of political economy advanced by the so-called Neue Marx-Lektüre (New Marx Reading)—mostly the works of Helmut Reichelt, Hans-Georg Backhaus, and Michael Heinrich since the 1970s.

49. Marx, *Capital*, 1: 103.

50. This is summed up nicely by Ernest Mandel in his introduction to *Capital* volume 1: "Precisely because Marx's dialectic is a materialist one, however,

it does not start from intuition, preconceptions or mystifying schemes, but from a full assimilation of scientific data. The method of investigation must differ from the method of exposition. Empirical facts have to be gathered first, the given state of knowledge has to be fully grasped. Only when this is achieved can a dialectical reorganization of the material be undertaken in order to understand the given totality. If this is successful, the result is a 'reproduction' in man's thought of this material totality: the capitalist mode of production" (19).

51. Ibid., 20.

52. Marx, *Capital*, 1: 744.

53. Maurice Merleau-Ponty, *Adventures of the Dialectic*, trans. Joseph Bien (Evanston, IL: Northwestern University Press, 1973), 63.

54. Evidence of this influence can be found throughout the "Chapter on Capital" in the *Grundrisse*, as documented in detail by Hiroshi Uchida in his *Marx's Grundrisse and Hegel's Logic* (London: Routledge, 1988).

55. Paul Lafargue, *The Right to be Lazy*, trans. Charles Kerr (Chicago: Charles Kerr, 1907), 9.

56. Ibid., 24.

57. See especially Mark E. Meaney, *Capital as Organic Unity: The Role of Hegel's Science of Logic in Marx's Grundrisse* (New York: Springer, 2003); Uchida, *Marx's Grundrisse and Hegel's Logic*.

58. Merleau-Ponty, *Adventures of the Dialectic*, 62–63.

59. Marx, *Grundrisse*, 101.

60. At the beginning of the *Science of Logic*, Hegel defines determinate negation as "*the negation of the determined fact* which is resolved, and is therefore determinate negation [. . .]. Because the result, the negation, is a *determinate* negation, it has a *content*. It is a new concept but one higher and richer than the preceding—richer because it negates or opposes the preceding and therefore contains it, and it contains even more than that, for it is the unity of itself and its opposite." Georg Wilhelm Friedrich Hegel, *The Science of Logic*, trans. George Di Giovanni (Cambridge: Cambridge University Press, 2010), 33. In as much as determinate negation implies "a determinate, 'contentful nothing' " (78), it should be considered as closely related to, but not identical with, Hegel's notion of "negation of negation," which is "concrete, *absolute* negativity" as opposed to the first negation, which is "on the contrary only *abstract* negativity" (89). The core of Hegel's dialectic is represented by this powerful figure of the negation of negation ("the infinite unity of negativity with itself"; 530), which inheres in, and enables, a determinate negation.

61. Marx, *Grundrisse*, 296.

62. See Marx, *Capital*, 1: 744.

63. Karl Marx, *Economic Manuscripts of 1861–63*, in *Karl Marx and Friedrich Engels: Collected Works*, vol. 30 (London: Lawrence and Wishart, 1988), 348. See also Karl Marx, *Theories of Surplus Value*, pt. 1 (London: Lawrence and Wishart, 1963), 40. In a letter to Engels of January 1868, Marx returns to this point by claiming that "in contrast to *all* former political economy, which *from the very*

outset treats the *different fragments of surplus value* with their fixed form of rent, profit, and interest as already given, *I first deal with the general form of surplus value*, in which all these fragments are still undifferentiated." Marx and Engels, *Selected Correspondence*, 186. However, my point is that Marx's Hegelian method here is not fully Hegelian, insofar as the logical relation between surplus-value in general and its particular forms needs to be theorized as *the defect of both*—the self-reflexive negativity that makes them both (universal and particular surplus-value) inconsistent. On this question see also Fred Moseley's essay "The Universal and the Particulars in Hegel's *Logic* and Marx's *Capital*," which has inspired my reasoning above (see Moseley and Smith, *Marx's Capital and Hegel's Logic*, 115–39).

64. Marx, *Capital*, 1: 323.

65. Ibid., 325 (my italics).

66. Marx, *Grundrisse*, 547.

67. Theodor W. Adorno, *Negative Dialectics* (London: Routledge, 2000), 190.

68. Marx, *Capital*, 1: 128.

69. In Marx's words: "It is no longer the worker who employs the means of production, but the means of production which employ the worker." Ibid., 425.

70. "On the one hand, all labour is an expenditure of human labour-power, in the physiological sense, and it is in this quality of being equal, or abstract, human labour that it forms the value of commodities. On the other hand, all labour is an expenditure of human labour-power in a particular form and with a definite aim, and it is in this quality of being concrete useful labour that it produces use-values." Ibid., 137. It seems to me that Marx's differentiation between abstract and concrete labor takes place against the backdrop of capitalist abstraction, in the precise sense that the notion of use-value is overdetermined by that of exchange-value, and thus by the logic of capitalist valorization. Put differently, in capitalism labor-power is already conceived "in a particular form" and "with a definite aim"; it is already "useful" insofar as it works as capital's presupposition. As Robert Kurz argues: "Not only can the concrete side not be separated from the abstract, but the former is subordinated to the latter. In other words: use-value is only *a form of representation* or *appearance* of abstract labour. Overarching both is the abstraction 'labour' as a real abstraction." *The Substance of Capital: The Life and Death of Capitalism*, trans. Robin Halpin (London: Chronos, 2016), 88 (my italics). For a similar approach, see Jean Baudrillard, *The Mirror of Production*, trans. Mark Poster (St. Louis, MO: Telos Press, 1975), 21–51.

71. Marx, *Capital*, 1: 134.

72. Georg Wilhelm Friedrich Hegel, *Phenomenology of Spirit*, trans. A. V. Miller (Oxford: Oxford University Press, 1977), 118.

73. André Gorz, *Reclaiming Work: Beyond the Wage-Based Society*, trans. Chris Turner (Cambridge, UK: Polity, 1999), 2.

74. Georg Wilhelm Friedrich Hegel, *System of Ethical Life and First Philosophy of Spirit*, trans. T. M. Knox (New York: State University of New York Press, 1979), 247.

75. Ibid., 246.

76. Thus, "whatever is truly universal in his particular skill is the *discovery of something universal, and the others learn it*; they cancel its particularity, and it becomes directly a universal good." Ibid.
77. Ibid., 249.
78. Ibid., 124.
79. Hegel, *Philosophy of Right*, 17.
80. Ibid., 104.
81. Ibid.

Chapter 2

1. Hegel, *Philosophy of Right*, 105.
2. Ibid.
3. Ibid., 107.
4. Ibid., 96.
5. Ibid., 98.
6. Ibid., 99.
7. Ibid., 99–100.
8. Ibid., 96.
9. Ibid., 109.
10. Ibid., 100.
11. Ibid., 99.
12. The vast critical literature on this topic includes Shlomo Avineri, *Hegel's Theory of the Modern State* (London: Cambridge University Press, 1972); Thom Brooks, *Hegel's Political Philosophy: A Systematic Reading of the Philosophy of Right* (Edinburgh: Edinburgh University Press, 2007); Robert R. Williams, *Beyond Liberalism and Communitarianism: Studies in Hegel's Philosophy of Right* (New York: State University of New York Press, 2001); Timothy C. Luther, *Hegel's Critique of Modernity: Reconciling Individual Freedom and the Community* (Lanham, MD: Lexington Books, 2010); Paul Franco, *Hegel's Philosophy of Freedom* (New Haven, CT: Yale University Press, 1999); Steven B. Smith, *Hegel's Critique of Liberalism* (Chicago: University of Chicago Press, 1991); Bruce Gilbert, *The Vitality of Contradiction: Hegel, Politics, and the Dialectic of Liberal-Capitalism* (Montreal: McGill-Queen's University Press, 2013).
13. Hegel, *Philosophy of Right*, xviii–xix.
14. Ibid., xix.
15. Ibid., xx.
16. Ibid., xlvii.
17. Ibid., xxix.
18. Ibid., xxx.
19. Georg Wilhelm Friedrich Hegel, *Introduction to the Lectures on the Philosophy of History*, trans. T. M. Knox and A. V. Miller (Oxford: Clarendon Press, 1985), 9.

20. Hegel, *Philosophy of Right*, xxxiii.
21. Ibid.
22. Ibid., xxxiv.
23. Ibid., 82.
24. Ibid., 200.
25. "The concept is the *free* [actuality; *das Freie*], as the *substantial power that is for itself*, and it is the *totality*, since *each* of the moments is *the whole* that *it* is, and each is posited as an undivided unity with it. So, in its identity with itself, it is what is *determinate in and for itself*." Georg Wilhelm Friedrich Hegel, *Encyclopedia of the Philosophical Sciences in Basic Outline*, pt. 1, *Science of Logic*, trans. and ed. Klaus Brinkmann and Daniel O. Dahlstrom (Cambridge: Cambridge University Press, 2010), 233.
26. Marcuse, "On the Philosophical Foundations of the Concept of Labour in Economics," 21.
27. Ibid., 25.
28. Ibid., 22.
29. Hegel, *The Science of Logic*, 656.
30. Ibid., 531. Here Hegel begins to articulate the theme of the double negation (*negation of negation*): what the concept as abstract universal negates is a negative concrete determination. However, "this double negation comes to be represented as if it were *external* to it, both as if the properties of the concrete that are left out were different from the ones that are retained as the content of the abstraction, and as if this operation of leaving some aside while retaining the rest went on outside them. With respect to this movement, the universal has not yet acquired the determination of *externality*; it is still in itself that absolute negation which is, precisely, the negation of negation or absolute negation" (ibid.). Acquiring self-externality entails an inward bending back upon itself, which is what turns abstract into concrete universality: "The truly higher universal is the one in which this outwardly directed side is redirected inwardly" (533). Here, then, is the truth about double negation: not simply the negation of a negative externality, which is excluded so that the concept acquires a positive identity, but "creative power as self-referring absolute negativity," which "differentiates itself internally" (ibid.); "the form with which the infinite concept clothes its differences—a form which is equally itself one of its differences" (534).
31. Ibid., 513.
32. Ibid., 574.
33. See Karl Marx and Friedrich Engels, *The Holy Family, or Critique of Critical Critique*, trans. R. Dixon (Moscow: Foreign Languages Publishing House, 1956), 78–83.
34. Hegel, *The Science of Logic*, 579.
35. Slavoj Žižek, *Incontinence of the Void: Economico-Philosophical Spandrels* (Cambridge, MA: MIT Press, 2017), 273.
36. It is worth quoting this key passage at length: "The disparity which exists in consciousness between the 'I' and the substance which is its object is the

distinction between them, the negative in general. This can be regarded as the *defect* of both, though it is their soul, or that which moves them. That is why some of the ancients conceived the void as the principle of motion, for they rightly saw the moving principle as the negative, though they did not as yet grasp that the negative is the self. Now, although this negative appears at first as a disparity between the 'I' and its object, it is just as much the disparity of the substance with itself. Thus what seems to happen outside of it, to be an activity directed against it, is really its own doing, and Substance shows itself to be essentially Subject." Hegel, *Phenomenology of Spirit*, 21.

37. See my previous work on this topic, e.g., Fabio Vighi, "Genie out of the Bottle: Lacan and the Loneliness of Global Capitalism," *Crisis and Critique* 6, no. 1 (2019): 391–415; "Capitalist Bulimia: Lacan on Marx and Crisis," *Crisis and Critique* 3, no. 3 (2016): 415–32; Heiko Feldner and Fabio Vighi, *Critical Theory and the Crisis of Contemporary Capitalism* (London: Bloomsbury, 2015).

38. See especially Baudrillard, *The Mirror of Production*; and Georges Bataille, *Theory of Religion*, trans. Robert Hurley (New York: Zone, 1989), 87–104; both originally published in 1973. See also Jacques Camatte's numerous contributions (since 1968) to the journal *Invariance*, which he continues to edit, although more and more sporadically.

39. See Hegel, *Philosophy of Right*, particularly 96–153, where Hegel repeatedly argues that through punishment, the law sublates crime as "negation of the negation" (100). In its mediating role, the law for Hegel does not merely treat crime as an exception to a naturally balanced situation, but rather engages with the crime-exception by granting it a foundational role that requires mediation.

40. Marx, *Capital*, 1: 302.

41. On this point see Hiroshi Uchida, *Marx's Grundrisse and Hegel's Logic*. From a Marxian angle, Uchida argues that the logical categories in Hegel's major work were themselves reflections of the productive processes of capitalist society.

42. Hegel, *Outlines of the Philosophy of Right*, 16.

43. See Jacques Lacan, "The Signification of the Phallus," in *Écrits*, 1st complete ed. in English (New York: Norton, 2006), 575–84 (581).

44. See David Graeber, *Bullshit Jobs: A Theory* (London: Penguin, 2018).

45. See Joseph Schumpeter, *Capitalism, Socialism, and Democracy* (London: Routledge, 2010).

46. Marx, *Capital*, 1: 531–33.

47. Gorz, *Reclaiming Work*, 145.

48. André Gorz, *Critique of Economic Reason*, 8.

49. Ibid., 200–201.

50. Ibid., 202.

51. Ibid., 206.

52. Ibid.

53. Ibid., 208.

54. Gorz, *Reclaiming Work*, 110.

55. Gorz, *Critique of Economic Reason*, 212.

56. Ibid., 214.

57. On this point see, for instance, Jonathan Crary, *24/7: Late Capitalism and the Ends of Sleep* (London: Verso, 2014); Peter Fleming, *Resisting Work: The Corporatization of Life and Its Discontents* (Philadelphia: Temple University Press, 2014); Mark Fisher, *Capitalist Realism: Is There No Alternative?* (Winchester, UK: Zero Books, 2009).

58. Marx, *Capital*, 1: 250.

59. Martin Ford, *Rise of the Robots: Technology and the Threat of a Jobless Future* (New York: Basic Books, 2015), lxv.

60. Robert Kurz, *Marx 2000* (London: Chronos, 2002), http://autonomies.org/2016/11/against-labour-against-capital-marx-2000-by-robert-kurz/.

61. In the words of Klaus Schwab, founder of the World Economic Forum: "The speed of current breakthroughs has no historical precedent. When compared with previous industrial revolutions, the Fourth is evolving at an exponential rather than a linear pace. Moreover, it is disrupting almost every industry in every country. And the breadth and depth of these changes herald the transformation of entire systems of production, management, and governance." "The Fourth Industrial Revolution: What It Means, How to Respond," *Foreign Affairs*, December 12, 2015, https://www.weforum.org/agenda/2016/01/the-fourth-industrial-revolution-what-it-means-and-how-to-respond/.

62. The issue of labor displacement and fall in the mass of profit was anticipated in the postwar period by a variety of thinkers including, among others, Hannah Arendt, *The Human Condition* (Chicago: University of Chicago Press, 1958); Ernest Mandel, *Late Capitalism* (London: New Left, 1975) and Wassily W. Leontief, "National Perspective: The Definition of Problems and Opportunities," in *The Long-Term Impact of Technology on Employment and Unemployment: A National Academy of Engineering Symposium, June 30, 1983* (Washington, DC: National Academy Press, 1983), 3–7.

63. Kurz, *Marx 2000*.

64. See http://www.oecd.org/sdd/productivity-stats/.

65. See Emre Tiftik and Khadija Mahmood, "Global Debt Monitor. Covid-19 Lights a Fuse," *Institute of International Finance*, April 6, 2020, https://www.iif.com/Portals/0/Files/content/Research/Global%20Debt%20Monitor_April2020.pdf.

66. See Ryan Banerjee and Boris Hofmann, "The Rise of Zombie Firms: Causes and Consequences," *BIS Quarterly Review*, September 2018, 67–78. See also John Detrixhe, "Zombie Companies Are Hiding an Uncomfortable Truth about the Global Economy," *Quartz*, March 9, 2020, https://qz.com/1812705/zombie-companies-are-spreading-as-interest-rates-fall/.

67. I have developed this point in Fabio Vighi, "A Self-Fulfilling Prophecy: Systemic Collapse and Pandemic Simulation." *The Philosophical Salon*, August 16, 2021, http://thephilosophicalsalon.com/a-self-fulfilling-prophecy-systemic-collapse-and-pandemic-simulation/.

68. See for example Aaron Bastani, *Fully Automated Luxury Communism: A Manifesto* (London: Verso, 2019); Aaron Benanav, *Automation and the Future of Work* (London: Verso, 2020).

69. Ulrich Beck, *The Brave New World of Work*, trans. Patrick Camiller (Cambridge: Polity, 2000), 63.

70. See Jean Baudrillard, *In the Shadow of the Silent Majorities, Or, the End of the Social, and Other Essays*, trans. Paul Foss, John Johnston, and Paul Patton (New York: Semiotext(e), 1983), 58–61.

71. Inspired by Dostoevsky's remarks in his 1864 novella *Notes from the Underground*, Sloterdijk refers to the Crystal Palace—the Great Exhibition of 1851 in London—as a metaphor for "the world interior of capital," "a hothouse that has drawn inwards everything that was once on the outside." "In this horizontal Babylon, being human becomes a question of spending power, and the meaning of freedom is exposed in the ability to choose between products for the market—or to create such products oneself." According to Sloterdijk, it is in this image of a self-enclosed and self-sufficient civilization ruled by capital, and the sense of domesticity it creates, that "the motif of the 'end of history' began its triumph": "The visionaries of the nineteenth century, like the communists of the twentieth, already understood that after the expiry of combatant history, social life could only take place in an expanded interior, a domestically organized and artificially climatized inner space." *In the World Interior of Capital: Towards a Philosophical Theory of Globalization*, trans. Wieland Hoban (Cambridge, UK: Polity, 2013, 170–71).

72. Ibid., 175.

73. These are lines from the Eagles' famous song "Hotel California," released in 1976.

74. Sloterdijk, *In the World Interior of Capital*, 176.

Chapter 3

1. Jacques Lacan, *D'un autre à l'autre*, bk. 16 of *Le séminaire de Jacques Lacan* (Paris: Seuil, 2006).

2. Jacques Lacan, *The Other Side of Psychoanalysis*, trans. Russell Grigg, bk. 17 of *The Seminar of Jacques Lacan* (New York: Norton, 2007), 110.

3. Here is the well-known passage: "[T]he revolutionary aspiration has only a single possible outcome—of ending up as the master's discourse. This is what experience has proved. What you aspire to as revolutionaries is a master. You will get one" (ibid., 202).

4. Jeremy Rifkin, *The Zero Marginal Cost Society: The Internet of Things, the Collaborative Commons, and the Eclipse of Capitalism* (London: Palgrave 2014), 2–4.

5. Gorz, *Reclaiming Work*, 1.

6. Karl Marx, *Capital: A Critique of Political Economy*, vol. 3, trans. David Fernbach (London: Penguin, 1981), 358.

7. In Leo Rauch, ed., *Hegel and the Human Spirit: A Translation of the Jena Lectures on the Philosophy of Spirit (1805–6) with Commentary* (Detroit: Wayne State

University Press, 1983), 104. On this point see also Slavoj Žižek, *Less Than Nothing: Hegel and the Shadow of Dialectical Materialism* (London: Verso, 2012), 510–11.

8. Jacques Lacan, "Du discours psychoanalytique," in *Lacan in Italia, 1953–1978*, ed. Giacomo B. Contri (Milan: La Salamandra, 1978), 36.

9. Slavoj Žižek, *Like a Thief in Broad Daylight: Power in the Era of Post-human Capitalism* (London: Allen Lane, 2018), 6. In truth, in the first chapter of his book Žižek develops a deeper reading of the explosive contradictions that are leading us toward "posthuman capitalism." The progressive decomposition of our sociosymbolic order, however, is only briefly correlated with the unstoppable devaluation that is affecting and afflicting contemporary capitalist societies. While Žižek mentions in passing the effects of technological unemployment, he does not develop the analysis of the cause, namely, capitalism's obdurate reliance on the valorization fetish (wage labour) despite its increasingly catastrophic ineffectiveness vis-à-vis automation.

10. Cioran, *A Short History of Decay*, 53.

11. See Jacques Lacan, "Du discours psychanalytique," 32–55; "Television," *October*, no. 40 (1987): 6–50.

12. On this point see especially Todd McGowan, *The End of Dissatisfaction? Jacques Lacan and the Emerging Society of Enjoyment* (New York: State University of New York Press, 2003).

13. Georg Simmel, *The Philosophy of Money*, 3rd enl. ed., trans. Tom Bottomore and David Frisby (London: Routledge, 2004), 258.

14. See for instance Samo Tomšič, *The Capitalist Unconscious: Marx and Lacan* (London: Verso, 2015); Adam Kotsko, *Neoliberalism's Demons: On the Political Theology of Late Capital* (Stanford, CA: Stanford University Press, 2018); Wendy Brown, *In the Ruins of Neoliberalism: The Rise of Antidemocratic Politics in the West* (New York: Columbia University Press, 2019).

15. See, among others, Serge Lesourd, *Comment taire le sujet? Des discours aux parlottes libérales* (Toulouse: Erès, 2006); Frédéric Declercq, "Lacan on the Capitalist Discourse: Its Consequences for Libidinal Enjoyment and Social Bonds," *Psychoanalysis, Culture and Society* 11, no. 1 (2006): 74–83; Bert Olivier, "Lacan on the Discourse of Capitalism; Critical Prospects," *Phronimon* 10, no. 1 (2009): 25–42; Marie-Jean Sauret, *Malaise dans le capitalisme* (Toulouse: Presses Universitaires du Mirail), 2009; Todd McGowan, *The End of Dissatisfaction?*; *Capitalism and Desire: The Psychic Cost of Free Markets* (New York: Columbia University Press, 2016); Paul Verhaeghe, *What about Me? The Struggle for Identity in a Market-Based Society* (Melbourne: Scribe, 2014); Julio Cesar Lemes de Castro, "The Discourse of Hysteria as the Logic of Mass Consumption," *Psychoanalysis, Culture and Society* 21, no. 4 (2016): 403–21; Matthias Pauwels, "The Most Hysterical of Masters: Lacan's Capitalist Discourse and Contemporary Styles of Interpellation," *Psychoanalysis, Culture and Society* 24, no. 1 (2019): 53–71.

16. Jean-Pierre Dupuy, *The Mark of the Sacred*, trans. M. B. DeBevoise (Stanford, CA: Stanford University Press, 2013), xiii.

17. Ibid., 63.

18. Jacques Lacan, "The Knowledge of the Psychoanalyst" (*Seminar XIX-bis*, unpublished, lesson of November 4, 1971).

19. See also Lacan, "Du discours psychoanalytique," 36.

20. Gorz, *Farewell to the Working Class*, 54.

21. Ibid., 52.

22. Cornelius Castoriadis, *The Imaginary Institution of Society* (Cambridge, UK: Polity, 2005), 16.

23. Lacan, *D'un autre à l'autre*, lesson of February 26, 1969.

24. I have developed this point in Fabio Vighi, *On Žižek's Dialectics: Surplus, Subtraction, Sublimation* (London: Continuum, 2010), 39–58.

25. Gorz, *Farewell to the Working Class*, 46.

26. Arendt, *The Human Condition*, 79–135.

27. Gorz, *Critique of Economic Reason*, 14.

28. Ibid., 15.

29. Ibid., 21.

30. Lacan, *The Other Side of Psychoanalysis*, 168.

31. Baudrillard, *The Mirror of Production*, 17.

32. Ibid., 36.

33. Ibid., 18–19.

34. Ibid., 19.

35. It is worth noting that the *social* dimension of capital ("the quantity of labour necessary for its [the commodity's] production in a given state of society, under certain social average conditions of production, with a given social average intensity, and average skill of the labour employed") is alien to the classical theory of value (e.g., Ricardo's), which therefore remains broadly asocial. Karl Marx, *Wage Labour and Capital and Value, Price and Profit* (New York: International Publishers, 1975), 33.

36. Lacan, *The Other Side of Psychoanalysis*, 149.

37. Marx, *Capital*, 1: 1029.

38. Gorz, *Reclaiming Work*, 55.

39. Lacan, *The Other Side of Psychoanalysis*, 177.

40. The difference between the "esoteric" and "exoteric" Marx was first proposed by the *Neue Marx-Lektüre* (New Marx Reading) in the 1970s and then reaffirmed by proponents of value-critique. See for instance Robert Kurz, *Marx lesen: Die wichtigsten Texte von Karl Marx für das 21. Jahrhundert* (Frankfurt: Eichborn Verlag, 2010), whose introduction is available here in English translation: https://libcom.org/library/reading-marx-21st-century-robert-kurz.

41. As A. Kiarina Kordela put it: "In truth, only surplus-value is differential substance, in the proper sense of the word, that is, a purely differential (non-)

substance." *Surplus: Spinoza, Lacan* (New York: State University of New York Press, 2007), 43.

42. Lacan, *The Other Side of Psychoanalysis*, 177–78.

43. See Lacan's "Signification of the Phallus," in *Ecrits*, 575–584.

44. See the formula of fantasy in the lower part of Lacan's discourse of the Master.

45. "What distinguishes the discourse of capitalism is this: the *Verwerfung*, the rejection, the rejection outside of all the fields of the symbolic with what I already said this has as a consequence: the rejection of what? Of castration." Lacan, *Seminar XIX-bis*, unpublished, lesson of November 4, 1971.

46. See Max Horkheimer and Theodor W. Adorno, *Dialectic of Enlightenment*, trans. John Cumming (London: Verso, 1997), 106.

47. See Alfred Sohn-Rethel, *Das Geld, die bare Münze des Apriori* (Berlin: Wagenbach, 1990).

48. Marx, *Capital*, 1: 575.

49. Ibid., 163–65.

50. Ibid., 280.

51. Ibid., 279–80.

52. Gorz, *Farewell to the Working Class*, 15.

53. Lacan, *The Other Side of Psychoanalysis*, 50.

54. Ibid., 49.

55. Ibid.

56. Ibid., 50.

57. Ibid., 77.

58. Ibid., 50.

59. Marx, *Grundrisse*, 288–89.

60. Marx, *Grundrisse*, 296, 298.

61. Marx, *Capital*, 1: 142. Incidentally, the metaphor of the fluidity of labour-power as a substance that is external to the value it coagulates into brings us back to Thales, the pre-Socratic philosopher for whom water, owing to its fluidity, was the substance of everything.

62. Marx, *Capital*, 1: 133.

63. Lacan, *The Other Side of Psychoanalysis*, 107–8.

64. Karl Marx and Friedrich Engels, *The Communist Manifesto* (Scotts Valley, CA: CreateSpace Independent Publishing Platform, 2015), 7.

65. Marx, *Grundrisse*, 255.

66. Ibid., 256.

67. Ibid., 257.

68. Ibid., 263.

69. Ibid.

70. Ibid., 266.

71. Ibid., 272.

72. Ibid.
73. Ibid., 274.
74. Marx, *Capital*, 1: 451.
75. What comes to mind here is Lacan's notion of sexual difference, where the impossibility of the relationship is sustained by a particular fantasy, a fictional formula whose purpose is to bridge the universal gap of sexuality.
76. Marcuse, "On the Philosophical Foundations of the Concept of Labour in Economics," 25.
77. Žižek, *Less Than Nothing*, 251.
78. Ibid., 250.
79. Marx, *Capital*, 1: 92.
80. Ibid., 274–76.
81. Ibid., 188.
82. See Immanuel Kant, *Critique of Pure Reason*, trans. Marcus Weigelt (London: Penguin, 2007), 176–83.
83. See for instance Slavoj Žižek, *The Ticklish Subject: The Absent Centre of Political Ontology* (London: Verso, 1999), 9–69.
84. Ibid., 36.
85. The same passage from the tautological definition of labour-power to the description of its exploitation is reiterated by Marx in his 1865 text "Value, Price and Profit." Here, Marx concludes that "the *value of labouring power* is determined by the *value of the necessaries* required to produce, develop, maintain, and perpetuate the labouring power." Marx, *Wage Labour and Capital and Value, Price and Profit*, 38. From this, he then presents his theory of surplus-value. Again, the problem is that if the value of labour is the value of necessaries required to reproduce it, these necessaries are themselves the product of labour, and so we are going around in circles.
86. "During the second period of the labour process, that in which his labour is no longer necessary labour, the worker does indeed expend labour-power, he does work, but his labour is no longer necessary labour, and he creates no value for himself. He creates surplus-value which, for the capitalist, has all the charms of something created out of nothing. This part of the working day I call surplus labour-time, and to the labour expended during that time I give the name of surplus labour." Marx, *Capital*, 1: 325.
87. "I depict the capitalist as the necessary functionary of capitalist production and demonstrate at great length that he not only 'deducts' or '*robs*' but enforces the *production of surplus value*, thus first helping to create what is to be deducted." Karl Marx and Frederick Engels, *Karl Marx and Frederick Engels: Collected Works*, vol. 24 (New York: International Publishers, 1989), 535.
88. Ibid., 270.
89. Ibid., 279.
90. Henry, *From Communism to Capitalism*, 58.

Chapter 4

1. Lacan refers to the gap as a dialectical notion in Seminar 11, when he claims that the relation between subject and Other is "entirely produced in a process of gap." *The Four Fundamental Concepts of Psychoanalysis*, trans. Alan Sheridan [Seminar, bk. 11] (London: Hogarth, 1977), 206. See also 21–22.

2. Baudrillard, *The Mirror of Production*, 104.

3. Lacan, *The Four Fundamental Concepts of Psychoanalysis*, 273.

4. Jacques Lacan, "L'insu que sait de l'une bévue, s'aile a mourre," *Ornicar?*, no. 17/18 (1979): 21; excerpt translated in Paul Verhaeghe and Frédéric Declercq, "Lacan's Analytic Goal: Le Sinthome or the Feminine Way," *Psychoanalytische Perspectieven* 34, no. 4 (2016): 336–57.

5. Gorz, *Farewell to the Working Class*, 43.

6. Cioran, *The Temptation to Exist*, 210.

7. Herbert Marcuse, *One-Dimensional Man: Studies in the Ideology of Advanced Industrial Society* (London: Routledge, 2002), 237.

8. Ibid., 250.

9. Marx, *Capital*, 1: 254.

10. See Karl Marx, "'Notes' on Adolph Wagner," in *Marx: Later Political Writings*, ed. Terrell Carver (Cambridge: Cambridge University Press, 1996), 227–57.

11. Marx, *Capital*, 1: 255.

12. Lacan, *The Four Fundamental Concepts of Psychoanalysis*, 167–68.

13. Lacan, *Ecrits*, 722.

14. Lacan, *The Other Side of Psychoanalysis*, 108.

15. This well-known passage is from the preface to the first edition of *Capital*. See Marx, *Capital*, 1:90.

16. Cornelius Castoriadis, "General Introduction," in *Cornelius Castoriadis: Political and Social Writings*, vol. 1, *1946–1955: From the Critique of Bureaucracy to the Positive Content of Socialism*, ed. David A. Curtis (Minneapolis: University of Minnesota Press, 1988), 26.

17. This central contradiction within Marx's thought can also be framed, of course, as a conflict between his materialistic critique of Hegel's speculative idealism, which he derived from Feuerbach, and his tendency not to jettison Hegel's dialectical method of enquiry into the self-development of humankind. There exists a vast critical literature on this theme, which for reasons of space cannot be discussed here.

18. Adorno, *Negative Dialectics*, 19.

19. Lacan, *The Four Fundamental Concepts of Psychoanalysis*, 176.

20. Marx, *Grundrisse*, 254.

21. Hegel, *The Science of Logic*, 73. And "this emptiness, is therefore simply as such the beginning of philosophy" (78).

22. At the start of book 2 of the *Logic*, Hegel makes it clear that "*reflective determinations* are of a different kind than the merely immediate determinations of

being. These last are more readily admitted to be transient, merely relative, confined to the reference to another. The reflective determinations have instead the form of a being which is in-and-for-itself. They claim the status, therefore, of *essential determinations*, and instead of passing over into their opposites, they appear rather as absolute, free, and mutually indifferent. They stubbornly resist, therefore, their movement; their *being* is the self-identity which they possess in their determinateness, and by virtue of it, though indeed presupposing each other, in this referring to the other they nonetheless maintain themselves as totally separate." *The Science of Logic*, 351.

23. Ibid., 389.
24. Ibid., 407–8.
25. Ibid.
26. Ibid., 746.
27. See Theodor W. Adorno, *Hegel: Three Studies* (Cambridge, MA: MIT Press, 1993); *Negative Dialectics*, especially 135–60.
28. Insofar as essence is "the *negation* of the sphere of being in general," it confronts being "not merely as an unessential determinate being," but as "a *non-essence, illusory* being." *The Science of Logic*, 395.
29. Ibid., 390.
30. Ibid., 409.
31. Ibid., 400.
32. Ibid., 409.
33. Ibid., 478.
34. Ibid., 477.
35. This logic whereby the impossibility of a notion becomes its condition of possibility is perfectly captured in film noir. The self-destructive dimension of the noir character (whether *femme fatale* or private eye) speaks not only for their self-relating negativity, but especially for the reproduction of the noir universe as such, which ultimately is the universe of capitalist exploitation.
36. Not to mention the fact that that the single take was reworked fully in postproduction, inclusive of object removal, colour and focus correction, reframing, and time-warping (slowing down and acceleration).
37. This point is central to Slavoj Žižek's Hegelianism, where epistemological limitation (the inherent limit of positing and external reflection) is read as ontological self-difference. See, for instance, *Less Than Nothing*, 239.
38. Hegel, *Phenomenology of Spirit*, 383–409.
39. See Sigmund Freud, *The Future of an Illusion*, in vol. 21 of *The Standard Edition of the Complete Psychological Works of Sigmund Freud*, ed. James Strachey (London: Hogarth, 1961).
40. Sigmund Freud, "The Theme of the Three Caskets," in vol. 12 of *The Standard Edition of the Complete Psychological Works of Sigmund Freud*, ed. James Strachey (London: Hogarth, 1958), 299. For an excellent discussion of Freud's determinism, see Ruda, *Abolishing Freedom*, 131–64.

41. Cioran, *A Short History of Decay*, 28.

42. See François Truffaut, *Hitchcock* (London: Secker and Warburg, 1968), 138.

43. In his discussion of interest-bearing capital in *Capital* volume 3, as well as in parts of *Theories of Surplus Value*, Marx unwittingly gets very close to describing the automatic dimension of capitalism *per se*, while attributing it to fictitious capital, where the relationship between capital and labor "reaches its most superficial and fetishized form" and is therefore an "automatic fetish" (Marx, *Capital*, 3: 515–16). Money-capital here appears as a mysterious creature capable of self-expansion without the mediation of labour-power.

44. In cinema, the ultimate decoy is George Kaplan, the nonexistent CIA agent in Hitchcock's *North by Northwest* (1959). Like Kaplan, the decoy works by not being there, that is, as an absent cause of narrative development.

45. Indeed, the theme of the retroactivity of signification via the temporal short circuit of the passage from contingency to necessity has been central to Žižek's project since its inception. The subject's empirical activity, Žižek contends in *The Sublime Object of Ideology*, "is possible only if he structures his perception of the world in advance in a way that opens the space for his intervention—in other words, only if he retroactively posits the very presuppositions of his activity, of his 'positing.' This 'act before the act' by means of which the subject posits the very presuppositions of his activity is of a strictly formal nature; it is a purely formal 'conversion' transforming reality into something perceived, assumed as a result of our activity." *The Sublime Object of Ideology* (London: Verso, 1989), 218.

46. Baudrillard, *The Mirror of Production*, 30.

47. Poster in ibid., 11.

48. Cioran, *A Short History of Decay*, 89.

49. Poster in Baudrillard, *The Mirror of Production*, 15. Baudrillard writes that "[t]here is *neither a mode of production nor production* in primitive societies. There is *no dialectic* and *no unconscious* in primitive societies. These concepts analyze only our own societies, which are ruled by political economy" (49).

50. Ibid., 46.

51. Kurz, *The Substance of Capital*, 37.

52. Baudrillard, *The Mirror of Production*, 66.

53. Ibid., 33.

54. Wassily W. Leontief, "The Distribution of Work and Income," *Scientific American* 247, no. 3 (September 1982): 188–204.

55. See for example Daniel Saros, *Information Technology and Socialist Construction: The End of Capital and the Transition to Socialism* (London: Routledge, 2014), where the author devises a socialist economic model that is not based on central planning but on socially coordinated feedback information on consumption needs and production.

56. Shoshana Zuboff, *The Age of Surveillance Capitalism: The Fight for a Human Future at the New Frontier of Power* (New York: Public Affairs Books, 2019), 353.

57. Ibid., 354.

58. Žižek, *The Sublime Object of Ideology*, 40.
59. Cioran, *A Short History of Decay*, 63.
60. See Dan DeFrancesco, "Here's a Breakdown of How Much US Banks Are Spending on Technology," *Business Insider*, March 28, 2019.
61. Evgeny Morozov, *To Save Everything, Click Here: Technology, Solutionism and the Urge to Fix Problems That Don't Exist* (London: Penguin, 2014), viii.
62. See, for example, Nicholas Stern, *Why Are We Waiting? The Logic, Urgency, and Promise of Tackling Climate Change* (Boston: MIT Press, 2015).
63. For instance, in *Capital* volume 1 Marx argues that "the capitalist mode of production is a historically necessary condition for the transformation of the labour process into a social process" (453).

Chapter 5

1. See Michael Hudson, *Killing the Host: How Financial Parasites and Debt Bondage Destroy the Global Economy* (Petrolia, CA; Counterpunch, 2015).
2. Gorz, *Reclaiming Work*, 37–38.
3. Hyman P. Minsky, "The Relevance of Kalecki: The Useable Contribution," *PSL Quarterly Review* 67, no. 265 (2013): 95–106.
4. Marx, *Capital*, 3: 516.
5. See Scott Hirst and Lucian A. Bebchuk, "The Specter of the Giant Three," *Boston University Law Review* 99, no. 6 (2019): 721–41.
6. Ernst Lohoff and Norbert Trenkle, "The Great Devaluation—Introduction," *Krisis*, July 4, 2012, http://www.krisis.org/2012/the-great-devaluation-introduction/. See also Ernst Lohoff and Norbert Trenkle, *Die große Entwertung* (Münster: Unrast Verlag, 2012).
7. See https://www.reuters.com/business/global-debt-is-fast-approaching-record-300-trillion-iif-2021-09-14/.
8. See Deborah Summers, "No Return to Boom and Bust: What Brown Said When He Was Chancellor," *Guardian*, September 11, 2008, https://www.theguardian.com/politics/2008/sep/11/gordonbrown.economy.
9. Arjun Appadurai, *Banking on Words: The Failure of Language in the Age of Derivative Finance* (Chicago: University of Chicago Press, 2016), 155.
10. See Michael Roberts, *The Long Depression: How It Happened, Why It Happened, and What Happens Next* (Chicago: Haymarket, 2016), 97–98.
11. OECD source quoted in Roberts, *The Long Depression*, 107.
12. Susan Lund et al., "A Decade after the Global Financial Crisis: What Has (and Hasn't) Changed?," Our Insights, August 29, 2018, McKinsey and Company, https://www.mckinsey.com/industries/financial-services/our-insights/a-decade-after-the-global-financial-crisis-what-has-and-hasnt-changed.
13. Ibid.

14. Jeremy Rifkin, *The End of Work: The Decline of the Global Labor Force and the Dawn of the Post-Market Era* (New York: Putnam, 1996), 17.

15. As summarized by Samir Amin: "He [Marx] said explicitly that capitalist accumulation destroyed the natural bases on which it was founded: human beings (the alienated, exploited, dominated and oppressed worker) and the land (symbol of natural wealth given to humanity)." *The Implosion of Capitalism* (London: Pluto, 2014), 131.

16. Marx, *Grundrisse*, 706.

17. Robert Kurz, *Marx 2000*.

18. Gorz, *Reclaiming Work*, 49.

19. "We are being afflicted with a new disease of which some readers may not yet have heard the name, but of which they will hear a great deal in the years to come—namely, *technological unemployment*. This means unemployment due to our discovery of means of economising the use of labour outrunning the pace at which we can find new uses for labour." John Maynard Keynes, *Essays in Persuasion* (London: Norton, 1964), 364.

20. Kurz, *Marx 2000*.

21. Martin Ford puts it rather mildly: "Despite the evidence suggesting that a huge percentage of Western consumers simply don't have sufficient income to create adequate demand for the products and services produced by their economy, there is no general agreement among economists that income inequality is creating a substantial drag on economic growth." *Rise of the Robots*, 197.

22. Neil Irwin, "Aughts Were a Lost Decade for U.S. Economy, Workers," *Washington Post*, January 2, 2010.

23. "Human anatomy contains the key to the anatomy of the ape." Marx, *Grundrisse*, 105.

24. "For me, perhaps the central insight is that the recent crisis, despite its many exotic features, was in fact a classic financial panic—a systemwide run of 'hot money' away from assets whose values suddenly became uncertain. In that respect, the crisis was akin to many other financial crises faced by governments and central banks—including that most venerable of central banks, the Bank of England—over the centuries." Ben Bernanke, "Monetary Policy and the Global Economy," London School of Economics, March 25, 2013, http://www.federalreserve.gov/newsevents/speech/bernanke20130325a.htm.

25. Paul Krugman, *End This Depression Now!* (London: Norton, 2012), 22. On this point Krugman draws on Keynes's famous metaphor of the "magneto trouble" in a car from his essay "The Great Slump of 1930": "But because we have magneto trouble, we need not assume that we shall soon be back in a rumbling waggon and that motoring is over." Keynes, *Essays in Persuasion*, 139.

26. John Maynard Keynes, *The General Theory of Employment, Interest and Money* (New York: BN Publishing, 2008), 103.

27. See David Harvey, *The Limits to Capital* (London: Verso, 2018); *The Enigma of Capital and the Crises of Capitalism* (London: Profile, 2010); *Seventeen Contradictions and the End of Capitalism* (London: Profile, 2014); John Bellamy Foster, *The Theory of Monopoly Capitalism: An Elaboration of Marxian Political Economy* (New York: Monthly Review Press, 2014). For a discussion of these and other responses to the 2008 crisis, see Feldner and Vighi, *Critical Theory and the Crisis of Contemporary Capitalism*, especially 1–31.

28. *Levy Institute Report*, quoted in Harman, *Zombie Capitalism*, 278.

29. See for instance Jean-Claude Michéa, *Les mystères de la gauche: De l'idéal des Lumières au triomphe du capitalisme absolu* (Paris: Flammarion, 2014); *Notre ennemi le capital* (Paris: Flammarion, 2018).

30. Karl Marx, *Theories of Surplus Value*, pt. 3, trans. Jack Cohen (London: Lawrence and Wishart, 1972), 455.

31. Rosa Luxemburg, *The Accumulation of Capital* (Oxford: Routledge, 2003), 426–27.

32. Hegel, *Phenomenology of Spirit*, 185–210.

33. Peter Fleming, *The Death of Homo Economicus: Work, Debt and the Myth of Endless Accumulation* (London: Polity, 2017), 85.

34. See Fabio Vighi, "A Self-Fulfilling Prophecy: Systemic Collapse and Pandemic Simulation." *The Philosophical Salon*, August 16, 2021, http://thephilosophicalsalon.com/a-self-fulfilling-prophecy-systemic-collapse-and-pandemic-simulation/.

35. Anatole Kaletsky, "Averting Economic Disaster Is the Easy Part," *Project Syndicate*, March 19, 2020, https://www.project-syndicate.org/commentary/government-compensation-for-covid-19-losses-by-anatole-kaletsky-2020-03.

36. For Heidegger, technology as "enframing" (*Gestell* in German means "frame" or "skeleton") indicates that everything for us makes sense only through the frame of technology. Everything we encounter in the world is framed in advance by technology.

37. See Fisher, *Capitalist Realism*.

38. Franco Berardi, *After the Future* (Edinburgh: AK Press, 2011), 40.

39. Han, *Psychopolitics*, 63, 65.

40. Gorz, *Reclaiming Work*, 42.

41. See ibid., 43.

42. Han, *Psychopolitics*, 8.

43. Phoebe Moore and Andrew Robinson, "The Quantified Self: What Counts in the Neoliberal Workplace," *New Media and Society* 18, no. 11 (2015): 2774–92.

44. Gorz, *Critique of Economic Reason*, 83.

45. Gorz, *Reclaiming Work*, 40–41.

46. Ibid., 41.

47. Lacan, *The Other Side of Psychoanalysis*, 197–208.

48. Jacques Lacan, *Problèmes cruciaux pour la psychanalyse*, Seminar, bk. 12, unpublished, 1965, session of June 9. Baudrillard makes a similar point about the scientific discourse: "The phantasm of science is double: on the one hand, there is an 'epistemological break' that relegates all other thought to a senseless prehistory of knowledge and, simultaneously, on the other hand, there is a linear accumulation of knowledge, hence of truth as a final totalization." *The Mirror of Production*, 114.

49. Lacan, *Problèmes cruciaux pour la psychanalyse*, session of May 5, 1965.

50. Ibid., session of May 12, 1965.

51. Ibid.

52. Maurizio Lazzarato, *Governing by Debt* (South Pasadena, CA: Semiotext(e), 2015).

53. Appadurai, *Banking on Words*, 127–28.

54. As Žižek put it, "in populism, the enemy is externalized or reified into a positive ontological entity (even if this entity is spectral), whose annihilation would restore balance and justice." Slavoj Žižek, "Against the Populist Temptation," *Critical Inquiry* 32, no. 3 (2006): 555.

55. Robert Kurz, "Politische Ökonomie des Antisemitismus," *Krisis*, no. 16/17 (1995), https://www.exit-online.org/link.php?tabelle=autoren&posnr=18.

56. See Baudrillard, *The Mirror of Production*, 114–15.

57. Far from being the guru of postmodernism, as he was often wrongly labeled, Baudrillard provides one of the most scathing critiques of our postmodern condition.

58. Jean Baudrillard, *Symbolic Exchange and Death*, rev. ed., trans. Iain Hamilton Grant (Los Angeles: Sage, 2017), 29.

59. Ibid., 30.

60. Ibid., 44.

61. Baudrillard, *In the Shadow of the Silent Majorities*, 35.

62. See Marcel Mauss, *The Gift: The Form and Reason for Exchange in Archaic Societies* (London: Routledge, 1990).

63. Baudrillard, *Symbolic Exchange and Death*, 58. See also Jean Baudrillard, *For a Critique of the Political Economy of the Sign*, trans. Charles Levin (New York: Telos Press, 1981), 164–84.

64. On the ideology of philanthrocapitalism see, among others, Linsey McGoey, *No Such Thing as a Free Gift: The Gates Foundation and the Price of Philanthropy* (London: Verso, 2015); Nicole Aschoff, *The New Prophets of Capital* (London: Verso, 2015); Vandana Shiva, *Oneness vs. the 1%* (New Delhi: Women Unlimited, 2018).

65. For Baudrillard, the counter-gift haunts the system as the agent of its potential destruction or destabilization. This may come in various forms (potlach, expenditure, refusal, sacrifice, suicide, inertia, hyperconformity, etc.), all of which would seem to bear some elementary structural resemblance with the Freudian "return of the repressed": a disruptive violence that necessarily accompanies all symbolic systems. While Baudrillard sees the counter-gift as a subjective challenge to existing

power relations, his definition of what a counter-gift might entail changes with the progression of his work.

66. See Marshall McLuhan, *Understanding Media: The Extensions of Man* (Abingdon, UK: Routledge, 2001).

67. Jean Baudrillard, *Simulations*, trans. Paul Foss, Paul Patton, and Philip Beitchman (New York: Semiotext(e), 1983), 3.

68. Jean Baudrillard, *The Perfect Crime*, trans. Chris Turner (London: Verso, 2008).

69. Baudrillard, *Symbolic Exchange and Death*, 81.

70. Jean Baudrillard, *Seduction*, trans. Brian Singer (London: Macmillan, 1990).

71. Baudrillard, *In the Shadow of the Silent Majorities*, 71.

72. Ibid., 77.

73. Ibid., 96.

74. Robert Epstein and Ronald E. Robertson, "The Search Engine Manipulation Effect (SEME) and Its Possible Impact on the Outcomes of Elections," *Proceedings of the National Academy of Sciences* 112, no. 33 (2015), https://www.pnas.org/content/112/33/E4512.

75. Baudrillard, *Simulations*, 70.

76. Ibid., 152.

77. Ibid., 135–37.

78. Jean Baudrillard, *The Conspiracy of Art*, trans. Ames Hodges (New York: Semiotext(e), 2005), 202.

79. See Edward Luce, "The Great American Disconnect," *Financial Times*, March 29, 2015, https://www.ft.com/content/00b4937c-d47b-11e4-8be8-00144feab7de; Deniz Igan, Divya Kirti, and Soledad Martinez Peria, *The Disconnect between Financial Markets and the Real Economy*, Special Notes Series on COVID-19, August 26, 2020, International Monetary Fund, https://www.imf.org/-/media/Files/Publications/covid19-special-notes/en-special-series-on-covid-19-the-disconnect-between-financial-markets-and-the-real-economy.ashx.

80. Jean Baudrillard, *Screened Out*, trans. Chris Turner (London: Verso, 2002), 31–32 (my italics).

Epilogue

1. See Klaus Schwab and Thierry Malleret, *COVID-19: The Great Reset* (Cologny, Switzerland: World Economic Forum, 2020). See also Hilary Sutcliffe, "COVID-19: The 4 Building Blocks of the Great Reset," Agenda, August 11, 2020, World Economic Fourm, https://www.weforum.org/agenda/2020/08/building-blocks-of-the-great-reset/.

2. "Prince Charles Says Pandemic a Chance to 'Think Big and Act Now,'" Royal Family Channel, June 5, 2020, YouTube video, https://www.youtube.com/watch?v=BucTwPegW5k.

3. See World Economic Forum, *The Reshaping of the World: Consequences for Society, Politics and Business—World Economic Forum 2014*; "We Need to Press Restart on the Global Economy," Agenda, November 10, 2015, World Economic Forum, https://www.weforum.org/agenda/2015/11/we-need-to-press-restart-on-the-global-economy/; "How to Reboot the Global Economy," Talks, World Economic Forum, https://www.weforum.org/open-forum/event_sessions/how-to-reboot-the-global-economy; Homi Kharas and John W. McArthur, "We Need to Reset the Global Operating System to Achieve the SDGs. Here's How," Agenda, January 13, 2017, World Economic Forum, https://www.weforum.org/agenda/2017/01/we-need-to-upgrade-the-sustainable-development-goals-here-s-how/.

4. "Clade X Exercise," Center for Health Security, Bloomberg School of Public Health, Johns Hopkins University, https://www.centerforhealthsecurity.org/our-work/events/2018_clade_x_exercise/index.html.

5. Event 201 website, https://www.centerforhealthsecurity.org/event201/.

6. "When it is threatened today, by simulation (the threat of vanishing in the play of signs), power risks the real, risks crisis, it gambles on remanufacturing artificial, economic, political stakes. This is a question of life and death for it. But it is too late." Baudrillard, *Simulations*, 44.

7. Jean Baudrillard, *Fragments: Conversations with François L'Yvonnet*, trans. Chris Turner (London: Routledge, 2004), 71. As William Pawlett put it, quoting from *Symbolic Exchange and Death*, "Baudrillard's conviction is that people will never acquiesce to the system and resign themselves to being merely 'the capitalist of their own lives.'" *Jean Baudrillard* (London: Routledge, 2007), 66.

8. See Baudrillard, *Fragments*, 64.

9. Marx, *Capital*, 1: 926.

10. Slavoj Žižek, *Pandemic! 2: Chronicles of a Time Lost* (New York: OR Books, 2020), 28.

11. Max Weber, *Political Writings* (Cambridge: Cambridge University Press, 1994), 310–11.

12. Baudrillard, *Simulations*, 64.

13. Ibid., 27.

14. "In a society which seeks—by prophylactic measures, by annihilating its own natural referents, by whitewashing violence, by exterminating all germs and all of the accursed share, by performing cosmetic surgery on the negative—to concern itself solely with quantified management and with the discourse of the Good, in a society where it is no longer possible to speak Evil, Evil has metamorphosed into all the viral and terroristic forms that obsess us." Jean Baudrillard, *The Transparency of Evil*, trans. James Benedict (London: Verso, 1993), 81.

15. Baudrillard, *Simulations*, 29.

16. Paul Mason, "The Italian Crisis Shows Why the European Left Must Break with the Neoliberal EU," *New Statesman*, May 30, 2018, https://www.newstatesman.com/politics/economy/2018/05/italian-crisis-shows-why-european-left-must-break-neoliberal-eu.

17. "For workers, it is no longer a question of freeing themselves *within* work, putting themselves in control of work, or seizing power within the framework of their work. The point now is to free oneself *from* work by rejecting its nature, content, necessities and modalities. But to reject work is also to reject the traditional strategy and organisational forms of working-class movement. It is no longer a question of winning power as a worker, but of winning the power no longer to function as a worker. The power at issue is no longer the same as before." Gorz, *Farewell to the Working Class*, 67.

18. Gorz, *Reclaiming Work*, 8.

19. "The lack of an overall conception of future society fundamentally distinguishes the new post-industrial proletariat from the class which, according to Marx, was invested with a historical mission. The neo-proletariat has nothing to expect *of* contemporary society nor of its subsequent evolution. [. . .] The logic of capital, which, after two centuries of 'progress,' has led to this outcome through the accumulation of ever more efficient means of production, can offer no more and no better. More precisely, productivism and industrial society can only continue by offering more and worse—more destruction, more waste, more repairs to destruction, more programming of the most intimate facets of industrial life. 'Progress' has arrived at the threshold beyond which plus turns into minus. The future is heavy with menace and devoid of promise. The forward march of productivism now brings the advance of barbarism and oppression." Gorz, *Farewell to the Working Class*, 73.

20. Ibid., 75.

Works Cited

Adorno, Theodor W. *Hegel: Three Studies*. Cambridge, MA: MIT Press, 1993.
———. *Negative Dialectics*. London: Routledge, 2000.
Althusser, Louis. *Philosophy of the Encounter: Later Writings, 1978–87*. London: Verso, 2006.
Amin, Samir. *The Implosion of Capitalism*. London: Pluto, 2014.
Appadurai, Arjun. *Banking on Words. The Failure of Language in the Age of Derivative Finance*. Chicago: University of Chicago Press, 2016.
Arendt, Hannah. *The Human Condition*. Chicago: University of Chicago Press, 1958.
Arthur, C. J. *Dialectics of Labour: Marx and His Relation to Hegel*. Oxford: Blackwell, 1986.
———. *The New Dialectic and Marx's Capital*. Leiden: Brill, 2002.
Aschoff, Nicole. *The New Prophets of Capital*. London: Verso, 2015.
Avineri, Shlomo. *Hegel's Theory of the Modern State*. London: Cambridge University Press, 1972.
Banerjee, Ryan, and Boris Hofmann. "The Rise of Zombie Firms: Causes and Consequences." *BIS Quarterly Review*, September 2018.
Bastani, Aaron. *Fully Automated Luxury Communism: A Manifesto*. London: Verso, 2019.
Bataille, Georges. *Theory of Religion*. Translated by Robert Hurley. New York: Zone, 1989.
Baudrillard, Jean. *For a Critique of the Political Economy of the Sign*. Translated by Charles Levin. New York: Telos Press, 1981.
———. *Fragments: Conversations with François L'Yvonnet*. Translated by Chris Turner. London: Routledge, 2004.
———. *In the Shadow of the Silent Majorities, Or, the End of the Social, and Other Essays*. Translated by Paul Foss, John Johnston, and Paul Patton. New York: Semiotext(e), 1983.
———. *The Mirror of Production*. Translated by Mark Poster. St. Louis, MO: Telos Press, 1975.

———. *The Perfect Crime*. Translated by Chris Turner. London: Verso, 2008.
———. *Screened Out*. Translated by Chris Turner. London: Verso, 2002.
———. *Simulations*. Translated by Paul Foss, Paul Patton, and Philip Beitchman. New York: Semiotext(e), 1983.
———. *Symbolic Exchange and Death*, rev. ed., trans. Iain Hamilton Grant. Los Angeles: Sage, 2017.
———. *The Transparency of Evil*. Translated by James Benedict. London: Verso, 1993.
Beck, Ulrich. *The Brave New World of Work*. Translated by Patrick Camiller. Cambridge: Polity, 2000.
Bellofiore, Riccardo. "Marx after Hegel: Capital as Totality and the Centrality of Production." *Crisis and Critique* 3, no. 3 (2016): 31–64.
Benanav, Aaron. *Automation and the Future of Work*. London: Verso, 2020.
Berardi, Franco. *After the Future*. Edinburgh: AK Press, 2011.
Brooks, Thom. *Hegel's Political Philosophy: A Systematic Reading of the Philosophy of Right*. Edinburgh: Edinburgh University Press, 2007.
Brown, Wendy. *In the Ruins of Neoliberalism: The Rise of Antidemocratic Politics in the West*. New York: Columbia University Press, 2019.
Castoriadis, Cornelius. *The Imaginary Institution of Society*. Cambridge, UK: Polity, 2005.
Cioran, Emil. *A Short History of Decay*. Translated by Richard Howard. New York: Arcade, 2012.
———. *The Temptation to Exist*. Translated by Richard Howard. Chicago: University of Chicago Press, 1998.
Contri, Giacomo B., ed. *Lacan in Italia, 1953–1978*. Milan: La Salamandra, 1978.
Crary, Jonathan. *24/7: Late Capitalism and the Ends of Sleep*. London: Verso, 2014.
Curtis, David A., ed. *Cornelius Castoriadis: Political and Social Writings*. Vol. 1, *1946–1955: From the Critique of Bureaucracy to the Positive Content of Socialism*. Minneapolis: University of Minnesota Press, 1988.
Declercq, Frédéric. "Lacan on the Capitalist Discourse: Its Consequences for Libidinal Enjoyment and Social Bonds." *Psychoanalysis, Culture and Society* 11, no. 1 (2006): 74–83.
DeFrancesco, Dan. "Here's a Breakdown of How Much US Banks Are Spending on Technology." *Business Insider*, March 28, 2019.
Deleuze, Gilles, and Guattari, Felix. "Capitalism: A Very Special Delirium." In *Hatred of Capitalism. A Reader*, edited by Chris Kraus and Sylvère Lotringer, 215–221. Los Angeles: Semiotext(e), 2001.
Dupuy, Jean-Pierre. *The Mark of the Sacred*. Translated by M. B. DeBevoise. Stanford, CA: Stanford University Press, 2013.
Epstein, Robert, and Ronald E. Robertson. "The Search Engine Manipulation Effect (SEME) and Its Possible Impact on the Outcomes of Elections." *Proceedings of the National Academy of Sciences* 112, no. 33 (2015), https://www.pnas.org/content/112/33/E4512.

Feldner, Heiko, and Fabio Vighi. *Critical Theory and the Crisis of Contemporary Capitalism*. London: Bloomsbury, 2015.
Fisher, Mark. *Capitalist Realism: Is There No Alternative?* Winchester, UK: Zero Books, 2009.
Fleming, Peter. *The Death of Homo Economicus: Work, Debt and the Myth of Endless Accumulation*. London: Polity, 2017.
———. *Resisting Work: The Corporatization of Life and Its Discontents*. Philadelphia: Temple University Press, 2014.
Ford, Martin. *Rise of the Robots: Technology and the Threat of a Jobless Future*. New York: Basic Books, 2015.
Foster, John Bellamy. *The Theory of Monopoly Capitalism: An Elaboration of Marxian Political Economy*. New York: Monthly Review Press, 2014.
Franco, Paul. *Hegel's Philosophy of Freedom*. New Haven, CT: Yale University Press, 1999.
Freud, Sigmund. *The Future of an Illusion*. In *The Standard Edition of the Complete Psychological Works of Sigmund Freud*, edited by James Strachey, vol. 21. London: Hogarth, 1961.
———. "The Theme of the Three Caskets." In *The Standard Edition of the Complete Psychological Works of Sigmund Freud*, edited by James Strachey, vol. 12. London: Hogarth, 1958.
Gilbert, Bruce. *The Vitality of Contradiction: Hegel, Politics, and the Dialectic of Liberal-Capitalism*. Montreal: McGill-Queen's University Press, 2013.
Gorz, André. *Critique of Economic Reason*. Ttranslated by Gillian Handyside and Chris Turner. London: Verso, 1989.
———. *Farewell to the Working Class. An Essay on Post-industrial Socialism*. Translated by Michael Sonenscher. London: Pluto, 1982.
———. *Reclaiming Work: Beyond the Wage-Based Society*. Ttranslated by Chris Turner. Cambridge, UK: Polity, 1999.
Graeber, David. *Bullshit Jobs: A Theory*. London: Penguin, 2018.
Harman, Chris. *Zombie Capitalism: Global Crisis and the Relevance of Marx*. London: Bookmarks, 2009.
Harvey, David. *The Enigma of Capital and the Crises of Capitalism*. London: Profile, 2010.
———. *The Limits to Capital*. London: Verso, 2018.
———. *Seventeen Contradictions and the End of Capitalism*. London: Profile, 2014.
Han, Byung-Chul. *Psychopolitics: Neoliberalism and New Technologies of Power*. Translated by Erik Butler. London: Verso, 2017.
Hegel, Georg Wilhelm Friedrich. *Encyclopedia of the Philosophical Sciences in Basic Outline*. Pt. 1, *Science of Logic*, translated and edited by Klaus Brinkmann and Daniel O. Dahlstrom. Cambridge: Cambridge University Press, 2010.
———. *Introduction to the Lectures on the Philosophy of History*. Translated by T. M. Knox and A. V. Miller. Oxford: Clarendon Press, 1985.

———. *Outlines of the Philosophy of Right*. Translated by T. M. Knox. Oxford: Oxford University Press, 2008.

———. *Phenomenology of Spirit*. Translated by A. V. Miller. Oxford: Oxford University Press, 1977.

———. *System of Ethical Life and First Philosophy of Spirit*. Translated by T. M. Knox. New York: State University of New York Press, 1979.

Heller, Henry. *The Birth of Capitalism: A 21st Century Perspective*. London: Pluto, 2011.

Henry, Michel. *From Communism to Capitalism: Theory of a Catastrophe*. Translated by Scott Davidson. London: Bloomsbury, 2014.

Hirst, Scott, and Lucian A. Bebchuk. "The Specter of the Giant Three." *Boston University Law Review* 99, no. 6 (2019): 721–41.

Horkheimer, Max, and Theodor W. Adorno. *Dialectic of Enlightenment*. Translated by John Cumming. London: Verso, 1997.

Hudson, Michael. *Killing the Host: How Financial Parasites and Debt Bondage Destroy the Global Economy*. Petrolia, CA; Counterpunch, 2019.

Irwin, Neil. "Aughts Were a Lost Decade for U.S. Economy, Workers." *Washington Post*, January 2, 2010.

Johannessen, Jon-Arild. *Automation, Innovation and Economic Crisis: Surviving the Fourth Industrial Revolution*. London: Routledge, 2018.

Kaletsky, Anatole. "Averting Economic Disaster Is the Easy Part." *Project Syndicate*, March 19, 2020. https://www.project-syndicate.org/commentary/government-compensation-for-covid-19-losses-by-anatole-kaletsky-2020-03.

Kant, Immanuel. *Critique of Pure Reason*. Translated by Marcus Weigelt. London: Penguin, 2007.

Keynes, John Maynard. *Essays in Persuasion*. London, Norton, 1964.

———. *The General Theory of Employment, Interest and Money*. New York: BN Publishing, 2008.

Kordela, A. Kiarina. *Surplus: Spinoza, Lacan*. New York: State University of New York Press, 2007.

Kotsko, Adam. *Neoliberalism's Demons: On the Political Theology of Late Capital*. Stanford, CA: Stanford University Press, 2018.

Krugman, Paul. *End This Depression Now!* London: Norton, 2012.

Kurz, Robert. *Marx 2000*. London: Chronos, 2002. http://autonomies.org/2016/11/against-labour-against-capital-marx-2000-by-robert-kurz/.

———. *Marx lesen: Die wichtigsten Texte von Karl Marx für das 21. Jahrhundert*. Frankfurt: Eichborn Verlag, 2010.

———. "Politische Ökonomie des Antisemitismus." *Krisis*, no. 16/17 (1995). https://www.exit-online.org/link.php?tabelle=autoren&posnr=18.

———. *The Substance of Capital: The Life and Death of Capitalism*. Translated by Robin Halpin. London: Chronos, 2016.

Lacan, Jacques. *D'un autre à l'autre*. Bk. 16 of *Le séminaire de Jacques Lacan*. Paris: Seuil, 2006.

---. *Écrits*. 1st complete ed. in English. New York: Norton, 2006.
---. *The Four Fundamental Concepts of Psychoanalysis*. Translated by Alan Sheridan. [Seminar, bk. 11.] London: Hogarth, 1977.
---. "The Knowledge of the Psychoanalyst." Seminar 19-bis. Unpublished, 1971.
---. "L'insu que sait de l'une bévue, s'aile a mourre." Seminar, bk. 24. Unpublished, 1976–77.
---. *The Other Side of Psychoanalysis*. Translated by Russell Grigg. Bk. 17 of *The Seminar of Jacques Lacan*. New York: Norton, 2007.
---. "Problèmes cruciaux pour la psychanalyse." Seminar, bk. 12. Unpublished, 1964–65.
---. "RSI." Seminar, bk. 22. Unpublished, 1974–75.
---. "Television." *October*, no. 40 (1987): 6–50.
Lafargue, Paul. *The Right to be Lazy*. Translated by Charles Kerr. Chicago: Charles Kerr, 1907.
Lazzarato, Maurizio. *Governing by Debt*. South Pasadena, CA: Semiotext(e), 2015.
Lemes de Castro, Julio Cesar. "The Discourse of Hysteria as the Logic of Mass Consumption." *Psychoanalysis, Culture and Society* 21, no. 4 (2016): 403–21.
Leontief, Wassily W. "The Distribution of Work and Income," *Scientific American* 247, no. 3 (September 1982): 188–204.
---. "National Perspective: The Definition of Problems and Opportunities." In *The Long-Term Impact of Technology on Employment and Unemployment: A National Academy of Engineering Symposium, June 30, 1983*. Washington, DC: National Academy Press, 1983.
Lesourd, Serge. *Comment taire le sujet? Des discours aux parlottes libérales*. Toulouse: Erès, 2006.
Lohoff, Ernst, and Norbert Trenkle. *Die große Entwertung*. Münster: Unrast Verlag, 2012.
---. "The Great Devaluation—Introduction." *Krisis*, July 4, 2012. http://www.krisis.org/2012/the-great-devaluation-introduction/.
Losurdo, Domenico. *Liberalism: A Counter-history*. Translated by Gregory Elliott. London: Verso, 2014.
Luther, Timothy C. *Hegel's Critique of Modernity: Reconciling Individual Freedom and the Community*. Lanham, MD: Lexington Books, 2010.
Luxemburg, Rosa. *The Accumulation of Capital*. Oxford: Routledge, 2003.
Mandel, Ernest. *Late Capitalism*. London: New Left, 1975.
Marcuse, Herbert. "On the Philosophical Foundations of the Concept of Labor in Economics." *Telos*, no. 16 (Summer 1973): 9–37.
---. *One-Dimensional Man: Studies in the Ideology of Advanced Industrial Society*. London: Routledge, 2002.
Marx, Karl. *Capital: A Critique of Political Economy*. Vol. 1, translated by Ben Fowkes. London: Penguin, 1990.

———. *Capital: A Critique of Political Economy*. Vol. 3, translated by David Fernbach. London: Penguin, 1981.

———. *Economic and Philosophic Manuscripts of 1844*. Translated by Martin Milligan. Radford, VA: Wilder, 2011.

———. *Grundrisse*. Translated by Martin Nicolaus. London: Penguin, 1993.

———. "'Notes' on Adolph Wagner." In *Marx: Later Political Writings*, edited by Terrell Carver, 227–57. Cambridge: Cambridge University Press, 1996.

———. *The Poverty of Philosophy*. In *Karl Marx and Friedrich Engels: Collected Works*, vol. 6. New York: International Publishers, 1976.

———. *Theories of Surplus Value*. Pt. 1, translated by Emile Burns. London: Lawrence and Wishart, 1963.

———. *Theories of Surplus Value*. Pt. 3, translated by Jack Cohen. London: Lawrence and Wishart, 1972.

———. *Wage Labour and Capital and Value, Price and Profit*. New York: International Publishers, 1975.

Marx, Karl, and Friedrich Engels. *The Communist Manifesto*. Scotts Valley, CA: CreateSpace Independent Publishing Platform, 2015.

———. *The Holy Family, or Critique of Critical Critique*. Translated by R. Dixon. Moscow: Foreign Languages Publishing House, 1956.

———. *Karl Marx and Friedrich Engels: Collected Works*. Vol. 24. New York: International Publishers, 1989.

———. *Karl Marx and Friedrich Engels: Collected Works*. Vol. 30. London: Lawrence and Wishart, 1988.

———. *Selected Correspondence*. Moscow: Progress Publishers, 1975.

Mason, Paul. "The Italian Crisis Shows Why the European Left Must Break with the Neoliberal EU." *New Statesman*, May 30, 2018. https://www.newstatesman.com/politics/economy/2018/05/italian-crisis-shows-why-european-left-must-break-neoliberal-eu.

Mauss, Marcel. *The Gift: The Form and Reason for Exchange in Archaic Societies*. London: Routledge, 1990.

McGoey, Linsey. *No Such Thing as a Free Gift. The Gates Foundation and the Price of Philanthropy*. London: Verso, 2015.

McGowan, Todd. *Capitalism and Desire: The Psychic Cost of Free Markets*. New York: Columbia University Press, 2016.

———. *The End of Dissatisfaction? Jacques Lacan and the Emerging Society of Enjoyment*. New York: State University of New York Press, 2003.

McLuhan, Marshall. *Understanding Media: The Extensions of Man*. Abingdon, UK: Routledge, 2001.

Meaney, Mark E. *Capital as Organic Unity: The Role of Hegel's Science of Logic in Marx's Grundrisse*. New York: Springer, 2003.

Merleau-Ponty, Maurice. *Adventures of the Dialectic*. Translated by Joseph Bien. Evanston, IL: Northwestern University Press, 1973.

Michéa, Jean-Claude. *Les mystères de la gauche: De l'idéal des Lumières au triomphe du capitalisme absolu*. Paris: Flammarion, 2014.
———. *Notre ennemi, le capital*. Paris: Flammarion, 2018.
Minsky, Hyman P. "The Relevance of Kalecki: The Useable Contribution." *PSL Quarterly Review* 67, no. 265 (2013): 95–106.
Moder, Gregor. *Hegel and Spinoza: Substance and Negativity*. Evanston, IL: Northwestern University Press, 2017.
Moore, Phoebe, and Andrew Robinson. "The Quantified Self: What Counts in the Neoliberal Workplace." *New Media and Society* 18, no. 11 (2015): 2774–92.
Morozov, Evgeny. *To Save Everything, Click Here: Technology, Solutionism and the Urge to Fix Problems That Don't Exist*. London: Penguin, 2014.
Moseley, Fred, and Tony Smith, eds. *Marx's Capital and Hegel's Logic: A Reexamination*. Leiden: Brill, 2014.
Olivier, Bert. "Lacan on the Discourse of Capitalism; Critical Prospects." *Phronimon* 10, no. 1 (2009): 25–42.
Pauwels, Matthias "The Most Hysterical of Masters: Lacan's Capitalist Discourse and Contemporary Styles of Interpellation." *Psychoanalysis, Culture and Society* 24, no. 1 (2019): 53–71.
Pawlett, William. *Jean Baudrillard*. London: Routledge, 2007.
Polanyi, Karl. *The Great Transformation: The Political and Economic Origins of Our Time*. London: Beacon, 2002.
Rauch, Leo, ed. *Hegel and the Human Spirit: A Translation of the Jena Lectures on the Philosophy of Spirit (1805–6) with Commentary*. Detroit: Wayne State University Press, 1983.
Rifkin, Jeremy. *The End of Work: The Decline of the Global Labor Force and the Dawn of the Post-Market Era*. New York: Putnam, 1996.
———. *The Zero Marginal Cost Society: The Internet of Things, the Collaborative Commons, and the Eclipse of Capitalism*. London: Palgrave, 2014.
Roberts, Michael. *The Long Depression: How It Happened, Why It Happened, and What Happens Next*. Chicago: Haymarket, 2016.
Ruda, Frank. *Abolishing Freedom: A Plea for a Contemporary Use of Fatalism*. Lincoln: University of Nebraska Press, 2016.
Saros, Daniel. *Information Technology and Socialist Construction: The End of Capital and the Transition to Socialism*. London: Routledge, 2014.
Sauret, Marie-Jean. *Malaise dans le capitalisme*. Toulouse: Presses Universitaires du Mirail, 2009.
Schumpeter, Joseph. *Capitalism, Socialism, and Democracy*. London: Routledge, 2010.
Schwab, Klaus, and Thierry Malleret. *COVID-19: The Great Reset*. Cologny, Switzerland: World Economic Forum, 2020.
———. "The Fourth Industrial Revolution: What It Means, How to Respond." *Foreign Affairs*, December 12, 2015.
Shiva, Vandana. *Oneness vs. the 1%*. New Delhi: Women Unlimited, 2018.

Simmel, Georg. *The Philosophy of Money*. 3rd enl. ed. Translated by Tom Bottomore and David Frisby. London: Routledge, 2004.
Sloterdijk, Peter. *In the World Interior of Capital: Towards a Philosophical Theory of Globalization*. Translated by Wieland Hoban. Cambridge, UK: Polity, 2013.
Smith, Jason E. *Smart Machines and Service Work: Automation in an Age of Stagnation*. London: Reaktion, 2020.
Smith, Steven B. *Hegel's Critique of Liberalism*. Chicago: University of Chicago Press, 1991.
Sohn-Rethel, Alfred. *Das Geld, die bare Münze des Apriori*. Berlin: Wagenbach, 1990.
———. *Intellectual and Manual Labour: A Critique of Epistemology*. Translated by Martin Sohn-Rethel. London: Macmillan, 1978.
Stern, Nicholas. *Why Are We Waiting? The Logic, Urgency, and Promise of Tackling Climate Change*. Boston: MIT Press, 2015.
Tomšič, Samo. *The Capitalist Unconscious: Marx and Lacan*. London: Verso, 2015.
Tronti, Mario. "I 'grilli' della merce." In *Figure del feticismo*, edited by Stefano Mistura, 103–22. Turin: Einaudi, 2011.
Truffaut, François. *Hitchcock*. London: Secker and Warburg, 1968.
Uchida, Hiroshi. *Marx's Grundrisse and Hegel's Logic*. London: Routledge, 1988.
Verhaeghe, Paul. *What about Me? The Struggle for Identity in a Market-Based Society*. Melbourne: Scribe, 2014.
Verhaeghe, Paul, and Frédéric Declercq. "Lacan's Analytic Goal: Le Sinthome or the Feminine Way." *Psychoanalytische Perspectieven* 34, no. 4 (2016): 336–57.
Vighi, Fabio. "Capitalist Bulimia: Lacan on Marx and Crisis." *Crisis and Critique* 3, no. 3 (2016): 415–32.
———. "Genie out of the Bottle: Lacan and the Loneliness of Global Capitalism." *Crisis and Critique* 6, no. 1 (2019): 391–415.
———. *On Žižek's Dialectics: Surplus, Subtraction, Sublimation*. London: Continuum, 2010.
———. "A Self-Fulfilling Prophecy: Systemic Collapse and Pandemic Simulation." *The Philosophical Salon*, August 16, 2021, http://thephilosophicalsalon.com/a-self-fulfilling-prophecy-systemic-collapse-and-pandemic-simulation/.
Weber, Max. *Political Writings*. Cambridge: Cambridge University Press, 1994.
Williams, Eric. *Capitalism and Slavery*. Chapel Hill: University of North Carolina Press, 1994.
Williams, Robert R. *Beyond Liberalism and Communitarianism: Studies in Hegel's Philosophy of Right*. New York: State University of New York Press, 2001.
Žižek, Slavoj. "Against the Populist Temptation." *Critical Inquiry* 32, no. 3 (2006): 551–74.
———. *Incontinence of the Void: Economico-Philosophical Spandrels*. Cambridge, MA: MIT Press, 2017.
———. *Less Than Nothing: Hegel and the Shadow of Dialectical Materialism*. London: Verso, 2012.

———. *Like a Thief in Broad Daylight: Power in the Era of Post-human Capitalism.* London: Allen Lane, 2018.

———. *Pandemic! COVID-19 Shakes the World.* New York: OR Books, 2020.

———. *Pandemic! 2: Chronicles of a Time Lost.* New York: OR Books, 2020.

———. *The Sublime Object of Ideology.* London: Verso, 1989.

———. *The Ticklish Subject: The Absent Centre of Political Ontology.* London: Verso, 1999.

Zuboff, Shoshana. *The Age of Surveillance Capitalism: The Fight for a Human Future at the New Frontier of Power.* New York: Public Affairs Books, 2019.

Index

Adorno, Theodor W., 20, 35, 93, 96
Althusser, Luis, 7–8, 153n
Amin, Samir, 170n
Appadurai, Arjun, 116, 136
Arendt, Hannah, 61, 160n
Aristotle, 1, 4
Arthur, Christopher, 4, 11

Badiou, Alain, 8
Bataille, Georges, 33
Baudrillard, Jean, ix, 33, 62, 86, 106–107, 139–146, 156n, 159n, 168n, 172n, 174n
Beck, Ulrich, 47
Bellofiore, Riccardo, 12, 153n
Bentham, Jeremy, 67, 109
Bernanke, Ben, 122
Biden, Joe, 124
Blair, Tony, 124
Brown, Gordon, 115
Buffett, Warren, 140

Castoriadis, Cornelius, 59, 92
Cioran, Emil, xii, 87, 103, 106, 109
von Clausewitz, Carl, 111
Clinton, Bill, 124, 140
Cohen, Leonard, 101

Deleuze, Gilles, 4, 8, 62
Dostoevsky, Fyodor, 48, 161n

Dupuy, Jean-Pierre, 57

Engels, Friedrich, 15, 20, 31, 71, 107, 155–156n, 165n
Epicurus, 8
Epstein, Robert, 142

Fleming, Peter, 37–38, 126
Ford, Martin, 44, 170n
Foster, John Bellamy, 123
Franklin, Benjamin, 3
Freud, Sigmund, 8, 46, 90, 102
Friedman, Milton, 111, 128

Gates, Bill, 46, 140, 145
Gorz, André, ix, 10, 12, 21, 39–41, 53, 59, 87, 119, 13, 149, 175n
Graeber, David, 38
Greenspan, Alan, 122
Grotius, Hugo, 3

Hardt, Michael, 133
Harvey, David, 123
Hayek, Friedrich, 111
Hegel, Georg Wilhelm Friedrich, ix, xi, xii, 1–3, 13–18, 20–23, 25–31, 34–36, 42, 52–53, 67, 74–75, 85, 91, 93–103, 125–126, 152n, 154n, 155n, 158n, 159n, 166n
    Beautiful Soul, 102

Hegel, Georg Wilhelm Friedrich
  (*continued*)
  concrete and abstract universality,
    18, 21, 31–33, 35, 83, 98, 158n
  cunning of reason, 52–53
  dialectic, 14–17, 30, 33–35, 42, 68,
    94, 97, 103, 154n, 155n, 166n
  Encyclopedia, 30, 158n
  *Introduction to the Lectures on the
    Philosophy of History*, 157n
  love, 29–30
  negation of negation, xi, 18, 68,
    96–97, 155n, 158n, 159n
  particular and universal, 15, 21,
    25–29, 31–33, 98–99, 156n,
    157n
  political economy, 20–23
  positing/presupposing, 9–10, 13,
    20, 37, 74, 76, 87, 95–98, 154n,
    167n, 168n.
  Phenomenology of Spirit, 21, 33, 126,
    159n
  Philosophy of Right, xii, 3, 23,
    25–30, 159n
  Science of Logic, 14–17, 31, 95,
    154n, 155n, 158n, 166n, 167n
  spirit is a bone, 126
  *System of Ethical Life and First
    Philosophy of Spirit*, 156n
Henry, Michel, 11, 83
Hitchcock, Alfred, 104, 168n
Hobbes, Thomas, 147
Horkheimer, Max, 66
Hudson, Michael, 111
Hume, David, 2

Kaletsky, Anatole, 128
Kant, Immanuel, 29, 78–80, 101
Kautsky, Karl, 20
Keynes, John Maynard, 120, 122–123,
  170n
Kordela, A. Kiarina, 163n

Krugman, Paul, 123, 170n
Kurz, Robert, 39, 44–45, 114, 119,
  138, 156

Lacan, Jacques, ix, 8, 33–34, 36, 49,
  51–60, 63–71, 85, 87, 90–93,
  104, 108, 134–135, 142, 161n,
  164n, 166n
  big Other, 49, 52, 64, 66, 67, 70,
    102, 108–109, 132.
  Capitalist discourse, 54–55, 60, 66,
    142
  discourse theory, 55–58, 60–66, 83,
    91–92, 126–127, 135, 142, 161n,
    164n
  drive, xiv, 4, 57, 66, 80, 86, 90–91,
    124
  Écrits, 159n, 164n
  fantasy, xiv, 6, 86, 164n, 165n
  jouissance (including *surplus-
    jouissance*), 33–34, 54, 60, 63–66,
    68–71, 80, 85, 87, 91, 104,
    123–124
  objet a, 65
  phallus, 36, 65
  savoir-faire, 33–34, 59–64, 82
  Seminar 11, 90, 166n
  Seminar 12, 134
  Seminar 16, 51, 63, 132
  Seminar 17, 52, 68–69
  Seminar 22, xiv
  Seminar 24, 87
  signifier of lack, xiii, xiv, 65, 70
  surplus-value (critique of), 54–55,
    57–58, 64–70, 85, 91, 93
  symbolic castration, xiv, 64
  symptom, xiv, 69–70, 85, 123–126
Lafargue, Paul, 17
Lazzarato, Maurizio, 136
Leontief, Wassily, 108
Locke, John, 3
Lohoff, Ernst, 114

INDEX

Losurdo, Domenico, 3
Lucretius, 19
Luxemburg, Rosa, 125

Mandel, Ernest, 154n, 160n
Mann, Michael, 34
Marcuse, Herbert, 5, 31, 75, 88–89
Marx, Karl, ix, xiii–xiv, 1–8, 9–21, 27, 31, 35, 38, 42, 45, 53, 59, 62–64, 67–68, 70–78, 80, 83, 85–87, 90–95, 101, 103–107, 111, 117–119, 121–124, 126, 134, 138, 143, 146–147, 151n, 152n, 154n, 156n
  automatic subject, 90
  Capital (vol. 1), 6, 15–20, 38, 63, 67, 70, 76, 77, 82, 94, 146, 154n, 169n
  Capital (vol. 3), 45, 117, 168n
  commodity fetishism, 67
  The Communist Manifesto, 71
  dialectics, 1–4, 14–17, 31, 35, 42, 68, 71–73, 75, 81, 92–95, 103, 105–106, 121
  Economic and Philosophic Manuscripts of 1844, 3, 152n, 155n
  finance, 111, 113
  The German Ideology, 92
  Grundrisse, 3, 4, 11, 15, 16, 18, 19, 70, 72, 94, 119, 121, 151n, 154n, 155n
  The Holy Family, 31
  labour, 5–6, 9–13, 17–19, 21, 38–39, 70, 73–78, 80–83, 85, 91, 93, 101, 105–107, 121–122
  mode of production, 67, 101, 110
  Notes on Adolph Wagner, 90
  positivism, 92
  The Poverty of Philosophy, 153n
  rate of profit, 45, 53, 117–119
  surplus-value, 20, 68, 70–71, 91, 93

Theories of Surplus Value, 168n, 171n
value-form, 14, 27, 64–65, 67, 76, 85–86
Wage Labour and Capital and Value, Price and Profit, 163n, 165n
Mauss, Marcel, 139
McGowan, Todd, 162n
McLuhan, Marshall, 140
Meaney, Mark, 154n, 155n
Merleau-Ponty, Maurice, 16, 17
Michéa, Jean-Claude, 124
Minsky, Hyman, 112, 123
von Mises, Ludwig, 111
Mitterrand, Francois, 124
Moore, Phoebe, 133
Morozov, Evgeny, 109
Moseley, Fred, 154n, 156n

Negri, Toni, 133
Newton, Isaac, 135

Obama, Barack, 124
Owen, Robert, 78

Paulson, Henry, 122
Pawlett, William, 174n
Polanyi, Karl, 152n
Poster, Mark, 106
Postone, Moishe, 39

Rifkin, Jeremy, 52, 118
Robinson, Andrew, 133
Ruda, Frank, 151n, 167n

Schmidt, Helmut, 124
Schumpeter, Joseph, 159n
Schwab, Klaus, 160n, 173n
Shiva, Vandana, 172n
Simmel, Georg, 56
Sloterdijk, Peter, 48, 161n
Smith, Adam, 2, 3, 22, 56
Smith, Tony, 154n, 156n

Sohn-Rethel, Alfred, 67, 151n
Sokurov, Alexander, 100
Soros, George, 140
Spinoza, Baruch, 8, 19

Trenkle, Norbert, 114
Tronti, Mario, 12

Uchida, Hiroshi, 155n, 159n

Vincent, Jean-Marie, 39

Wachowski brothers, 143
Warhol, Andy, 143
Weber, Max, 147
Williams, Eric, 153n
Woody, Allen, 48

Žižek, Slavoj, 8, 32, 54, 75, 79, 105, 106, 109, 147, 162n, 167n, 168n, 172n
Zuboff, Shoshana, 108–109
Zuckerberg, Mark, 140

www.ingramcontent.com/pod-product-compliance
Ingram Content Group UK Ltd.
Pitfield, Milton Keynes, MK11 3LW, UK
UKHW021833140426
5217IPUK00021B/1432